Blue Peter
50th Anniversary

hamlyn

BBC
Blue Peter
50th Anniversary

hamlyn

To Mandy, Rosy and Rupert

An Hachette Livre UK Company
www.hachettelivre.co.uk

First published in Great Britain in 2008 by
Hamlyn, a division of Octopus Publishing Group Ltd
2–4 Heron Quays, London E14 4JP
www.octopusbooks.co.uk

Copyright © Octopus Publishing Group Limited 2008

By arrangement with the BBC

The BBC logo is a trade mark of the British Broadcasting Corporation and is used under licence.

BBC logo © BBC 1996

All rights reserved. No part of this work may be reproduced or utilized in any form or by any means, electronic or mechanical, including photocopying, recording or by any information storage and retrieval system, without the prior written permission of the publisher.

ISBN 978-0-600-61793-8

A CIP catalogue record for this book is available from the British Library.

Printed and bound in China

10 9 8 7 6 5 4 3 2 1

CONTENTS

	Foreword	6
	Introduction	8
1	Setting Sail	10
	Fur and Feather	24
2	Now for Something Completely Different	36
	Blue Peter Flies the World	58
3	A Wonderful Splash of Colour	62
	In the Garden	84
	The *Blue Peter* Books	88
4	Fast Forward	90
	The *Blue Peter* Badge	118
5	Two to Three, Three to Four	122
	We Never Ask for Money	150
6	Flagship	156
	Famous Faces	178
	Index	186
	Acknowledgements	192

FOREWORD

The doorbell rings. Outside stands a courier, his face almost obliterated by a huge jiffy bag. 'Biddy Baxter?' I nod. 'I cried when Shep died', he said as he handed over the bag. He looked to be about early thirties. 'So did John', I replied, thinking the courier would have been five or six when he heard the announcement on the programme. Incredible that that memory had remained with him for over 20 years. But not uncommon – such was the total involvement so many children had with *Blue Peter*.

A powerful partnership: Edward Barnes and Biddy Baxter in the Blue Peter office. They used to paraphrase Dr Johnson, saying: 'He who is tired of Blue Peter is tired of television.'

How did this magic begin? How did this experiment, to find out whether children could empathize just as much by watching people and animals in a one-way medium as they could face to face with their families and friends, turn out to be the epitome of the Jesuits' maxim 'Give me a child until he is seven and I will give you the man'?

The challenge for Edward Barnes, Rosemary Gill and me was to make *Blue Peter* their – the viewers' – programme. To involve them in every possible way, first and foremost by using their ideas to the extent that by the 1980s 75 per cent of the content of each edition of *Blue Peter* came directly or indirectly from viewers' letters and phone calls. With a postbag of over 7,000 letters (including competition entries) per week we had a superb finger on the pulse of our audience – most of the five- to 12-year-olds in the country – although there were plenty who were younger and many teenagers as well as adults who were fans. But we were firmly committed to the prepubescent audience with their boundless enthusiasm, who soaked up information like blotting paper. 'I like *Blue Peter*,' they would write, 'because I never know what's going to happen next!'

To keep faith with our audience – whose parents were paying our salaries via the licence fee – we started an index of badge winners so that children never received a duplicated reply. Badges had to be won, but we devised a system that made it just as easy for a four-year-old to win as it was for their eight-year-old sister or 12-year-old brother. Contact with our viewers was an integral part of the plot and the fact that we had eight million stringers sending in suggestions for the programme from every corner of the UK meant that we were never Southern-centric.

The letters were also a shot in the arm for the production team. Anyone experiencing a low moment could wander into the Correspondence Unit and read gems like:

Dear John
You are good at climbing and kind to dogs and you help old ladies across the road, but please would you comb your hair.

Or

Dear Petra
My name is Nicholas and I am six years old. I only heard the other day that you are diabetic. I am diabetic as well as you and on May 29th my mummy is having a Jubilee party just for diabetic children so that we don't feel left out of the celebrations. I would like you to come to my party if it is possible. My mummy will give you your injection.
Lots of love,
Nicholas

And

Dear Lesley
I'm sorry you forgot your words on Monday. Were you nervous? I felt very nervous when I had to read Psalm 23 in chapel last Sunday.

Quite frankly, when Edward, Rosemary and I were planning the 'new' *Blue Peter* in 1962, if anyone had suggested it would still be in the *Radio Times* 50 years after those first 15-minute programmes pioneered by John Hunter Blair in 1958, we would have been utterly incredulous. How has it survived to celebrate its Golden Jubilee? A combination of the best viewers in the world – still largely prepubescent children – a succession of outstanding presenters and our successors in the Editor's chair: Lewis Bronze, Oliver Macfarlane, Steve Hocking and Richard Marson, all four of whom kept that magical ethos of the programme alive while bringing *Blue Peter* well and truly into the 21st century.

Whether children's programmes – let alone *Blue Peter* – will survive as we know them in this excitingly unpredictable age is a step into the unknown – only time will tell!

Biddy Baxter

Biddy Baxter

INTRODUCTION

I won my *Blue Peter* badge in 1972. To be honest, I've no memory of this achievement and suspect it may have had a lot to do with my older brother and sister, whose badges arrived on the same exciting morning, as I was only five and a half years old. I've still got the letter, in its utility brown BBC envelope, stamped with the *Blue Peter* ship. Sadly, the badge was lost in a playground many years ago.

We were a *Blue Peter* family. My favourite presenter was Lesley Judd. One year we were taken to the National Cat Club Show at Olympia, where our rescued moggy, Tiger, was 'highly commended'. Lesley was on duty at the *Blue Peter* stand and I queued for what seemed like hours to obtain her autograph. When I finally reached her, she smiled and asked, 'Do you watch *Blue Peter*?' But I found I was completely – and unusually – tongue-tied by the experience of actually meeting someone who was 'on television'. Lesley signed her photo-card for me and I was thrilled. Years later, I kept that prized photograph, the signature slightly smudged, in a frame in the corner of my office.

I went away to school and stopped watching the programme until one idle afternoon in the sixth form. I should have been revising, but I decided to watch *Blue Peter* instead. That day there was a film about the new presenter Janet Ellis joining the team. It was also a detailed behind-the-scenes look at the making of the programme. Then and there, I knew I'd found my dream job: Editor of *Blue Peter*.

Almost exactly 20 years later, I was given my chance. I'd made my way up from the studio floor to become first a producer and director and then Deputy Editor. By the time I left, in July 2007, I'd worked with most of the presenters past and present, directed over 100 films, edited over 500 programmes, won a BAFTA and cast three presenters, a gardener, two cats and a dog.

On *Blue Peter* no day is ever the same, good or bad, and at the end of series party there was a surprise. Biddy Baxter stepped out from the crowd and, after making a very generous speech, awarded me the programme's highest honour, a gold badge. It was an emotional evening. Two weeks later, at my own farewell, I laughed – and cried – throughout the screening of a special tape, full of out-takes and anecdotes from many of my closest colleagues, friends and presenters, among them Sarah Greene, who said: 'We first met way back in 1989. You were meant to be interviewing me about an ITV show but all we talked about was *Blue Peter* and *Going Live!* I knew exactly where you were headed and I was right. And by all accounts, you've been bloody brilliant at it.'

This is an insider's account of the world's longest-running children's television programme, the result of many months of research and interviewing, as well as years of personal experience. It's a celebration, but not, I hope, a whitewash.

So, if you ever won a *Blue Peter* badge, sent in a milk-bottle top, ran a bring-and-buy sale, entered a competition or just sat and watched, this book is for you.

Richard Marson

INTRODUCTION

1 8 September 2003: my first show as Editor – proof that dreams can come true.

2 Trying to out-pose the presenters during the making of our James Bond special. I worked with Konnie, Matt, Simon and Liz for over five years and we were a very close team.

3 The only autograph I've ever treasured: my reward for waiting to meet Lesley Judd at the 1972 National Cat Club show.

4 One of my happiest memories: producing the programme in which we dug up the boxes for the year 2000 and reunited the 'dream team' of Val, John and Peter.

1 Setting Sail
1958–1962

Today's children face an ocean of choice. There are over 20 television channels fighting a cut-throat competition to lure them in. But television is no longer the main attraction. Computer games are hugely popular, and both mobile phones and the internet offer hitherto undreamed of scope for social networking, which has understandably proved irresistible to youth. Thanks to technology, children can now consume or create an almost endless variety of content whenever the mood takes them. They take the rapidity of progress for granted. This is their world.

The very first presenters: Christopher Trace and Leila Williams. Chris was initially engaged for a fee of 19 guineas, while his co-presenter received 14.

All these facts only make the survival of *Blue Peter* in the 21st-century landscape all the more remarkable. It has endured through five decades of extraordinary and accelerated social change.

In many ways, the Britain to which *Blue Peter* first broadcast would be unrecognizable to most adults alive today, let alone children. In 1958, the cost of the average house was £2,390. Average weekly wages had just gone up to six pounds 14 shillings and petrol retailed at just under five 'bob' (old shillings), or 24 'new' pence, a gallon. A Conservative government, led by Prime Minister Harold Macmillan, was presiding over the death throes of the British Empire. We had yet to become a multi-racial society and there were still rigid divides of class.

Although the children of 1958 were more regimented and controlled than their 2008 counterparts, they enjoyed far greater freedom to roam, play and get their knees dirty. They had little disposable income and weren't ruthlessly targeted to gorge junk food, starve themselves thin or wear the 'right' clothes.

There were only two television channels, both in black and white. There were no videos, DVDs or PVRs, so the public had just one chance to tune in. Despite the limited airtime, there were plenty of children's programmes. *Watch With Mother* catered for the little ones, while shows such as *Crackerjack*, *Mr Pastry*, *Sooty* and *Billy Bunter* provided laughs, and there were improving quizzes and factual programmes like *All Your Own*, *Sketch Club* and *Studio E*. There were also lots of drama serials aimed at the whole family, most stirring adaptations of children's classics such as *The Splendid Spur*, *The Silver Sword* and *The Railway Children*. ITV, still in its infancy, offered glossier alternatives, such as the adventures of *Ivanhoe*, starring a young Roger Moore, and bought-in American film series.

Blue Peter was created to bridge a gap in the BBC Children's Department's output. The feeling was that five- to eight-year-olds were being short-changed – too old for *Watch With Mother* but not quite old enough for programmes like *Studio E*. Producer John Hunter Blair was given the job of doing something about it.

Into the blue

Hunter Blair was a large man, variously described by those who knew him as 'an absolute eccentric', 'extraordinarily kind', 'Bunterish', 'academic' and 'rumpled'. He lived alone and smoked a pipe. On one occasion, he banged his pipe into a wastepaper basket in the production gallery and nearly sent the whole place up in flames. He had a keen sense of humour and the absurd, and was a highly educated linguist with a passion for music, pretty girls and OO gauge model railways. His enthusiasm for the latter extended to having a large and complex layout running the length of an entire wall in his office. He would play with this while dictating scripts, letters and memos to his capable secretary Gilly Reilly, who recalls, 'He was very erudite, but he had this schoolboy streak in him.'

'We sat around for ages trying to think of a name. He came into the office one day and said, "Should we call it *Blue Peter*?" I said, "That's a jolly good name. I'm a sailor and I know the *Blue Peter* flag, but why *Blue Peter*?" He replied, "It just sounds a nice name and we're going off on a new adventure. We're going to sail off into the blue!" And that was it.'

One of the most persistent and repeated inaccuracies about *Blue Peter* is that it is named after the flag raised when a ship sets sail on a new adventure. In fact, the flag is actually lowered at the start of a voyage. On 16 October 1958 the BBC announcer introduced the very first edition with these words: 'If you stand on a dockside looking at the ships, you may see flying from the masthead of one of them a blue and white flag. That means that the ship is about to leave. Within a few hours, perhaps a few minutes, the ship will be off on a new voyage. Today Christopher Trace is waiting in the studio to introduce a new programme which bears the same name as that flag – *Blue Peter*.'

This was the cue to run the film of the opening titles, which were organized by Gilly Reilly. On 30 September 1958, cameraman John Turner filmed just over 15 seconds of the *Blue Peter* flag being lowered on the *Cutty Sark* at Greenwich. This footage was married with an aerial stock shot of a tall ship from the BBC film library, looped to make it long enough for the sequence. As well as the theme, 'Barnacle Bill', Hunter Blair would always instruct sound to 'add seawash' as these titles were played out.

Blue Peter shared Studio E at the BBC's Lime Grove – a ramshackle former film studio in West London that had been taken over by the BBC and converted for television – with other children's programmes such as *Sketch Club* and *Junior Sportsview*, and went out at five o'clock every Thursday afternoon, running for 15 minutes. Chris Trace spoke the

1 John Hunter Blair, ciné camera in hand, the man who unwittingly created the world's longest-running children's programme.

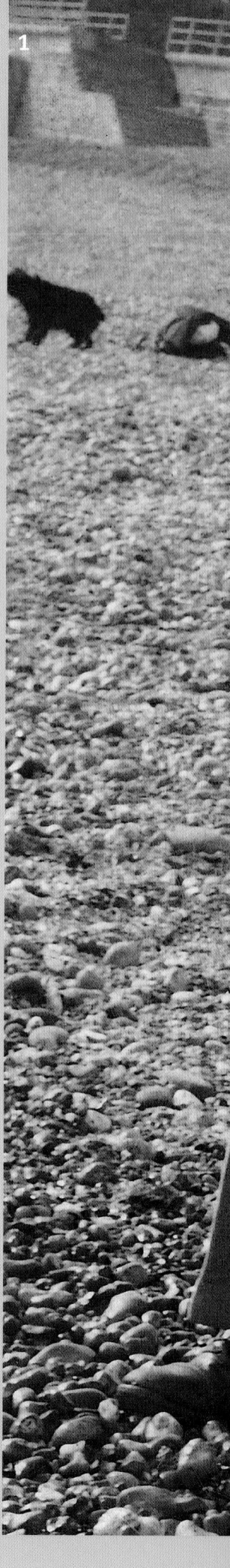

2 Although ill health forced him to retire, Hunter Blair did live long enough to see his programme grow and flourish.

1 The popularity of Christopher Trace kept *Blue Peter* afloat during a troubled era of changing producers and differences of approach.

2 Over the years, Chris gradually relaxed his look and began to favour open-necked shirts and jumpers.

3 Trace was in his element showing off anything mechanical, from the *Blue Peter* train layout to heavy machinery like this tractor.

opening words, the first of many millions since: 'Hello! Well, our *Blue Peter* is lowered and we're off on the first voyage of our new programme. One of the things we're going to do is to show you what's new in the things which specially interest you younger viewers, boys and girls.'

Chris then revealed the *Blue Peter* model railway layout and explained that 'the fun of having a model railway is to collect things for it, and during the next few weeks, I'm going to show you a lot of things you can get for your model railway.' On film, there was a bought-in cartoon called *Sparky and the Talking Train*. Chris introduced Leila Williams, who announced, 'While Chris and the boys are building up their model railway each week, we girls will try to collect a really nice set of things for our dolls.' Role reversal was still a long way off. The final item was a demonstration of a mind-reading magic trick with the assistance of child actor David Langford. In a twist of fate, 20 years to the day after this first programme, Langford was in the gallery, directing the 20th-birthday edition, having become one of the programme's most talented and prolific directors.

After the first programme, an audience research report found that, in the target age group of eight- to 11-year-olds and below, '…almost without exception they found this programme very enjoyable to watch'. Chris's trains were 'an especial attraction' for boys, while an eight-year-old girl remarked that Leila was 'lovely'. Owen Reed, the Head of Children's Programmes, scribbled a note to Hunter Blair: 'I think this is very encouraging. You spotted a need and look like fulfilling it.'

Full steam ahead

The new arrival never looked back. Indeed, transmission continued on a weekly basis for the next seven years with only very occasional gaps, for instance on the day the royal wedding of Princess Margaret and Antony Armstrong-Jones overran in May 1960, and when BBC technicians went on strike in April 1961, and to make room for the Budget in April 1962.

The ceaseless schedule meant that Chris and Leila couldn't present every programme. Sometimes they covered for each other to allow for holidays, and on one occasion actress Ann Taylor held the fort. Leila was absent for a whole six weeks from November 1959. Hunter Blair wrote to her to explain: 'Please don't think you are being dropped for any "sinister" reasons. The fact is the shape of the programme is being altered for a few weeks and there is just not enough work for two compères.'

During this period, the artist Tony Hart presented two editions by himself. He'd made his first contribution the previous year, on the sixth programme, illustrating a story about a dog. Soon, as well as providing the pictures, he was telling his own stories about Packi, the little white elephant: 'He trotted around the world trying to find somebody to take him in, but nobody wants a white elephant, you see! He was called Packi because elephants are pachyderms – thick-skinned creatures – although our Packi wasn't thick-skinned at all.' Tony Hart featured frequently throughout the first four years, and reflects, '*Blue Peter* was my first realization that people could work like a family.'

By now, the programme had built up a steady and loyal audience. Owen Reed had been sceptical about whether competitions would work for this audience, but, again, Hunter Blair proved him wrong when 1,500 girls aged between five and eight sent in their votes for their favourite dolls. Other simple yet popular competitions soon followed. Meanwhile, Hunter Blair also created his own serial based on the studio's model railway layout, set in a fictional Ruritanian land called San Marco, the stories inspired by his extensive travel across Europe.

The content gradually expanded to include mini-series and items about small animals, woodwork, coins, the Brownies, life in the RAF and the Brigade of Guards, flags, national anthems, music and songs. There were cartoons such as *Dreamy Daniel*, a quaintly titled bought-in film series called *How Other Children Live*, as well as a series of African stories, told by Hugh Tracey. By 1960, trains and dolls were no longer the mainstay of the programme. There was still virtually no filming, although in November 1961 Chris and Leila did appear in a short sequence shot at the British manufacturers' toy fair.

Challenging times

The founding quartet of Producer, secretary and presenters worked happily together until Hunter Blair developed a debilitating heart problem. He took a break, leaving *Blue Peter* in caretaker hands, often incompetent or uninterested. Inevitably, this resulted in some terrible ideas and dreadful programmes. A few months later Hunter Blair was back, but it was a temporary reprieve, and on 12 June 1961 he produced his last programme. The programme's creator would never return.

The first person intended to be a successor rather than a mere caretaker was Clive Parkhurst. Unfortunately, he was resented and disliked by the rest of the team. He dropped Leila Williams altogether. However, to everyone's relief, he followed her out the door just a few weeks later. His replacement, John Furness, cast Anita West to replace Leila, but neither of these new arrivals proved to have staying power either. There was now a miasma of crisis hanging over *Blue Peter*. The audience had stayed faithful through all the chopping and changing, but how long would their patience hold?

Interview boards were held to find a new, permanent Producer to commit to the show. With only one BBC channel, producer positions were like gold dust and competition was keen. Many of the candidates were talented, ambitious and experienced. Edward Barnes, a production assistant who'd worked as a floor manager on several early editions of the programme, was one of them. The envelopes containing the results of the boards arrived in the department administrator's office. He held them up to the light: 'If it was a small square it was a rejection slip. Mine was a small square slip and so were all the others. Only one had a neatly folded letter. This chit of a girl from radio had got it.'

Her name was Biddy Baxter.

1 August 1962: Chris Trace interviews Peter Reilly about sailing's international cadet class. Reilly's daughter was Gilly Reilly, John Hunter Blair's PA.

2 Artist Tony Hart, the designer of the *Blue Peter* ship and a regular in the early years, with Peter Palette, whose adventures he wrote and narrated in the summer of 1962.

3 Gilly Reilly worked on *Blue Peter* throughout the 1960s, becoming an assistant producer. Here she is showing Prince Edward how to make sugar mice.

Presenter Profile
CHRISTOPHER TRACE

JOINED: 16 October 1958

LEFT: 24 July 1967

MEMORABLE MOMENTS: Training the puppy Petra; model making; running the *Blue Peter* model railway; trips to Basle, Nuremberg, Norway, Singapore and Borneo

1 Chris was the very first person to appear on the programme. For nearly nine years he was the face of *Blue Peter*.

It is no exaggeration to say that without Christopher Trace there would have been no *Blue Peter*. His attractive, authoritative personality helped to define the programme, providing crucial continuity in its most formative period. His importance cannot be underestimated and, like all the great presenters, he was wildly popular with children. Before *Blue Peter*, Chris had spent seven years in the army. He then became an actor and was Charlton Heston's stand-in in the movie *Ben Hur*.

Gillian Reilly vividly remembers him arriving in John Hunter Blair's office: 'Chris saw the train set. That was the end of the interview. They just played trains!' It got him the job and also proved a useful skill, as model railways were to be such a major ingredient in the early years. He was less skilled with magic tricks, which were another frequent item at the beginning.

Leila Williams recalled: 'They never, ever went right on transmission and we always used to have to start the next programme with him getting out of the problem he'd got into the week before! There was one card trick and I had to show the card I'd picked to camera. He shuffled the pack and said, "This is the card you chose." And I looked and said, "But it's not." So we started the next programme with this card trick again. Only this time all the cards were the same – he cheated!'

Holding the fort

If it hadn't been for Chris, it is doubtful whether the show would have survived the grim period between John Hunter Blair's enforced retirement and the arrival of Biddy Baxter, the catalyst for the future. Biddy, in partnership with Edward Barnes and later Rosemary Gill, used Chris as the bedrock on which they could build their new *Blue Peter*. The combination of Chris and Valerie Singleton, who joined as his co-presenter in 1962, was an immediate success and grew more so after the programme went twice-weekly in 1964. Chris, on the other hand, found the strain of the new schedule harder and harder to cope with, especially as he carried the bulk of the location filming.

He didn't suffer in silence and actually resigned on more than one occasion. After a freezing shoot at Camber Sands, he told Edward Barnes: 'Get someone else to share this bloody agony or I'm leaving for good.' On Whit Monday 1965, following one of these 'resignation' incidents, Edward Barnes wrote to Biddy: 'I think he is genuinely unhappy with the present set-up and that if he could find another way of making a living he'd take it. It would mean starting with someone entirely new and Val. This makes me feel very vulnerable and I don't much fancy Trace holding a pistol to our heads any time he feels a little fed up. Are we justified in keeping all our eggs in such a flimsy basket? Whilst we are in a winning position with the kids, ought we not to introduce a second man? If we find someone good, we would have someone ready made to take over. Not suddenly someone new, which could be disastrous. Chris himself could have no complaint about this – it would be taking a little of the pressure from him. But he would have no doubt at all what the implications would be and that wouldn't be a bad thing.'

2 Ex-army officer Trace, back in uniform to tell the story of the Victoria Cross and looking every inch the part in his Victorian scarlet tunic.

3 Chris with the first *Blue Peter* guide dog Honey, paid for with funds raised from silver paper collected by *Blue Peter* viewers in 1965.

4 Chris rehearsing with Valerie Singleton and 'second man', John Noakes, who was brought in to share the pressure of the twice-weekly schedule.

5 A chilly day at Camber Sands with Petra. This shoot, which Trace had to spend freezing in his swimming trunks, was the trigger for one of his threatened resignations.

6 As if he'd never been away – Chris looks relaxed during rehearsals for the 25th birthday programme.

On 30 December 1965, the 'second man', John Noakes, joined the team. He was willing to do all the exciting and physical films that Edward Barnes wanted to make, but that Chris's fear of heights ruled out. Although his schedule was now less demanding, Chris was clearly tiring of the programme. During an expedition to Norway, he'd had an extra-marital affair and there was the strain of the resulting divorce which brought unwelcome publicity too.

In January 1967, out of the blue, Chris finally announced that he wanted to leave. This time there was no going back. On his last show, he told viewers he was leaving to work on a film and do some writing. There is no record of his last appearance. It was one of the very few editions from this era to be destroyed, perhaps an indication of the undoubted nervousness surrounding his departure. Ursula Eason, the Deputy Head of Children's Programmes, wrote to various BBC figures saying: 'We have planned his departure from *Blue Peter* very carefully and do not want to provoke complaints. We are banking on the fact that children's memories are short and that, with the popularity of Val and John, his departure will not be too much noticed.'

To thank him for his work, Eason requested and received authorization to hold a simple party after transmission on 17 July, with 'champagne and potato crisps'.

A few days later, Chris wrote to thank her: 'It brought back many happy memories, especially meeting Leila again. I hope sincerely that *Blue Peter* will carry on without me. It's such a worthwhile programme. I am only sorry I lack the stamina to see it out.'

Life post-*Blue Peter* wasn't always easy for him. The film project failed and, although he continued to work on radio and in Norwich for the BBC's *Look East*, in 1973 Trace was declared bankrupt. But he always remained an optimist. He worked as a taxi driver and in a factory, and was filmed there for the 1980 television programme *Where Are They Now?* He returned to *Blue Peter* to celebrate its 20th birthday and brought with him an idea of his own – an award for Outstanding Endeavour. These awards, solid bronze medallions engraved with the *Blue Peter* ship, were made by the factory in which he worked and were presented every October from 1979 to 1990. Over that time recipients included Musical Youth for becoming the youngest band to reach number one in the pop charts, and Bob Geldof for Band Aid, Live Aid and Sport Aid.

In 1992, aged just 59, he developed cancer. On 3 September, Valerie Singleton, Biddy Baxter and Edward Barnes visited him in hospital to reminisce about the old days. He died just two days later.

Presenter Profile
LEILA WILLIAMS

JOINED: 16 October 1958

LEFT: 8 January 1962

MEMORABLE MOMENTS: Presenting the very first *Blue Peter* and the very first 'make'

1 Leila Williams was the programme's first female presenter – and first beauty queen.

Originally, Leila Williams had set her heart on an acting career. Entering beauty contests was just a means to an end. She used the cash from winning Miss Blackpool to pay for elocution lessons and to fund a year at drama school. She carefully eradicated her natural Black Country accent, which in the days of ubiquitous received pronunciation would have stopped her getting work. Leila entered Miss Great Britain three times and was placed third and then second before finally winning the competition in 1957.

This enabled her to come to London, where she made a few commercials and got the job of hosting the seminal BBC pop programme *Six-Five Special* alongside Jim Dale. It was on *Six-Five Special* that she met her future husband, singer Fred Mudd from The Mudlarks.

When her agent called her about a new BBC children's programme, it was just another interview, the latest in a long line. She duly set off for the *Blue Peter* office in Shepherd's Bush Green, where she found 'queues and queues of people – every girl in London from every agency'. She had another appointment and couldn't wait, so she persuaded the commissionaire to let her jump the queue and meet John Hunter Blair and his secretary Gilly Reilly.

They had a quick chat and Leila left a couple of photographs. Soon her agent was back in touch. Leila had been recalled to report for an audition at Broadcasting House. This threw her a little, as she knew that Broadcasting House was the home of radio and she really didn't want to work in radio. So she nearly didn't go, but in the end '...thought it would be rude not to. Thank goodness I did!'

This time she had to read a story and then John Hunter Blair asked her to interview his secretary. Leila asked her what she did when she wasn't being a secretary and was told all about Gilly's passion for sailing: 'I learnt an awful lot about sailing that morning!'

She got the job and was told she was there to act as assistant to Christopher Trace. This was an unlikely twist of fate. Leila had actually met Chris before, when they'd both appeared in an amateur play in her home town of Walsall. As co-presenters, they quickly struck up a strong rapport with each other and their tiny two-strong production team: 'It was a little happy family. We rehearsed in the office. Chris and I could both speak in a Black Country accent, so after we'd read through for timing and got it all word perfect, we used to read the script in Black Country. And that used to make John [Hunter Blair] cry with laughter. We were all shrieking. In fact, there was always laughter coming from that office. Someone complained about the noise!'

Leila still has vivid memories of the very first programme: 'We were doing a photographic session for publicity, and I just happened to glance to the side and I saw this monitor. There was this pair of legs. And I thought, "That's odd." I carried on doing the pictures and I looked again and I thought, "They're my legs!" So I not only had the nerves of a first programme, I had this leg-happy cameraman as well. I spent the day pulling my skirt down!'

2 Reunited with Chris Trace and back on the *Blue Peter* seat unit after 16 years, Leila rehearses the 20th-birthday programme.

3 The 20th-birthday line-up in 1978 included all the *Blue Peter* presenters so far, with the exception of John Noakes.

4 For the 35th birthday, Leila helped to present a video vote for favourite *Blue Peter* moment. The winner was Yvette Fielding screaming on a Blackpool rollercoaster!

The first 'make'

Both Chris and Leila made regular contributions to the content of the fledgling *Blue Peter*. Leila's landlady had a daughter whose pride and joy was her doll's pram. Leila had tried to buy a mattress, sheets, pillows and blankets for this pram, but with no luck, so in the end she made them herself. The crowning glory was a patchwork quilt created from the hem of an old dress: 'John sent me scuttling home and said, "You bring me that pram and show me." And that became the first *Blue Peter* make. John wanted it to be like a magazine where you turn the pages and there is something different, something going on all the time. He was a very clever man.'

The *Blue Peter* 'family' were so close that when Leila got married, she asked John Hunter Blair to give her away. When ill health forced him to leave, the programme fell into the hands of a succession of caretaker producers. Both presenters were now coming up with a lot of the show's content themselves. Then, in September 1961, a new Producer was appointed. His name was Clive Parkhurst.

Leila recalls: 'He suddenly produced this wall chart and we had to fill in what we were going to do. We had to have nine weeks' programmes planned. And he used to come in and say, "Oh, she can't do that, that won't work, that's too expensive." Really it became impossible because I was too busy. It wasn't my only job – I was doing small parts in films, adverts and I worked at ATV as a weathergirl, and on an early talent show called *Bid For Fame*.'

A difficult and unpleasant autumn followed. In October, Leila was dropped from six editions, returning for one final month. 'We were like two raw wires and we just exploded. I was rather rude to him [Clive] over the telephone and gave him his opportunity. He went upstairs and said he couldn't find anything for me to do. It was absolutely true, he'd never found me anything to do. I'd found it myself. My contract was on a monthly basis, so at the end of the month that was it. I was very, very saddened because I did love that programme.'

Not long after her abrupt and unhappy departure, Leila discovered she was pregnant and she left show business altogether to bring up her daughter. She stayed in touch with *Blue Peter*, however, returning on several memorable occasions, including the 20th-, 35th- and 40th-birthday programmes. 'I never thought, never ever in my wildest dreams, that it would go on for as long as it has. *Blue Peter* is a very apt title, as we did start on an adventure that's still going.'

Presenter Profile
ANITA WEST

1 Anita West, who stayed just four months and became the 'lost' presenter, was chosen in preference to Valerie Singleton.

JOINED: 7 May 1962

LEFT: 3 September 1962

MEMORABLE MOMENTS: Getting the job over Valerie Singleton; re-emerging to appear in the 40th-birthday programmes

For many years, Anita West was the forgotten presenter, omitted from the official numbering system and never mentioned in articles or on anniversaries. *Blue Peter* has always had a good written archive, but soon after I joined at Christmas 1997, I suggested it would be a sensible idea to create a searchable computer database as an alternative to wading through decades' worth of paper. During the process, up came Anita West's name, in scripts and the *Radio Times*. But who was she and why had she vanished?

Back in April 1962, Anita was an actress, keen to make her mark, but with little experience apart from a handful of commercials and a few weeks on a film shot in Yugoslavia. She was married to *The Goon Show*'s band leader Ray Ellington and had two small children. When her agent sent her to audition for *Blue Peter*, she found herself up against three other candidates, among them a BBC announcer called Valerie Singleton.

These auditions still exist. They are the earliest existing footage of *Blue Peter*. Working alongside Christopher Trace, each artist had to read a story, complete a make and interview a studio guest, the eminent children's producer Joy Harington. Anita remembers: 'I'd read the story to the children, so it was familiar, but I didn't expect to get it and I was so nervous. At one point my mouth dried up and my lip stuck to my teeth.'

Despite her anxieties, Anita did easily the best audition, and a few weeks later, she made her first appearance. Tony Hart was on the same show: 'She really was a dish, most beautiful. The Producer brought her into the studio and I remember there was a sort of move among all the men to get a bit closer!'

Anita made a confident start and looked fantastic on camera, but soon she was feeling under pressure: 'I was so involved with it. You had to make all the things yourself. There wasn't a team of people. Tony was really helpful and kind, and taught me a lot of things to do, cutting out and how to do patterns. You did it all yourself with papier mâché or whatever you'd got and the creativity came from you. And I ran out of ideas.'

Leaving the show

At the same time, Anita's private life was not going well: 'Ray was having an affair with a singer in the band. There was going to be a divorce. In those days, anything in your private life that might have got in the way of your public life was not good news. I wasn't sure how the divorce was going to go. If it was a messy one, it would have been embarrassing for the programme. I didn't want bad publicity. I didn't want to lose the children. I wanted them around and I wanted to be there for them. I spent hours in tears before I had to go on air and I was worried I'd mess things up in front of the camera.'

For a time, she kept her problems to herself. Pleased with her performance, the BBC asked her to sign a full-time contract, offering to train her as an announcer alongside her weekly *Blue Peter* commitment of one day's rehearsal and

2 The BBC issued this formal publicity shot to promote Anita's arrival as a new presenter.

3 In 1998, Anita played presenter Stuart Miles' primary-school teacher in the 40th-anniversary special, 'Back In Time For Christmas'.

4 A rare 'tele-snap' of Anita, taken directly from the screen as she presented one of her 16 editions of *Blue Peter*.

one day's studio. They were taken aback when her reaction was to hand in her notice: 'I thought I just can't do that. I had to go to the Producer and say, "I'm really sorry, I can't continue any more. I'm giving a month's notice." I was really upset and I know they were with me. Probably because they didn't know the background. I didn't tell them because in those days you kept your private life private. Perhaps they thought I was being a little bit unprofessional.'

On her last show, Anita handed over to the beneficiary of her resignation, the runner-up from the auditions of a few months before, Valerie Singleton. Anita certainly had all the charisma to have been a very successful and long-running presenter. If the circumstances had been different and she'd stayed, it's strange to think of what might have been – a *Blue Peter* without Valerie Singleton, who became one of its most iconic figures.

Life after *Blue Peter*

Anita continued to juggle the demands of motherhood with taking occasional acting jobs. Over the years, she cropped up in everything from *Danger Man* and *The Saint* to *Space: 1999* and *Crossroads*. For a time, she went behind the camera to work as a PA for a company making commercials.

My rediscovery of Anita West couldn't have been more timely. In 1998, the programme was celebrating its 40th anniversary. This story was obviously newsworthy. I passed on the information to Lucy Bowden, who was producing the main documentary for BBC2's '*Blue Peter* Theme Night'. She tracked Anita down and persuaded her to be interviewed. Anita was surprised and delighted at being invited back into the fold. Afterwards she wrote to me succinctly: 'Thank you for finding me!'

As well as appearing in the documentary, Anita was invited to take her place in the grand presenter parade on the actual anniversary edition of the programme. I also asked if she wanted to be involved in that year's Christmas entertainment, which I was writing and producing. It was called 'Back In Time For Christmas', a kind of *Doctor Who* time-slip story, enabling lots of ex-presenters to make cameo appearances. In the plot, the current trio all ended up stuck in different stages of their own pasts. Stuart Miles was trapped in the day of his 1973 nativity play. Anita played his teacher. She was fantastic and I suggested to the editor, Oliver Macfarlane, that it would be more accurate to include Anita in the official roll-call of presenters. He agreed and she's now officially, and rightly, one of the family.

Special Assignment

FUR AND FEATHER

The animal stars of *Blue Peter* are, if anything, more famous and fondly remembered than their human counterparts. Biddy Baxter had a favourite saying, 'Fur and feather are more popular than flesh' – a concise, if not very tactful, way of reminding presenters of their relative place in the scheme of things.

It was Edward Barnes's wife, Dorothy Smith, who first suggested that the programme might have a dog of its own. It was a brilliantly topical idea. The 1960s fashion for high-rise housing meant that millions of children were being deprived of pet ownership. *Blue Peter*'s dog would be a dog for everyone. It would be featured on every edition and taken on location wherever possible.

On 17 December 1962, the nameless mongrel puppy selected made its first and only appearance. Soon after transmission, it died. Rather than upset viewers, Biddy and Edward combed the streets of London to find a lookalike replacement. At the 11th hour they struck lucky, although for a time the make-up department added a distinctive white marking so that the substitute matched the unfortunate original. This was gradually faded out as the weeks passed.

On 7 January 1963, the puppy was named Petra. A mongrel with a strong Alsatian streak and permanently pricked ears, she eventually lost most of her teeth through distemper, had poor eyesight and later developed diabetes. Petra vigorously defended her territory, the studio, when other animals were around, but was loved fiercely and unconditionally by the growing *Blue Peter* audience. Every aspect of her training was covered on the shows and this approach became the template for all the *Blue Peter* dogs that followed.

Peter Purves took responsibility for Petra soon after he joined: 'It was thought that if she lived with me, maybe she'd like the studio more. It was a good idea, and to a large extent it worked. You had to keep her under control. She had an aggressive streak in her and was neurotic, but she was immensely popular, a famous, famous dog. Once, I lost her in the Lake District for about four hours. It was a frightening experience. I was absolutely sweating, "I've lost the nation's favourite pet." Eventually she came back, completely bedraggled. I loved that dog and she loved me back.'

A tortoise and a Siamese

Petra wasn't alone for long. A tortoise called Fred arrived on 21 October 1963 and Jason, a seal-point Siamese cat, was introduced on 1 June 1964. Biddy knew they were on to a winner: 'Children are so used to being told what to do. Having a share in taking care of something even more defenceless than them was empowering.'

Jason, who was very nearly christened Jumbo, turned out to be the perfect television cat, sitting so still that some viewers wondered if he was stuffed. Directors could reliably plan shots with him as foreground

1 Just like their human co-stars, the pets had their own publicity cards. The following pages feature a selection. This card shows Rags, bought with the proceeds of the 1975 Clothes Horse Race Appeal.

2 Honey, *Blue Peter*'s first guide dog, was bought by viewers who collected silver paper which was melted down into aluminium ingots and sold.

Special Assignment FUR AND FEATHER

3 Chris looked after Petra, while Jason was Val's responsibility. Once they had to apologize for mistakenly suggesting that you bathe your cat's eyes with boracic acid!

4 Jack and Jill were twin silver tabbies who first appeared in 1976. Jill died of heart failure on 30 May 1983 and Jack also died suddenly on 20 April 1986.

5 In 1974 Freda starred in her own *Blue Peter* film, taking part in a tortoise race at Oxford University. Out of seven competitors, she came last.

BLUE PETER BARNEY

BLUE PETER JACK AND JILL

BLUE PETER FREDA

BLUE PETER GOLDIE

6 Barney, the *Blue Peter* parrot. Says Biddy Baxter, 'They were the most boring birds – they never *did* anything!'

7 Goldie was donated to *Blue Peter* by the Guide Dogs' Association. She had two litters, in 1981 and 1986.

BLUE PETER 50th Anniversary

interest. Just like Petra, Fred and Jason had their own fan photos, which were sent out in their thousands.

There were two highlights in the tortoise's annual calendar that never varied: going into and out of hibernation. In the days before political correctness, part of the process of bringing the tortoise out of hibernation was the careful touching up of its name, which was painted on the shell. Thanks to an eagle-eyed viewer, it eventually transpired that 'he' was actually 'she', and so on 12 June 1967, an 'a' was added to Fred. Freda, restored to the dignity of her correct sex, survived until 1979.

She was followed by a tortoise double act. They first appeared on 1979's Election Day, and so viewers were inspired to name them Maggie and Jim, after the then Leader of the Opposition and Prime Minister.

Although a few of the dogs lived with the presenters, the others, plus assorted cats and tortoises, had to be looked after by expert animal handlers. They tended to be ladies of a certain age, ever present in the studio and what used to be known as 'the salt of the earth'. Their service was inestimable. As well as the tedious trek to and from their suburban homes, they would take the animals to the vets whenever necessary. At weekends and during the holidays, they would escort their celebrity charges all over Britain to personal appearances at fêtes, shows and children's wards. For many years, until her death in 1994, the doyenne of these ladies was Edith Menezes. Edith held court from a chair in her own corner of the studio, where she'd gossip or read a seemingly endless supply of Mills and Boon romances in between swiftly recapturing any animal who dared to make a dash for it.

1 Patch lived with John Noakes. All presenters who looked after dogs full time received an extra fee. 'Me dog money', Noakes called it.

2 Petra's training included a whole series of films, some of them shot around the BBC Television Centre in West London.

3 For over 20 years, Edith Menezes looked after many of the pets, including Willow (seen here), Jason, Jack and Jill, Freda, George and, latterly, Shep.

4 When awake, the tortoise used to appear in every show. In recent years this policy changed to only having them in the garden.

5 Maggie and Jim – just like Freda, they were Southern European tortoises, the type best suited to the British climate.

MAGGIE and JIM
BLUE PETER

BLUE PETER GEORGE

6 On his first programme, Mark Curry trod on George: 'One minute he was sitting peacefully, the next he was breakdancing!'

Longest serving of them all

When Maggie and Jim perished in the bitterly cold winter of 1982, Edith offered her own tortoise, Pork Pie, as a replacement. He was rechristened George in honour of *Blue Peter*'s animal expert George Cansdale. Tortoises are low-risk co-stars, or so you'd think, but presenter Sarah Greene did have a problem with George: 'Whenever I wore these particular shoes, as soon as the programme started, I used to have this strange humping feeling on one of my feet. I realized that the tortoise thought my shoe was another tortoise and had fallen in love! One day I dared to look down and there he was, having a ball!'

George became the longest-serving pet of them all. When he eventually died in the spring of 2004, he made headlines, including the front page of *The Times*. I remember an Australian friend of mine shaking his head and saying, 'You Poms are such a bunch of weirdos!'

George shuffled off just after we had introduced a companion for him, Shelley, which was handy, as she became his replacement.

One of the advantages of having pets was that they enabled the programme to cover the facts of life and death. The dogs and cats were found mates and had litters. When they died, it was an opportunity to explore bereavement. For Peter Purves, '…one of the hardest things I ever had to do on the programme was to announce Petra's death'.

Patch, John Noakes's first *Blue Peter* dog, was one of Petra's puppies: 'He was a very friendly dog, he would go to anybody. I always needed someone to play off, but Pete wasn't there when I started, so I talked to the dog, as I later did with Shep.'

When Tony Hicks, the guitarist from The Hollies, demonstrated a new cordless electric guitar on the programme, Peter Purves remembers: 'He was wearing a velveteen suit and walking round the studio, playing the thing. Patch took a dislike to this and, during transmission, shot away from us. He'd have had a piece of Tony's bum if he could, but he actually just ripped his trousers. I knew Patch liked to boss like his mother, but I didn't know he was a music critic!'

Patch died after a filming trip on the canals. It is thought he ate some rat poison. Noakes was devastated and nearly in tears when he had to tell viewers.

One-man dog

On 16 September 1971, Patch's replacement, Shep arrived: 'All I had to do was say, "Sheep!" and he'd be up like a shot. He was super, but very much a one-man dog. He wouldn't go to anyone else', explained Noakes. 'You could talk to him and tell him all your problems. Dogs don't go off and sneak and tell them to somebody else!'

Shep showed his loyalty whenever he was co-opted into another presenter's link. Lesley Judd remembers: 'They'd always say, "Get an animal in with her, it's a boring shot without an animal." Great for one's ego! Often it would be Shep. I had to keep going as they counted me down into the film. All the time, you could feel Shep's upper lip trembling and

1 When pets' passports were introduced, Lucy and Mabel were taken on a trip to Brussels by Konnie Huq. She struggled to control them both.

2 Mabel was rescued by the RSPCA. The inspector looking after her had the initials M.A.B. and her kennel was marked M.A.B.1. This inspired her name.

hear a very low growling. He never bit, but it was most unnerving!' Shep became so famous that when John Noakes was turned into a Madame Tussauds waxwork, Shep was modelled too.

Like most of the programme's pets, Shep belonged to the BBC. On 27 November 1977, Noakes's wife Vicky wrote to Edward Barnes: 'John told me last week that you had decided to make him a present of Shep when he leaves the programme in June. A very kind gesture, I thought. It's strange how very attached one becomes to some animals and Mark [the Noakes' son] seems to have a particularly soft spot for Shep. But then I suppose we all do really. So from Mark and me, thanks for retiring Shep early. It really was a kind thought.'

When Edward Barnes told Biddy of the plan, she had one reservation: 'I thought it might be wise to ask for a written statement to the effect that John would not involve Shep in any kind of advertising. It would have been blatant exploitation of children. There was no contract involved, it was just a simple request.'

Noakes was informed of the condition and promptly hit the roof. There was a big row. On 2 February 1978, Edward wrote again to Vicky Noakes: 'I am not retracting from my decision to let Shep stay with John and the family. As I said to John, I have been asked to make sure that I am not making a present to our competitors at the same time. The only condition is that Shep will not be exploited for advertising.'

The relationship between Noakes and *Blue Peter* now descended into bitterness and acrimony. There was an uneasy truce until the spin-off programme *Go With Noakes* finally came to an end in 1983 when Noakes and Shep finished filming introductions to a series of repeats. Now the disagreement over Shep's ownership went public. Noakes gave angry interviews to the tabloids, the precursor of many to come over the next two decades.

The row over Shep's ownership seemed to crystallize all his resentment and frustration about the job he'd done so well and for so long. Edward was '...tremendously surprised. He wouldn't accept the condition, so he never had the dog. And it broke his heart.'

Shep retired to live with Edith Menezes, while John bought an identical black and white border collie, called it Skip and launched into a series of dog food commercials. It was a definite two fingers up at the BBC.

When Shep died in January 1987, Noakes gave the news on a children's programme called *Fax!*, breaking down in tears as he did so. Presenter Mark Curry was in charge of making *Blue Peter*'s announcement: 'Just as a joke, I said in rehearsal, "We'll be back on Thursday when I'll be stuffing Shep!" And of course the camera crew cracked up. Biddy came down and said, "Don't you ever, ever say things like that. That dog was a bigger star than you'll ever be!"'

Love my dog, love me

Mark had resisted all attempts to pair him with a dog. But this tactic of teaming a new presenter with a four-legged friend was based on simple psychology: 'Love me, love my dog' or rather 'Love my dog, love me'.

Special Assignment **FUR AND FEATHER**

3 Although well trained, Shep once attacked Roy Castle during transmission, disturbed by his frenetic playing of a range of musical instruments.

4 Andy helped to puppy-walk the guide dog Magic, but sadly, after months of training, she failed the rigorous health check.

5 Madame Tussaud's figures of Noakes and Shep – spot the genuine articles. The joke in the *Blue Peter* office was that Noakes should be displayed in the Chamber of Horrors! Both figures still survive in storage.

The responsibility for and relationship with a dog can also be a welcome distraction from the terrors of this exceptionally daunting job. It was the reason we gave Magic to Andy Akinwolere when he started in 2006, and in Simon Groom's awkward early days in the late 1970s, Goldie was his lifeline: 'Biddy said, "Would you like to join the programme?" When I replied yes, she was immediately very businesslike. "Right, tomorrow you're going with a photographer to a house in Rugby where you will collect a nine-week-old Golden Retriever puppy. You will join the programme with this puppy and look after it." Initially, it was a real help, but after leaving, it was a hindrance. That image was so strong, you were typecast. But I've no complaints and many happy memories.'

When Goldie left the programme with Simon, he accepted the same terms John Noakes had refused, writing to Biddy: 'Apart from the occasional non-commercial fête or charity function, I feel she has earned a long rest and gradual retirement.' Goldie died in 1992 and was buried on the Groom farm at Dethick. It didn't escape the notice of the presenters that her obituary was far longer than the tribute paid just weeks earlier after the death of *Blue Peter*'s very first presenter, Christopher Trace.

Parrot fashion

While the programme did well with cats, dogs and tortoises, it didn't have much luck with its parrots. Joey arrived in 1966 and Barney appeared from 1968. They made dull television, never learning to speak on camera, which might have redeemed them. This was despite the crew spending rehearsals and lunch breaks trying valiantly to coax them into saying, 'Who's a silly Biddy?' – and worse.

Joey's finest hour was guest-starring in an episode of the long-running BBC drama series *Dr Finlay's Casebook*. But both Joey and Barney died suddenly and after Barney's demise, *Blue Peter*'s parrot perch was left unoccupied.

As well as the regular pets, there were also animals that appeared on *Blue Peter* as a result of appeals. The 1976 Clothes Horse Race paid for Rags, the *Blue Peter* pony, given to the Riding for the Disabled Association but whose progress was followed on the programme. When Rags died in 1987, that year's appeal was named in her honour and provided a successor, Jet, who is still working for the Riding for the Disabled Association today.

The most famous of the animals bought by *Blue Peter* viewers was a string of guide dogs, all of whose training was covered in detail until the red-letter day when it was time to hand them over to their new owners. Honey and Cindy began the tradition in the 1960s. Buttons arrived in 1975 and Prince in 1981. The programme's latest guide dog, Magic, was the result of the *Blue Peter* Bark In The Park, a fund-raising dog walk to mark the 75th anniversary of the Guide Dog Association.

Sadly, after several months' training, Magic was discovered to be prone to seizures, probably caused by a form of epilepsy. This made her unsuitable as a guide dog after all. Instead, she was found a home and became a family pet.

1 The ill-fated Joey. 'I was against having a parrot,' says Edward Barnes, 'It was Biddy and Rose's mistake!'

2 The longest-serving cats, Kari and Oke, never had their own photo-card. They had to share one with Liz Barker, just as Meg later shared one with Matt.

3 It was decided not to breed from Willow and she became the first *Blue Peter* pet to be spayed, in April 1989.

4 Socks is placid enough to take part in everything from perching on a studio camera to coming out of the TARDIS with Freema Agyeman from *Dr Who*.

Cats' claws

When the ever-stoical Jason died in January 1976, he was replaced by two kittens, Jack and Jill. They were nicknamed 'the disappearing cats', legging it with such consistency that a montage of these moments became a popular and much-requested item. As presenter Janet Ellis observed: 'They didn't like being on television. They weren't naturals. But they had to be in shot sometimes, so I'd assume a vice-like grip on them and they'd assume a vice-like grip on my thighs. I've still got the scars!'

Jill died in the summer of 1983 and Jack followed, after holding the fort on his own, in 1986.

Willow, who arrived in September 1986, was a beautiful Burmese kitten. She holds the distinction of being the only pet sacked by the programme. Unlike Jack and Jill, Willow could be seen. Unfortunately, she could be heard too. She was horribly noisy, howling at inopportune moments during transmissions. She could also be vicious, clawing anyone foolish enough to attempt a passing stroke. This was difficult for the presenters, who had no choice, and often ended up scratched and bleeding, with their clothes snagged and spoilt. It was impossible as far as children were concerned. Meeting the pets was always a highlight of a studio visit and it wasn't satisfactory having a potentially savage 'off-limits' cat. Edith Menezes would smother Willow's paws with copious quantities of cream cheese so that, on screen at least, the cat looked as if it was contentedly washing its paws.

After five seasons of trying to make it work and hoping for improvement, Willow was 'retired' in 1991, continuing to live with her successors, but being spared the pressure of public life. Willow remained *Blue Peter*'s responsibility, of course, and perhaps to spite us, mellowed into a sweet-natured creature that lived to an extremely expensive old age. She finally expired in 2005.

Kari and Oke were *Blue Peter*'s next feline double act. Unlike their predecessors, they were rescue cats, their names inspired by that year's summer expedition to Japan. They joined at a time when studios were becoming busier and noisier, and steadily less cat-friendly. The constant turnaround of presenters, most of them uninterested in pets of any kind, didn't help. Nonetheless, they remained in situ until they had exceeded the venerable Jason's epic run, and by then I thought it was only fair that we retired them. We were also about to transmit five times a week and I realized a cute new kitten would probably be good box office.

Smudge made such a good start. He was a handsome, friendly, curious cat, taken from a rescued litter. It was each studio producer's responsibility to work out how and in what way the cat could be involved in the programme, and if there was going to be an alarming event, refuge could be readily provided in make-up or a dressing room.

This contingency slipped up badly on 7 February 2005, when there was a live interactive special called 'Brain of *Blue Peter*'. The studio was packed with hundreds of rowdy, excited children. Presenter Liz Barker attempted to hold Smudge, but he panicked, drew blood and leapt

BLUE PETER 50th Anniversary

1

1 Washing the dogs was a regular and always reliable item on *Blue Peter*. As well as being cheap to produce, it guaranteed a lot of fun in the studio as the wet dogs ran around, spraying the hapless presenters.

2 Willow lashes out at Bonnie, who was the gentlest of dogs and never seemed to mind the ill-treatment from her feline co-star.

3 Freda wakes up. *Blue Peter*'s tortoises were always guaranteed two items every year – being put into and taken out of hibernation.

4 Gethin Jones with Smudge, the cat who did so well until the day he ran amok in the studio. Worse was to follow.

5 Bonnie made one return appearance after she retired, to celebrate Mabel's birthday in February 2001. Bonnie died a few weeks later, on 17 April.

for freedom. He landed on a cable, which gave him a minor electric shock. It was a horrible moment and his devoted handler, Marina Cragg, was distraught.

Overnight, Smudge's personality changed. Now he was fretful and timid. Marina became increasingly protective, wanting to hand him over to a presenter only at the very last minute. This caused real tension for the presenters, who'd often make mistakes as a result of the stress over who could hold the cat and when. During the break between series, we found Britain's top cat therapist, Sarah Fisher. Her techniques seemed to work, but just as things were slowly improving, Marina called in floods of tears. Smudge had been run over in the road in front of her house.

The difficulties with Smudge really brought home the ethics of having animals in the studio. Some felt we should abandon the idea of having a cat at all. I asked the National Cat Club for advice. They suggested we choose a kitten from a Ragdoll litter. As a breed, Ragdolls are perfect for the job. They are attractive cats with the placid nature an animal needs to be genuinely content in a studio environment. There were a few grumbles from within the team, who thought, correctly, that a rescue cat sent a better message than a pedigree animal. But I didn't want to return to dragging an unhappy cat into a television studio twice a week just to be 'on message'.

Socks arrived on 9 January 2006 and has been *Blue Peter*'s happiest and most biddable pussy cat ever since, although a stray whiff of David Beckham's football boots did send him demented on one occasion!

On 25 September 2007 Socks was joined by Cookie, a second Ragdoll kitten, meaning that there was once again a feline double act on the show.

Dogs for everyone

The traditional rivalry between cats and dogs seems to have been largely absent on *Blue Peter*. A good-natured dog makes a huge difference. Bonnie, who took over from her mum Goldie in 1986, had the perfect temperament. She belonged more to the programme as a whole than to any individual. It was the same with Mabel and Lucy who followed her, and their collective staying power only increased their popularity.

Mabel was the programme's first rescue dog. She came from the RSPCA, and her unusual, quirky look and her uncanny ability to know when she was on camera quickly endeared her to children. She had been badly traumatized as a puppy, so there were a few problems in the early days. She was fond of darting in for a nip at the ankles of anyone dancing, marching or playing sport – all regular events in the *Blue Peter* studio. She hated balloons with a vengeance, which cast a dampener on the dogs' birthdays. The highlight of these is still the cake made from dog food. This may look delicious, but it smells atrocious. We always decorated the seating area with a display of viewers' homemade cards. Presenter Caron Keating once suggested to Biddy that the programme might celebrate the presenters' birthdays too: 'She said, "Darling, you'll never get as many cards as the dog!" She was absolutely right!'

Bonnie was retired in February 1999. On her last programme, we presented her with a specially made collar in which a gold badge had been embedded. It was the only time a pet was awarded a *Blue Peter* badge. Simon Thomas, who had just joined the team, was given the job of taking on Bonnie's successor, Lucy. It wasn't good casting. Simon liked dogs, but Lucy lived with Leonie Pocock, her handler, and only had eyes for her and her ever-ready supply of dog treats. The programme made a fundamental mistake in choosing a dog that had already outgrown the formative puppy stage, which was always hugely popular with the audience. Simon grew bored and frustrated trying to establish a relationship, and in the end, the pairing was quietly abandoned. Further disappointment followed when we discovered that Lucy was unable to have puppies herself.

It was a very different story with Matt Baker. Almost from the word go, in mid-1999, he angled to have a dog of his own. Matt was the first truly 'doggy' presenter since Simon Groom, and like Simon had grown up on a farm, with plenty of animals around. Despite reservations that three dogs was one too many, no one could resist his sheer enthusiasm and Meg, another Border Collie, arrived on 19 February 2001.

Like Shep, Meg was a one-man dog. While Matt was rehearsing, she would get bored and restless. She would hurtle round and round the seat unit, attempting to round it up. She would whine and ruin Matt's concentration. Once, in the middle of a recording, she suddenly leapt up and seized one of the cats by the throat. Only Matt's double-quick intervention prevented what could have been a disaster. Caring for Meg added considerably to his already stressful workload. Matt felt that '...looking back, Meg was completely the wrong breed to have on the show. I should have gone for something quirky – big, floppy and iconically different. Meg was so intelligent and it was hard for her. I felt guilty and bad, but I had to make it work. It was always a compromise and never easy.'

We protected Matt from repeated complaints by some of the crew that Meg was unmanageable and dangerous. This was unfair. She was simply responding to people in the studio who played with her when it suited them. It wasn't her fault that she didn't know when to stop. The Matt and Meg relationship made it all worthwhile. When she had puppies, Matt made the films himself, his eyes shining with love and pride.

In the *Blue Peter* garden at Television Centre, the statue of Petra, the 'dog for everyone', has pride of place. The statue is a tribute to the first of a dynasty of much-loved pets, and of a simple idea that helped to define the entire programme.

1 The studio prepares to 'go live' and celebrate Petra's 14th birthday in November 1976.

2 Petra was the first 'dog for everyone'. She appeared on over 1,100 programmes and formed a specially close bond with Peter Purves.

Special Assignment FUR AND FEATHER

3 The most recent *Blue Peter* doggy double act – woe betide anyone who came between One Matt and his Meg!

35

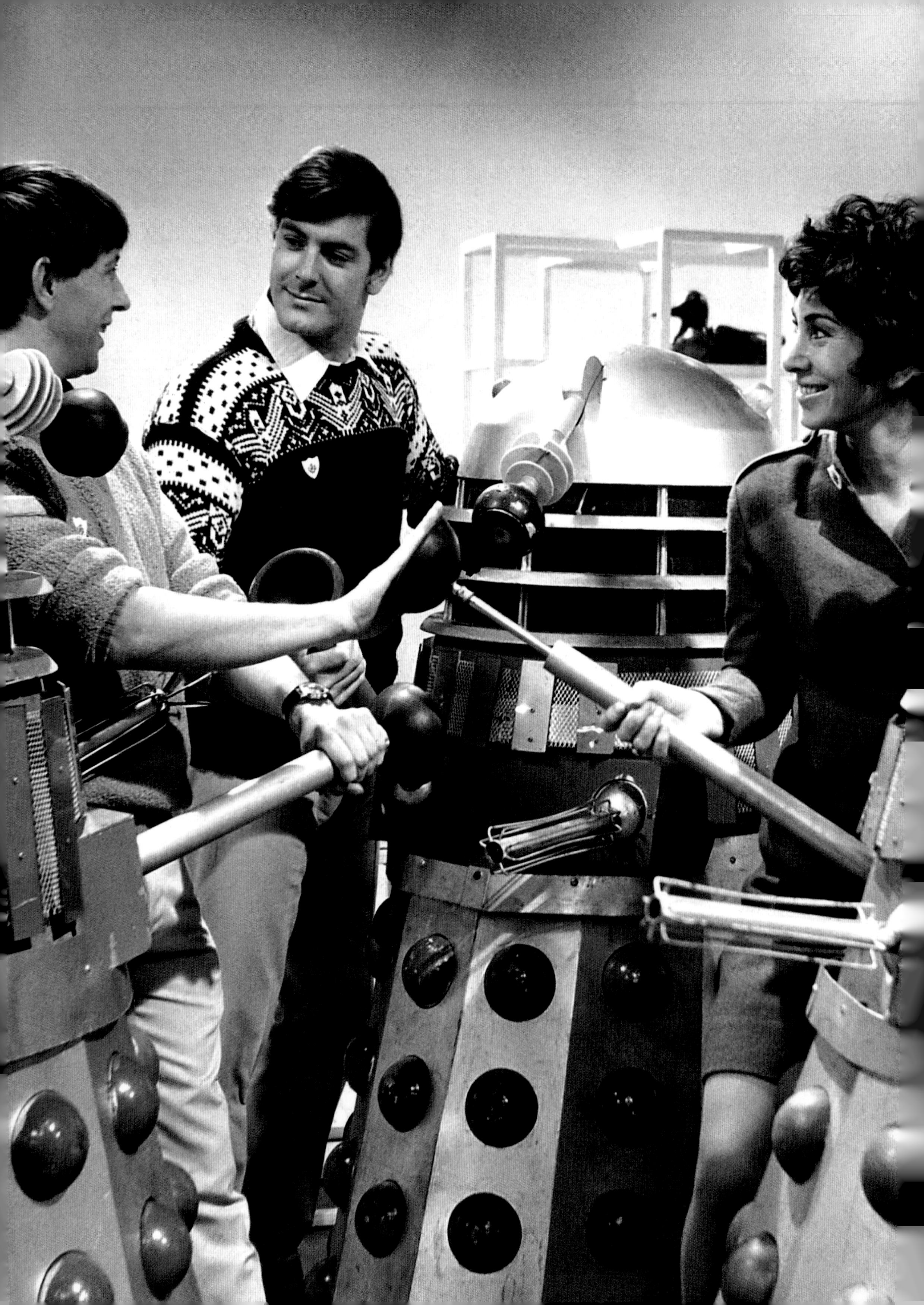

2 Now for Something Completely Different

1962–1969

Biddy Baxter was the last name on the *Blue Peter* credits for over 26 years. She was at least as famous as most of the presenters, and in many cases more so. Children found her unusual and alliterative name appealing. She was actually christened Joan. Biddy was a family nickname that derived from her own gobbledegook references to her infant self. The nickname might not have stuck except for the fact that there were several other Joans in the Beginners' class at the Wyggeston Grammar School for Girls and having one fewer made life easier for the teacher, Miss Lott.

Biddy joined the BBC in 1955, first as a trainee studio manager in radio before eventually becoming a producer in schools' programmes: 'I spent a lot of time going into primary schools, sitting at the back of the class. The first time I did, they were listening to a story I'd dramatized and I was absolutely distraught because they were fidgeting, picking their noses and playing with each other's hair. I thought, "This is utter disaster, I've failed and I'm not reaching the audience." When it ended, the teacher asked them questions and they had absolutely total recall. It taught me a very valuable lesson: that children are capable of doing many things at once.'

Biddy worked her way steadily through the BBC system, making the leap from radio to children's television. When the job of Producer on *Blue Peter* was advertised, to her 'shock, horror and amazement' she was appointed. Before she could take up her new position, she was committed to schools' programmes for a three further months. Owen Reed, the Head of Children's Programmes, suggested that Edward Barnes, one of the unsuccessful applicants who was already a member of the production team, could 'act up' until then. 'Biddy said, "You've got to be joking. He'll kill me when I get there!"', remembers Edward Barnes. 'She's about right too! We had a pretty dusty start.'

Instead, an experienced producer called Leonard Chase was appointed to smooth the transition until, at the end of October 1962, Biddy was finally free to start. 'I joined on a Wednesday and the next programme was the following Monday, so it was eyes down and think of what to put in it.'

John Noakes, Peter Purves and Valerie Singleton – the 'dream team' who first came together in 1967 when Purves joined the programme. Previously he had been best-known for his stint as a companion to Dr Who.

37

After an awkward and mutually suspicious beginning, the Baxter/Barnes partnership blossomed. She had an instinctive grasp of what children wanted; he had the skills to translate these instincts into good television. They learnt from each other and worked out their whole editorial policy in tandem. Biddy sensed that in *Blue Peter* they had '…this marvellous canvas. We wanted to do something that was really going to bring viewers into the programme, to involve them and use their ideas.'

This was a period of crisis for the BBC. It was being beaten at every turn by ITV opposition. Donald Baverstock had been appointed as Assistant Controller of Programmes to try to redress the balance. He went about it with a single-minded ruthlessness that left the television service quaking. It was a bad time for the spotlight to fall on children's programmes. Baverstock was unimpressed with Owen Reed. They were diametrically opposed: a textbook contrast between the new BBC – dynamic, ruthless and forward-thinking – and the old – considered, donnish and discreet.

In January 1963, it was announced that Reed was to be moved sideways to television training while his department was asset-stripped. The drama and variety were hived off to their adult counterparts. What little remained was amalgamated with women's programmes to form a dysfunctional new hybrid, Family Programmes, headed by the steely Doreen Stephens.

Blue Peter was safe, left to its own devices and free from the management spotlight, because it was delivering the goods. But the cynical dismantling of children's programmes left the survivors angry, with something to prove. Edward Barnes said: 'We believed that there was a job to be done, one that needed people with the specialization to do it. I think our venom came out in the programme. We were determined to show them that one day they'd be going on their knees for it. The programme obsessed us. We had this feeling that "We're the greatest!" It didn't endear us to the rest of the department.'

The three-headed monster

Biddy and Edward were joined by Rosemary ('Rose') Gill, who'd originally been brought in as temporary cover when Biddy was forced to undertake lengthy jury service. Rose stayed until 1976. Her enthusiasm, common sense and instant recall of her own happy childhood were the perfect qualifications for the new *Blue Peter* that had started to emerge. The 'triumvirate', as they were known, was a formidable alliance. Christopher Trace used to say '…it was like a three-headed monster coming at you'.

Together, Biddy, Edward and Rose provided the creative motor that powered *Blue Peter* through the innovations and expansions of the next few years. Long before the word 'interactive' was routinely bandied about, they set about doing all they could to transform a one-way medium into something that children could invest in and care about. As Biddy wrote in the *Radio Times* in September 1964: 'We often have letters from young viewers asking, "Can I join the *Blue Peter* Club?" The answer is that, if you watch *Blue Peter*, you are already a member.'

1 Biddy Baxter ran the programme from the apparent chaos of her desk, writing or rather rewriting most of the studio scripts. One producer recalls getting a script returned with only one word remaining from his original – 'the'!

2 Margaret Parnell, 'makes' genius, pictured during the programme's 35th anniversary with the household junk that she transformed into a litter of Bonnie's puppies.

Margaret's makes

Makes had featured since the earliest days of the programme, but they didn't really achieve their full prominence and distinctive *Blue Peter* quality until a Portsmouth-based housewife called Margaret Parnell wrote to Valerie Singleton in 1963: 'I had this idea for dolls' hats, made out of crêpe paper. I got them together with all the stages. And much to my surprise, she wrote back, said they liked them and were going to use them, and had I got any more ideas?'

She certainly had. One was how to turn your teddy into a guardsman, and on 10 August 1963, just before demonstrating this ingenious idea, Val wrote again: 'We all feel you've contributed so splendidly to the programme. Have you ever taught art work?' The answer was no. Margaret had no formal training but '…during the war, when you couldn't buy them, I used to make toys for my little sister. That started it off really.'

There were over 700 Margaret Parnell makes in all, many of which were revamped and repeated for years afterwards. Margaret was a genius, working away in the shed at the bottom of her garden, transforming household junk and old packaging into room settings for dolls and action figures, toys, jewellery, presents and games. There were makes for every season and special occasions like Mothering Sunday. The famous Advent Crown was Margaret's interpretation of a magical Christmas tradition remembered by Edward Barnes' wife, Dorothy, from her days in Vienna after the Second World War. It was Margaret who thought of using wire coat hangers as the basis for what became one of *Blue Peter*'s most enduring and charming makes. Margaret was also the brains behind the most successful make of them all, Thunderbirds' Tracy Island.

To avoid forbidden commercial references, all trade names on the packaging used had to be carefully concealed. The programme developed its own terms of reference for the materials. Smarties were 'chocolate button sweets', Sellotape was 'sticky tape', Biros were 'ballpoint pens', Plasticine was 'modelling clay' and of course Fablon was, most famously of all, 'sticky-backed plastic'.

Others have tried to follow in Margaret's footsteps, but the only one who has done so with any continuing success has been Gillian Shearing. Gill spent years working in the Correspondence Unit, dealing with viewers' letters. She started helping with 'cooks' and makes, and when Margaret retired, she began to provide almost all of them. Like Margaret, Gill has a particular ability to create a classy homemade version of an expensive high-street hit. Some of the most successful have included a wrestling ring for WWE (World Wrestling Entertainment) action figures, a Simpsons' living room, a TARDIS play space, a Black Pearl ship from the *Pirates of the Caribbean* films and a stadium for Beyblades spinning tops.

From September 2007, there was a different approach to makes and cooks, which now featured less frequently. They were split into different segments throughout a show and treated as a challenge for presenters and studio guests. Viewers who wanted to have a go themselves were pointed towards the details on the programme's website.

BLUE PETER 50th Anniversary

1

2 Noakes used his regular cooking slots as a chance to introduce more of his trademark slapstick and gently subversive humour.

1 The 'poison tasters' Lesley Judd and Peter Purves step into the culinary firing line to try another John Noakes creation.

3 The Advent Crown, one of the most famous makes of all, appeared on the programme every Christmas from 1964 to 2006.

4 In February 1986, rodent superstar Roland Rat hindered rather than helped Peter Duncan to cook one of the programme's favourite recurring recipes – Winter Warmer soup.

Poison tasters

In the 1960s the cooking was generally simple and sweet-toothed. Some of the concoctions, such as Fruit Cream Crunch (crushed-up ginger biscuits, cream, canned mandarin oranges and silver balls), would certainly cause complaints from today's fresh food/healthy eating lobby. By the 1980s, savoury was as important as sweet. Certain recipes became recurring favourites, for instance the Winter Warmer Soup, Sticky Witches (toffee apples with witches' hats and cloaks), Saucy Leeks, Crispy Mince Pies (made with bread rather than pastry) and the yearly variation on the pancake theme.

While the makes were shared out, the cooking was almost always the preserve of the male presenters. Biddy felt that it was '…marvellously encouraging for boys to see one of our boys doing the cooking. After all, some of the best chefs in the world are men.'

John Noakes turned his cooking into a comedy routine, referring to his co-presenters as his 'poison tasters!': 'I hate onion, cheese and tomato. And most of the cooking I used to do involved onion, cheese and tomato. I remember chopping up an onion and saying, "Oh life would be barren without an onion." I thought, "You lying so-and-so", but that was my sense of humour.'

Peter Duncan, who presented in the 1980s, was a happy but slapdash cook, who once had to apologize after suggesting that viewers might like to chop up a raw egg.

After royal butler Paul Burrell paid a visit to the *Blue Peter* studio in 1981, he wrote to thank Biddy for her gift of a *Blue Peter Book of Gorgeous Grub*, promising that it would have '…pride of place on our bookshelves. I wonder if *they* would appreciate Peter's kipper and egg flan?'

In 2007 *Blue Peter* held an extremely popular talent search called Can You Cook It? to find a viewer to become the show's cook for the rest of the year. Perhaps not surprisingly, considering the years of careful role reversal, the three finalists were all boys. Winner Jake Sawyers was so good that he was kept on into the following year.

The makes and cooks have always been hugely popular. They are relatively cheap, but that is not the principal benefit of featuring them. They are great pocket-money savers and anti-commercials. The Managing Director of the company that produced Action Man once wrote to the Director General of the BBC, complaining that *Blue Peter*'s home-made accessories for Action Man were harming his business! For the production team, they help with the light and shade of a programme, providing the quieter, more intimate moments in between big films and studio spectaculars. For presenters adept at the technique required, they are a chance to relax a little and invest their personality in the process. Latter 1980s presenter Caron Keating, who had loved them herself as a child, credited Biddy Baxter for realizing that '…at some point, even the most ham-fisted child would want to make a Christmas card or whatever else, before somebody said to them, "You're no good at drawing" or "You shouldn't be doing that".'

The audience's programme

The introduction of pets, badges, appeals and fabulous competitions, such as the chance to design the Christmas stamps, were the unfolding proof that *Blue Peter* was the audience's programme. It began to develop its own language and terminology. Wherever possible, *Blue Peter* was used as an adjective. Edward Barnes pinched from *Monitor*, the BBC's flagship arts programme, the idea of referring to *Blue Peter* 'cameras'. Enduring catchphrases, for example, 'And now for something completely different' and 'Here's one I made earlier', began to appear, although the former was dropped after its comic appropriation by *Monty Python*.

The distinctive logo used by Granada TV on everything from the idents at the start of their programmes to their letterheads inspired Edward to suggest something similar for *Blue Peter*. The ship logo, designed by Tony Hart, followed and was plastered everywhere, from the set to the stationery. Biddy was keen to get away from '…the standard carpet, chairs and desk set. In those days, sets were all like little rooms and we wanted something much sharper, much cleaner, much more open and bright. Somewhere that was magical, where we could have adventures and bring all kinds of extraordinary things into the studio.'

Designer Darrol Blake came up with the concept of a painted floor and backcloth or 'cyc', which, when combined with high-key lighting, would become a 'peak' white space, giving the illusion of infinity and making the most of whatever studio space was available. It was revolutionary and distinctive.

Biddy engaged in endless battles with the planning department over studio allocation. The programme was often forced into weeks of pre-recording shows. 'Live' injected adrenaline into the performances and there were no re-takes – a bonus when editing was cumbersome and time-consuming. Biddy's insistence, highly unusual at the time, on keeping all the programmes and films meant that increasingly the programme could make use of its own archive. Some of the best-remembered items were repeated many times.

Out of the studio and on location, Edward negotiated to swap the weekly allocation of one day of 35-mm filming (mute) for two days of 16-mm filming with sound. The film department thought this heretical, as 16-mm was a lower-quality format, but Edward knew that it would give him the flexibility to make proper action films, previously sorely missing from the programme. The action films proved very important, although film stock was extremely expensive. Each roll lasted only about ten minutes and the ratio was set strictly at five rolls per film. Woe betide any director who used more. This meant that the films had to be tightly planned and directed.

Away from the production office, Edward's wife Dorothy Smith was also hugely influential. Their three children adored their mongrel dog, Duff, inspiring Dorothy to suggest that *Blue Peter* might have 'a dog for everyone'. It was Dorothy who came up with the idea of a badge too. In 1979, when the programme wanted to raise money quickly for the

2 The fight to get access to big studios brought pressure on production to fill them with items like this giant patriotic balloon made for Expo '70.

NOW FOR SOMETHING COMPLETELY DIFFERENT

1 A rare 'behind-the-scenes' shot of The Hollies on *Blue Peter* in February 1964. Pop groups appeared regularly on the programme in the early to mid-60s until the success of *Top of the Pops* led to them being phased out.

3 High jinks in the studio as John Noakes tries to lose weight Victorian-style, following a sauna with a freezing shower.

1 'Peter the Great', 1974. Broomfield comments: 'To get the animation and drama of the story, you had to exaggerate features. A big nose was always useful!'

2 Dorothy Smith, *Blue Peter*'s historian from 1964 to 1990. She also wrote scripts for the *Special Assignments* and *Treasure Houses* spin-offs, and made key contributions to the development of the programme.

3 Val as Jane Austen in a 1973 film about the story of Bath, one of hundreds of scripts written by Dorothy Smith. She recalls: 'It was very much us [presenters] and them [production team]. I seem to remember being told a lot of times, "you'd be nothing without us."'

Cambodian Appeal, she suggested running bring-and-buy sales. All these notions had to be developed and put into practice by the production team, but they owe their genesis to her and they are part of her lasting legacy.

Bringing stories to life

As well as these strategic ideas, Dorothy became the programme's historian, researching and writing hundreds of items and films between 1964 and 1990. For several generations of children, myself included, it was her storytelling technique that inspired a love of history. As well as the parade of inspirational heroes and heroines, geniuses, inventors and monarchs, she scored a bull's-eye with material you'd never come across in school lessons. 'The Great Stink', 'The Frost Fair' and 'Dead As The Dodo' were just a few of their inviting titles.

Much of Dorothy's work came in the form of illustrated picture stories, sometimes narrated by actors ('John Nettleton tells the story'), sometimes by presenters. Biddy's experience in radio meant that the sound effects were excellent. She was especially fond of 'polar wind', a recording of a howling gale that never failed to add atmosphere. The actual pictures or 'captions' were the work of Robert ('Bob') Broomfield, who drew and painted literally thousands of them. They became a part of the landscape of *Blue Peter*, utterly distinctive in the best traditions of all famous children's illustrators. The best of them can still be seen in the *Blue Peter* annuals.

When Lewis Bronze became Editor in 1988, his boss Anna Home gave him one clear instruction – drop the picture stories. When I joined the programme ten years later, they returned, albeit less frequently than

4 'The Little Eagle', 1973. Broomfield recalls: 'I especially liked drawing the 18th and early 19th century. Edward Barnes said it was because I was *from* that period!'

in their heyday. Their advantage was that they enabled you to tell spectacularly strange but true stories, such as the one about Lord Minimus, the dwarf at the court of Charles I, which would have been impossible to dramatize. Bob eventually retired in 2006, when we screened the last of his stories, 'The Mechanical Turk'.

Dorothy and Bob were just two of a gradually expanding extended family of *Blue Peter* experts, many of whom made contributions for decades. There were animal experts such as George Cansdale, Mollie Badham and naturalist Grahame Dangerfield. Artist William Timyn drew the Bengo and Bleep and Booster stories, while Michael Bond, who had often worked on the studio crew when he was still a BBC cameraman, wrote a long series of Paddington meets *Blue Peter* stories for the *Blue Peter* annuals. Then there was the Puppy Walking Manager Derek Freeman, the reassuring presence over three generations of guide-dog training. And the redoubtable Peggy Spencer bossed the presenters into trying a new dance or two; children, so used to being bossed about themselves, just loved seeing the tables turned on the adults.

Flushed with their burgeoning success, Biddy, Edward and Rose suggested that they could transform *Blue Peter* into a daily offering. Donald Baverstock turned them down, telling Edward: 'It's a good programme, boy, but you don't want it every bloody night of the week.'

It was the Head of Family Programmes, Doreen Stephens, who suggested going twice weekly. On 28 September 1964, viewers were given the good news. The extra programme meant that Edward and Rose were promoted to producers, while Biddy became Editor. 'It was absolutely crucifyingly hard work…' is her recollection of that period.

For the time being, they continued with two presenters, although earlier that year they had come close to changing the line-up. Sandra ('Sandy') Michaels, with whom Edward had worked when she was a child actress, was tried out for two weeks in April, while Valerie Singleton was on holiday. 'She was very good…', according to Edward. 'I think we might well have been toying with replacing Val at that point, but Sandy decided it wasn't something she wanted to do, so we soldiered on and now I'm glad that we did.'

Shortly after the successful start of the twice-weekly schedule came some sad news. On 31 December 1964, Gillian Farnsworth, who worked on the programme, had paid a visit to the programme's founding father, John Hunter Blair. Despite his heart condition, he seemed quite contented and she left him watching *Blue Peter*. He died a few hours later. Jack Rich, Family Programmes' Organizer, wrote to his relatives: 'We feel he must have had some satisfaction in knowing that this programme, which he devised and initiated, has continued to maintain its popularity over the years.'

Blue Peter was buoyant and now the confident 'triumvirate' set its sights on older children. On 21 February 1967, Biddy sent Doreen Stephens a proposal for a *Blue Peter* spin-off, to be made by her team, and shown in an early evening slot: 'We would like an opportunity to extend the range of material, to provide more grit than we are able to include and cash in on the 12-plus audience.' Part of the proposal aimed to make more of John Noakes, who had been on the programme for just over a year: 'We have discovered he has a far greater potential for "off-beat", "zany enquiry" stories than can be exploited on *Blue Peter*.'

A dash of Carnaby Street

BBC1 liked the idea and commissioned a pilot programme. Rosemary Gill came up with a name, *John Bull*, and as well as Noakes on location, there were to be two studio presenters, Terence Edmond and Britt Allcroft. Young, blonde and with a typical 'swinging Sixties' look, Britt was actually working on the *Blue Peter* production team. Unfortunately, the whole pilot was a disaster. The tape still exists, an uncomfortable attempt to present an aged-up *Blue Peter* with a dash of Carnaby Street zeitgeist. Years after her stint on *Blue Peter* and her what-might-have-been brush with fame, Britt Allcroft enterprisingly bought the video rights to the *Thomas The Tank Engine* stories. She is now a multi-millionaire.

Work on the pilot meant that the request for a special Christmas Day *Blue Peter* had to be turned down. As Ursula Eason explained to the Controller of BBC1: 'We feel it is more realistic to express unwillingness. A morning edition would have to be recorded with all the consequent pretence that it's Christmas Day, when in fact it is not. Last year we recorded the programme for Boxing Day and we did not feel that it was a satisfactory edition.'

One satisfying development in 1967 was the relaunching of a proper Children's Department. Doreen Stephens left and the new Head, Monica Sims, was a great ally. Once Peter Purves joined as Christopher

Noakes and Purves aboard the 60532 *Blue Peter*. Named *Blue Peter* after the famous Derby winner of 1939, this Class A-2 Pacific Locomotive went into service in 1948. Saved from being scrapped in 1968, the loco's progress has been followed by the programme ever since. The renaming ceremony of the fully restored 532 took place in November 1970, when huge crowds threatened to engulf the presenters.

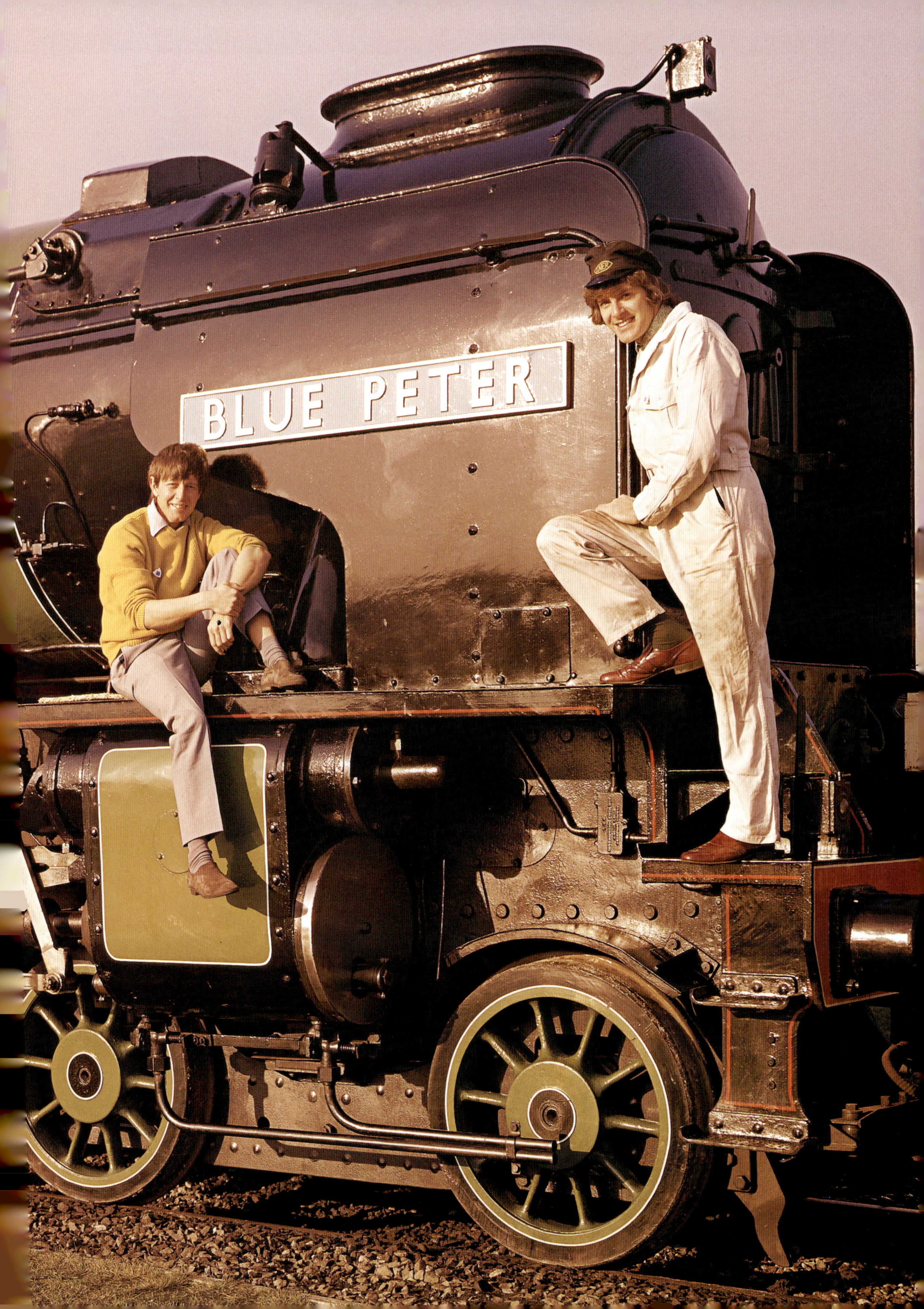
BLUE PETER

BLUE PETER 50th Anniversary

NOW FOR SOMETHING COMPLETELY DIFFERENT

1 July 1969 – Stephen Scott accompanies his baby brother, the pets and the presenters as they all drive out of the studio at the end of the last show of the season. Note the lack of safety belts!

2 Because of health and safety, an unusual picnic like this, part of the 1969 film about Daniel's day at the zoo, would be unthinkable today.

Trace's replacement, the 'dream team' of Peter, Valerie Singleton and John Noakes was in place. This trio became unquestionably the most famous presenting team in the show's history. The main worry was how long ITV would let *Blue Peter* continue unchallenged. Meanwhile, there was no let-up in the programme's energy.

Baby Daniel

One of Biddy's bravest ideas was made possible when Sylvia Scott, who looked after Jason the cat, discovered she was expecting her eighth child. The growth and development of baby Daniel Scott became a regular feature from 30 September 1968. The items had to be pre-recorded because of the strict rules governing the use of small children and infants in the studio but they appealed to Biddy because, 'It had never, ever been done before. My thinking was that even if you're three, you can be superior to a baby. But I thought it would be an absolute switch-off for an eight-year-old boy if they saw Valerie Singleton holding a baby, so the idea was that John and Peter would look after Daniel.'

This made great television, with John, in particular, using every opportunity to extract maximum comedy from his role as minder to his innocent infant co-star. Peter Purves, on the other hand, was less happy: 'My heart sank. I didn't like doing it and it didn't interest me.'

The programme 'retired' Daniel after his second birthday in the summer of 1970, so that he could grow up unaware of and unaffected by his juvenile television stardom. He made one brief return to the world of *Blue Peter* in 1993 during the 35th-anniversary documentary, talking about his troubled youth following his parents' divorce. He admitted dabbling with drugs and crime, which of course the press were only too delighted to regurgitate under lurid headlines.

In the same year that Daniel arrived, ITV finally launched their answer to *Blue Peter*. Thames Television's *Magpie* started once a week, but was soon given an extra edition. The name was apt. Many thought it was an almost ludicrously blatant carbon copy of its rival: three presenters, badges, makes, appeals and summer expeditions. About the only thing lacking was the pets. On 7 August 1969, Monica Sims, the Head of Children's Programmes, wrote to *The Times*: 'We much appreciate the sincere flattery of Thames Television for making their own *Magpie* such an exact imitation of *Blue Peter* and now look forward to seeing their new ideas for children's programmes.'

Unfairly or not, the programmes tended to be divided on the lines of *Magpie* – cool and working class; *Blue Peter* – square and middle class. As *Magpie* presenter, Tommy Boyd, remarked provocatively in a Radio 4 documentary about the competition between the two programmes: '*Magpie* viewers tended to watch it down the youth club with a can of Coke, whereas *Blue Peter* viewers tended to watch it in the parlour with their Boy Scout and Girl Guide uniforms on before they went off to the hall.'

The fierce rivalry between the programmes continued until *Magpie* was finally cancelled in the summer of 1980.

3 1968 – John and Peter in Norway chopping down the Christmas tree for Trafalgar Square. Says Noakes: 'We worked together so well and made some lovely films.'

4 John Noakes gets a lift from a friendly elephant during the 1969 summer expedition to Ceylon (now Sri Lanka).

1 The infamous Lulu the Elephant episode was directed by Paul Stone, later Head of BBC Children's Drama. Lulu herself made a return appearance the following March. This time there were no accidents.

2 Val cools off during the 1968 Safari to Morocco. During this trip, Val had a couple of narrow escapes, the first when she fell from a camel, the second when she had a close encounter with a deadly scorpion.

Get off me foot!

Even though it now looks politically incorrect, any live magazine programme would have killed for the moment that happened in the studio on 2 July 1969. Yet again, programme planning had forced the team to pre-record the day before transmission. This was the last show of the season, and as a trailer for that year's summer expedition, a baby elephant called Lulu had been brought to the Lime Grove studio from Chessington Zoo. What happened during the recording of that show has become legendary.

Biddy, concerned that the stick used to keep the elephant under control might look cruel, asked the keeper not to use it on transmission. The resulting chaos, with copious urination and defecation, has been shown thousands of times since. As ever, John Noakes hammed it up, taking the chance to cry out 'Get off me foot!' – actually the catchphrase of a comedian called Frank Randle, who had made him laugh when he visited Blackpool Pier with his dad.

Peter Purves still swears that it was live. The script, schedule and tape, with its clearly marked countdown clock, confirm that it was not, but you can understand his conviction. So many people, especially then, would have insisted on a retake. Some of those who worked on that edition say that this was discussed. But how ironic that the Rolls Royce of all live television mishaps was actually entirely on tape.

As the 1960s drew to a close, *Blue Peter* had been totally transformed. It had won its first prestigious SFTA (later BAFTA) award – industry recognition that Biddy, Edward and Rose were now in charge of the BBC's flagship children's programme.

Presenter Profile

VALERIE SINGLETON

JOINED: 3 September 1962

LEFT: 3 July 1972 (last regular appearance)

MEMORABLE MOMENTS: Taking a lion for a walk; dressing up to re-enact the lives of famous people such as Grace Darling and Mary, Queen of Scots; Royal Safari to Kenya; *Blue Peter Special Assignments* (including meeting the Pope); trips to Norway, Singapore, Jamaica, Morocco, Ceylon, Mexico and Iceland

It was often said that if a bomb dropped on the *Blue Peter* studio, Valerie Singleton would simply have stepped out of the rubble and carried on presenting. If Noakes was the quintessential male presenter, Val was without doubt his female counterpart. Her serious approach, her superb skill with the makes and her beautifully modulated voice were the perfect contrast to his anarchy. Viewers trusted that Val was in complete control, which meant that they could relax.

Valerie Singleton was the presenter who never formally left. From 1972 to 1975 she still made appearances in the studio and on film and her last series of *Special Assignments* wasn't until 1981.

Val had trained at RADA and, like so many presenters, had originally intended to spend her career acting. Then, in February 1962, during a strike of the actors' union Equity, she joined the BBC as an announcer: 'A friend suggested I go for it and I thought, "Why not?" I turned up at the audition and I was supposed to have prepared a script using the *Radio Times*. But I hadn't got hold of a copy the night before, so I just ad-libbed from one open in front of me. I think I got it because I didn't really care if I did or not!'

After work one day, she bumped into Christopher Trace in the BBC Club: 'He said, "We're looking for a new presenter." I auditioned and got a very nice letter saying they thought I was marvellous "…but you already have this job and we feel we'd like to give Anita a chance." It was a very elegant way of saying she'd done better than me!'

But when Anita West left after only four months, temporary Producer Leonard Chase offered Val the job. For the next two years, she was able to combine it with her continuity work, but when the twice-weekly schedule began, she had to choose: 'My parents were very worried – "You're giving up this prestigious job for a programme which nobody has ever heard of."'

Blue Peter made Val a household name. For her, one of the greatest satisfactions of the job was its opportunity to 'access all areas': 'I loved stepping over the rope that you get in stately homes and museums. I could sit at the Empress Elizabeth's desk in Vienna, I could handle the box that Florence Nightingale used at Scutari. One of my greatest memories was this stuffed horse called Ronald, which had led the Charge of the Light Brigade. I was stroking his nose in the studio and it was like stretching your hand out across history.'

Val didn't just sit in the studio telling stories. She bathed chimpanzees, flew a plane, excelled at water-skiing, fell off horses and a camel and was nearly killed in a powerboat accident on the Thames: 'They did ask me to stand strapped to the top of a biplane, but I said no to that.'

Special assignments

After the summer of 1972, Val moved on to presenting the spin-off series that had been specially created for her by Edward Barnes, *Blue Peter Special Assignments* and *Val Meets the VIPS*. For the next two and a half years, alongside these and her new role on the BBC's *Nationwide*, Val also continued to present occasional *Blue Peter* studios and films. By 1976, she had appeared in four seasons of *Special Assignments* and met Edward Barnes for lunch to discuss the next. 'But *Nationwide* had first call on Val and they really didn't want

1 Val with the *Blue Peter* stamp album. Items about newly issued stamps were a regular feature from the 1960s to early 2000s. Viewers designed the Christmas stamps in 1966 and 1981 and the first green stamps in 1992.

2 Edward Barnes directing Val during the shooting of the very first *Blue Peter Special Assignment* in Rome in the summer of 1972.

to know about the *Special Assignment* schedules which was costing me money as well as grief, because we were having to pay to fly her to and from London for their convenience, on a very tight budget – £6,000 per programme. Not unnaturally, the regular presenters also resented Val for getting all the "plums".'

Moving on

On 28 April, Edward wrote to Val: 'The general consensus is that [the next series] should be presented by someone immediately identifiable with the current programme. Also fairer to the current presenters to give them a chance at longer films which will be seen at the weekends. We honestly think you have now succeeded in throwing off the *Blue Peter* image and that you are very much and very firmly a *Nationwide* person. In view of this, we think it would be artificial for us to continue your association with *Blue Peter*.'

Val replied on 28 May 1976: 'Naturally, I am sad that our long association is to end, more especially as it was only a matter of a few weeks between our discussing plans for the future over lunch and the arrival of your letter. My commitments had not changed in any way in that time.'

Val remains convinced that Edward's decision was actually triggered by a minor dispute during the lunch involving what she was being paid for the use of her photograph in the annual. A few weeks earlier, there had also been a row over the fee demanded by Val's agent after she had taken part, at short notice, in Jason's obituary. Even if all this acrimony didn't prompt Barnes' decision, it can't have helped. It was time for a parting of the ways.

But it is a tribute to the colossal affection and regard in which she was held that Val never really left *Blue Peter*. There was no formal farewell celebration, and she continued to be invited back whenever there was a relevant excuse. In 1994, she was back to show the OBE she had just been awarded. The programme matched it with its own highest honour, a gold *Blue Peter* badge – she was the first presenter to receive one. She popped back to help with celebrity bring-and-buy sales, to show Simon Thomas how to make the Advent Crown and to give eyewitness reports on the work being done for *Blue Peter* appeal projects overseas.

In 2003, she played the eponymous Miss Singleton, the lady boss of an unlikely detective agency, in two series of the mini adventure serial *The Quest*. Miss Singleton was only ever seen obliquely, rather like Charlie in *Charlie's Angels*. To many parents, however, the voice was unmistakable and *The Quest*, shown in weekly instalments, made Val well known to yet another generation of viewers.

Presenter Profile VALERIE SINGLETON

3 Enjoying a rickshaw ride during the 1969 summer expedition to Ceylon (now Sri Lanka). Val reported from all over the world during her *Blue Peter* years.

Presenter Profile
JOHN NOAKES

1 John Noakes was the longest-serving presenter of all. He was 31 when he joined and 44 when he left, nearly 13 years later.

JOINED: 30 December 1965

LEFT: 26 June 1978

MEMORABLE MOMENTS: Climbing HMS *Ganges*' mast; setting a record for the highest civilian free-fall parachute jump; taking part in the St Moritz Run (bobsleigh) and the Cresta Run (toboggan); reporting from an erupting Mount Etna; climbing up Nelson's Column in Trafalgar Square; looking after the dogs Patch and Shep; trips to many exotic destinations including Jamaica, Morocco, Ceylon, Thailand, Turkey and Brazil

In 2005 a dinner was held with Edward Barnes and all five *Blue Peter* Editors. During the evening, talk turned inevitably to presenters past and present. The unanimous feeling around the table was that the greatest and most successful presenter of all time was John Noakes.

If it's true, as he later claimed, that his 12½-year marathon run was just a performance, then it was one of the greatest sustained feats in television acting ever. His bravery, his subversive sense of humour and his celebrated relationship with his four-legged friends, Patch and Shep, proved an irresistible combination. By the end of his extraordinarily long stint, Noakes had become *Blue Peter*'s superstar.

It all started in 1965 with the search for someone to join Christopher Trace and Valerie Singleton and share the workload. Biddy Baxter, Leicester-born, often returned to her home ground at weekends, where she frequently found items for the programme in the pages of the *Leicester Mercury*. She spotted a photograph of a young Noakes, appearing locally in the play *Hobson's Choice*. 'I did the audition and I was terrible, but I got the job anyhow!' John commented later.

On 9 December 1965, Doreen Stephens, Head of Family Programmes, asked BBC1 to authorize an increase of £50 per show to fund the third presenter. She explained that the programme had found '…a very promising man, John Noakes. He is young, attractive and unaffected, and a complete contrast to Christopher Trace.'

Noakes's introduction was deliberately low key. Biddy had warned her boss: 'The introduction of an additional personality will have to be done slowly and with tremendous subtlety if he is not to be resented as an intruder. I feel it would be dangerous to bring him in before Christmas, as it is a psychologically bad time to increase the family circle, but I want to start edging the new face in directly afterwards.'

It was just as well. Noakes had a distinctly rocky start: 'This glass eye, the camera, stripped me naked. I actually shook with fear, the voice tremoring as I said the words. The first few months were quite terrifying. I went through murder. I even went to a hypnotist and a faith healer to try to get me out of it.'

Daredevil Noakes

Noakes was nearly dropped, but in the event, although he was left out of the 1966 summer expedition, he was given another chance. Now he '…started to develop this idiot, who is not really the real John Noakes. I'd got rid of my Yorkshire accent at drama school. I brought it back and used it as part of a character. And being an actor, if I was in a racing car, I was the racing driver. If I was jumping out of an aeroplane, I was one of the Red Devils.'

He played his mistakes for laughs, and the fluffs and fumbles became part of the entertainment. Noakes would deliberately sabotage his own cooking, burning his fingers or dropping things. As well as acting the clown, he

Presenter Profile JOHN NOAKES

2 This classic 1977 film was not the first time that *Blue Peter* had sent Noakes to climb Nelson's column, but this second death-defying encounter totally eclipsed the 1968 version.

3 John had extraordinary stamina, one of the essential requirements for any successful *Blue Peter* presenter. Biddy's policy of 'No show – no dough' probably helped.

defined the role of the action presenter. He seemed utterly fearless, claiming that he had 'no imagination' and was only ever scared twice – once on a tree swing, the other up a circus sway pole.

Health and safety was still evolving in the 1960s. It was a mix of common sense and getting away with it. But repeated claims that presenters were never insured are not borne out by evidence in the BBC's written archives. Take this memo, sent by Biddy Baxter to Programme Contracts on 21 October 1966: 'We are making a film next Friday about steeplejacks, which will involve John Noakes climbing up the outside of a 180-foot [55-metre] tower. Will you please insure him for this?'

One early feat, which can still induce a dry mouth, was Noakes's attempt to climb the towering Royal Navy mast of HMS *Ganges*. It was extremely hazardous and not surprisingly the exercise was discontinued just a few years later. He nearly made it, but, totally exhausted, had to give in and change places with a cadet 127 feet (38.7 metres) from the ground. Biddy felt it '…was almost better than him getting there because it gave encouragement to all the viewers who never quite won the race or came top in the exam. Their hero, John, admitting defeat.'

There were no safety ropes for his famous ascent of Nelson's Column either: 'I could've murdered the assistant cameraman on that. He was new and full of enthusiasm. We started getting lightning and the steeplejack said, "If we get any more, I think we should go down." And if the natives say don't swim in the water, you don't swim in the water. In the meantime, this assistant cameraman was saying, "If you could get over that ledge just one more time." I thought, "If I get close enough to him, I'll push him off!"'

Another narrow escape was the time he came hurtling off a bobsleigh in St Moritz. On his return, his backside and legs were covered in bruises. Biddy, with her instinct for what would appeal to children, asked Noakes to drop his trousers and show the damage: 'I'd only got back the day before and said to the wife, "Have you got some clean knickers?" It was early morning and I put them on in the dark. When I unzipped my trousers live on air, I thought, "I've got my wife's black lace knickers on!"'

Noakes left *Blue Peter* in June 1978: 'Towards the end I was exhausted. The pressure was terrible. I'd done all these things and I don't think any of them really realized how difficult it was. It was a Peter Pan existence, a bit like an overgrown schoolboy's job. But it was a job. That's all it was.'

Presenter Profile
PETER PURVES

JOINED: 16 November 1967

LEFT: 23 March 1978

MEMORABLE MOMENTS: Driving a car through the side of a furniture van; climbing Black Crag in the Lake District; joining the White Helmets motorbike display team; climbing the Forth Road Bridge; looking after Petra; trips ranging from Morocco to Mexico, Thailand to Turkey and Brunei to Brazil

Before he joined the programme, Peter Purves had already had one brush with fame as the companion Steven in *Dr Who*. This role typecast him and afterwards he spent 18 months out of work. By the time he was called for interview by *Blue Peter*, he'd even been dropped by his agent. In his audition he had to cope with a moped that wouldn't work and then '…went to see them again. As I left the office and was about to get the lift, Biddy and Rosemary Gill came after me and said, "We'd like to offer you the job." I thought I would take it for six months and then go back to the serious business of acting!'

1 Peter looked after Petra, *Blue Peter*'s first dog. He later said that announcing her death was one of the hardest things he ever had to do.

He recalls, 'The first time I did the show, when the music started, I have never been so frightened in my life. Absolutely terrified.'

Biddy wanted Peter to assume the role of 'the heavy', as she put it – a straight man to John Noakes; someone who could be relied on to deliver the goods. Peter conquered his nerves and amply fulfilled her ambition. Like most straight men, being pigeonholed in this way did sometimes put his nose out of joint. He was hurt when programmes such as *Junior Points of View* sent him up, showing him as a cardboard cut-out. The criticisms were unkind, but the perception that he was less exciting than his co-presenters persisted.

In June 1970, he was given a rare right of reply when a viewer wrote in, asking why Peter never did anything brave. The response was another chance to see the film in which Peter joined the 'destruction squad', driving a car at speed through the side of a furniture van: 'These guys were lunatics. I was proud that I didn't chicken out of it, but it was total stupidity not to. That was a very scary moment.'

While items such as nature, science, trains and dogs became his particular forte, Peter tackled plenty of action assignments too, from racing and mountaineering to surfing and jousting. Climbing Black Crag in the Lake District with expert Chris Bonnington was '…such an achievement for me, as I was climbing beyond my capabilities', and his ascent of the Forth Road Bridge was equally stomach-churning: 'I was very proud of that. It was a fabulous, beautifully made film.'

Peter sometimes felt misunderstood by production: 'I have got a sense of humour. I would make gags on the set that were dead real. For instance, something would be taking a long time to set up and I'd say, "Oh for goodness sake, *come on!*" It was meant to be laughed at, to break the tension. But upstairs they always thought it was for real. In the gallery they'd be saying, "Oh God, he's off again!" But it was never, ever meant like that.'

There was one occasion when his dry sense of humour backfired: 'The World Cup had gone missing and was found by this dog called Pickles. Pickles was a hero. Some time later we had to announce that Pickles had been killed. He'd been chasing a cat, his lead caught on a gate and it broke his neck. Having said it was very sad, I came out with something like, "Mind you, it serves him right for

Presenter Profile PETER PURVES

2 One of his most spectacular assignments, climbing the Forth Road Bridge in 1975 was proof that Peter didn't always do the dull items.

3 Diving into *Blue Peter* – Purves at Crystal Palace during the shooting of his very first film in which he taught Val and John life-saving skills.

chasing cats." All hell broke loose in the gallery. Biddy was furious. It was a terrible, unforgivable comment.'

During the 1972 summer expedition, Peter suffered a serious accident while making a film about laying railway tracks in a Fijian sugar plantation: 'I dropped a metal sleeper on my ankle. My foot was pouring blood and it was just the most excruciating pain. I was rushed off to have stitches. Luckily, I was wearing one of the first kind of trainers, with a built-up back, and that cushioned it. Otherwise I'd have torn the Achilles' tendon.'

A dispute followed when the production team refused to allow him to continue filming: 'The story as told was that I had to rest up while John and Lesley [Judd] went on to Tonga to make a film about rugby. I actually went with them. There was no reason why I couldn't have been there too, but I had to keep out of shot on crutches. It was dishonest, but in retrospect maybe they were right. You're doing films about holidays, you don't want to upset people. But I was very upset and depressed, and having sat about in Tonga for a week not being able to work, I went and said, "I'm going home on the next plane." The following day I was filming.'

An amicable parting

By the summer of 1977, Peter had been there for nearly a decade: 'I stayed too long. I should have left two years earlier. It was too good a job. I came back from my summer holiday and went in to see Edward Barnes, the Head of Children's Programmes. I said, "I've been thinking it's time I had a change." And he said, "Well, it's funny you should say that, we had been thinking it's about time we should have a change here as well." So that was a nice mutual consensus. It was a very amicable departure.'

Edward created several follow-up projects for Peter, including *Stopwatch* and two series of *Special Assignments*. Many years later, Peter returned to *Blue Peter* to make guest appearances in *The Quest*. He looks back with pride: 'I'm very happy to be associated with one of television's great programmes. The job was just too good not to enjoy. If you rocked the boat, you were cutting off your nose to spite your face. It would be wrong to say we were the closest of friends because we didn't socialize much. But we got on great and we understood each other. We dropped in on a regular basis to the very best bits of other people's lives. It's the best fun you can have. That's why I stayed with it so long.'

Special Assignment

BLUE PETER FLIES THE WORLD

Blue Peter's very first overseas filming trip was in 1964 when Valerie Singleton flew to Lagos in Nigeria. It was a 'freebie' from an airline and it was a big success. Short hops to Boulogne and Basle followed. These were the first steps towards the programme's regular 'window on the world' – the summer expedition.

In July 1965, after seven years of continuous transmission, there was the first-ever summer break. This was the chance to shoot a whole series of overseas films at a time when travelling abroad was the exception rather than the rule. Thanks to a deal with airline Dan-Air, the programme set off to make six films in Norway. These enterprising deals were all against the BBC's rules. Edward Barnes remembers: 'I was asked once by someone high up, "Are you sure you can afford this?" I started to tell him that I was going to do a deal. "I don't want to hear about that. You can afford it. That's all I need to know!"'

In 1966, thanks to a friend in the upper ranks of the RAF, Edward Barnes managed to organize an exciting expedition to Singapore and Borneo. Emboldened by their success, from now on each year the programme began to pitch for extra funds to cover the summer trip. A bit of subtle blackmail always helped. On 10 June 1969, the Head of Children's Programmes, Monica Sims, sent a memo to the man holding the purse strings, Controller of BBC1 Paul Fox: 'I am afraid if they are not able to go [to Ceylon], we shall probably have to content ourselves with three or four seaside stories from Cornwall or perhaps a climb up the Eiffel Tower. I feel this would be very humdrum after the high standard *Blue Peter* have set themselves in previous years. Neither Edward Barnes nor the presenters are particularly anxious to undertake this onerous filming, but we all feel that the hard work and discomfort is worth it for the sake of the audience and *Blue Peter*'s success in the autumn. I hope you will agree.'

He did, but refused the extra expense of shooting in colour. Ironically, when it was repeated two years later, Fox complained to Edward about having to show black and white material on a colour channel!

Trouble in paradise

In the end, the summer expedition became an accepted essential in the budget. At first they were called 'holidays on screen', until increasing sensitivity about the use of public money meant that the term 'holiday' was dropped. In fact, holiday is the last thing they are. The trips involve constant travelling within each location, much of it off screen, in budget conditions and in extremes of temperature. Bugs, bites, sunburn and upset stomachs can't hold up the relentless schedule. For the presenters, tired at the end of a long run, there is little privacy or time off. Inevitably, tensions emerge. For part of the 1970 trip to Mexico, Valerie Singleton and Peter Purves weren't on speaking terms. 'Johnny [Noakes] was the intermediary', remembers Peter, '…Val would say, "John, will you tell Peter?" And I would go back via John. I mean, how childish can you get!'

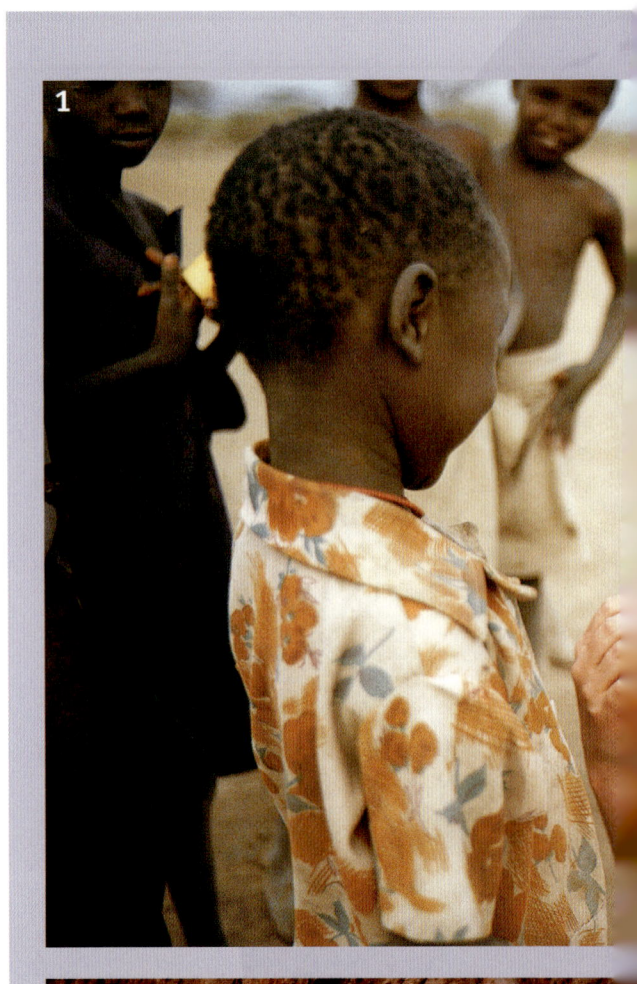

Special Assignment BLUE PETER FLIES THE WORLD

1 Janet Ellis in Kenya in 1984. During this trip, the programme returned to Starehe school, the beneficiary of the 1971 dormitory appeal.

2 The 1968 Safari to Morocco. All the expeditions were shot on film until the 1989 trip to Zimbabwe when video took over.

3 John Leslie and Yvette Fielding by the Victoria Falls. Some expeditions, like this 1989 trip to Zimbabwe, didn't feature all the presenting team of the time.

Blue Peter expeditions

1965	Norway – Christopher Trace and Valerie Singleton
1966	Singapore and Borneo – Christopher Trace and Valerie Singleton
1967	Jamaica and New York – Valerie Singleton and John Noakes
1968	Morocco – Valerie Singleton, John Noakes and Peter Purves
1969	Ceylon – Valerie Singleton, John Noakes and Peter Purves
1970	Mexico – Valerie Singleton, John Noakes and Peter Purves
1971	Iceland, Norway and Denmark – Valerie Singleton, John Noakes and Peter Purves
1972	San Francisco, Fiji and Tonga – John Noakes, Peter Purves and Lesley Judd
1973	The Ivory Coast – John Noakes, Peter Purves and Lesley Judd
1974	Thailand – John Noakes, Peter Purves and Lesley Judd
1975	Turkey – John Noakes, Peter Purves and Lesley Judd
1976	Brunei – John Noakes, Peter Purves and Lesley Judd
1977	Brazil – John Noakes, Peter Purves and Lesley Judd
1978	USA – Lesley Judd and Simon Groom
1979	Egypt – Simon Groom, Christopher Wenner and Tina Heath
1980	Malaysia – Simon Groom and Sarah Greene
1981	Japan – Simon Groom, Sarah Greene and Peter Duncan
1982	Canada – Simon Groom, Sarah Greene and Peter Duncan
1983	Sri Lanka – Simon Groom, Peter Duncan and Janet Ellis
1984	Kenya – Simon Groom and Janet Ellis
1985	Australia – Simon Groom and Janet Ellis
1987	Soviet Union – Mark Curry, Caron Keating and Yvette Fielding
1988	West Coast USA – Caron Keating and Yvette Fielding
1989	Zimbabwe – Yvette Fielding and John Leslie
1990	The Caribbean – Yvette Fielding, John Leslie and Diane-Louise Jordan
1991	Japan – John Leslie and Diane-Louise Jordan
1992	New Zealand – Yvette Fielding; Hungary – Anthea Turner
1993	Argentina – Anthea Turner and Diane-Louise Jordan
1994	New England USA – Diane-Louise Jordan, Tim Vincent and Stuart Miles
1995	South Africa – Diane-Louise Jordan, Tim Vincent, Stuart Miles and Katy Hill
1996	Hong Kong and China – Tim Vincent, Stuart Miles, Katy Hill and Romana D'Annunzio
1997	Canada – Stuart Miles, Katy Hill, Romana D'Annunzio and Richard Bacon
1998	Mexico – Stuart Miles, Katy Hill, Richard Bacon and Konnie Huq
1999	Australia – Katy Hill, Konnie Huq, Simon Thomas and Matt Baker
2000	Spain – Konnie Huq, Simon Thomas, Matt Baker and Liz Barker
2001	Vietnam – Konnie Huq, Simon Thomas, Matt Baker and Liz Barker
2002	Morocco – Konnie Huq, Simon Thomas, Matt Baker and Liz Barker
2003	Brazil – Konnie Huq, Simon Thomas, Matt Baker and Liz Barker
2004	India – Konnie Huq, Simon Thomas, Matt Baker and Liz Barker
2005	Japan – Konnie Huq, Matt Baker, Zöe Salmon and Gethin Jones
2006	Southern States USA – Konnie Huq, Zöe Salmon, Gethin Jones and Andy Akinwolere
2007	Bolivia – Konnie Huq, Zöe Salmon, Gethin Jones and Andy Akinwolere

1 When *Blue Peter* returned to Sri Lanka in the summer of 1983, the stories which had been shown in 1969 were simply remade. **2** The 2004 expedition to India – the first time all the presenters were on location throughout a trip since 1990. Liz Barker needed medical clearance as she was four months pregnant.

Special Assignment BLUE PETER FLIES THE WORLD

3 Janet Ellis suffered a debilitating asthma attack as she attempted to climb Ayers Rock with Simon Groom in Australia in 1985.

4 John, Val and Peter board another plane during the 1970 Mexico expedition. Tensions often built up thanks to the claustrophobic nature of these trips.

5 Val and Peter attempt to stay cool during the blistering heat of the 1968 Safari to Morocco.

It was the same story during the 1990 Caribbean expedition, this time the friction flaring up between Yvette Fielding and Diane-Louise Jordan. Often schedules have been staggered so that presenters overlap, but only spend the minimum amount of time cooped up together.

Setting up and filming a summer expedition is a major operation. It must have been tougher in the old days with much more primitive communication and infrastructure as well as cumbersome technology. It always helps if the host country is on side. Sometimes trips fell through because of lack of cooperation – as was the case with Japan in 1969 and Australia in 1971. If there are problems with bureaucracy and corruption, it can be very difficult indeed. During the 1973 expedition to the Ivory Coast, the only way to get anything done was to use bribes – and even then, the team met with constant hostility and obstruction.

Sometimes the problem is back at base. There was no trip in 1986 because of budget cuts. Lewis Bronze remembers that '…instead we decided to phase Simon [Groom] out by making some countryside specials. Peter [Duncan] was filming *Duncan Dares* that summer and we didn't feel that Simon and Janet [Ellis] in Australia had any special on-screen chemistry together, so we were not minded to spend very limited resources on an uncertain outcome.'

In 2005, we had to have a rapid re-think and postpone our journey to the Southern States of the USA because of the danger of overlapping stories with a CBBC series called *Only In America*.

Today, foreign travel is much more routine and the programme travels widely through the year, not just in summer. But the expeditions have endured. They still offer an excitement and sense of adventure all of their own. They may be tough for the presenters and crew, but they are an unrivalled opportunity to see a country, close up and jumping the queue. As Peter Purves points out, 'It is unpurchasable pleasure. Unless you are the richest of the rich, you could never afford to travel like that yourself.'

6 During the 1975 expedition to Turkey, the presenters explored a church built deep underground. Most expeditions highlighted the chosen country's religious culture.

61

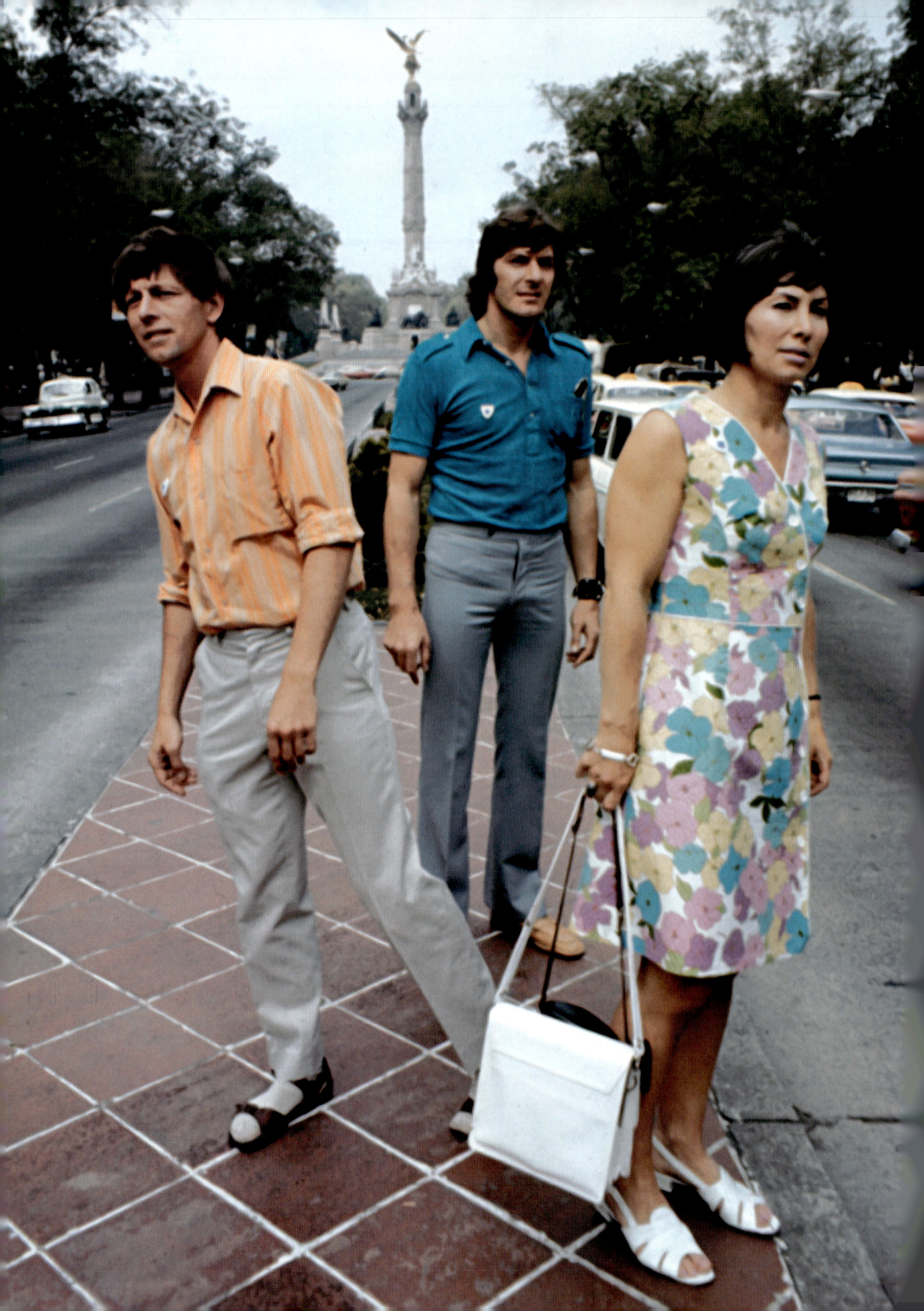

3 A Wonderful Splash of Colour

1970–1979

Blue Peter burst into colour on 14 September 1970. It had been a long time coming. Colour had been introduced by the BBC in 1967, but the new colour cameras needed more technical line-up time and Biddy was concerned that this would eat away at precious rehearsals. Another issue was that colour film took longer to process. Consequently, in May 1970, as an experiment, director John Adcock took all three presenters to make a colour film on board the liner *Queen Elizabeth II*. Although it was transmitted in black and white, this film proved that the new system could work.

July 1970. In the heat and pollution of Mexico City, John, Valerie and Peter film the first summer expedition to be shot in colour. The destination was chosen because of the interest generated by that year's World Cup.

The coming of colour brought some major advantages. The studios equipped to cope with it were the larger, more modern ones at BBC Television Centre. Until now, these had only rarely been available to the programme, but now they became routinely so. Over the next four years, whenever a suitable studio was lacking, there were occasional lapses back into monochrome, but the very last black and white *Blue Peter* was transmitted on 24 June 1974.

For the presenters, colour meant the unexpected but welcome introduction of a clothing allowance. Valerie Singleton '…had a lovely time shopping with someone from wardrobe. We had £200 to spend, so we earmarked all these things. The next day the poor wardrobe lady called me to say, "I'm dreadfully sorry, I've made a terrible mistake. It is £200 to share between you!"'

As plans for colour were finalized, Edward Barnes was preparing for his new role as Deputy Head of Children's Programmes. However, he continued to attend weekly planning meetings and studio run-throughs, and in the summer of 1970 he scheduled a swansong shoot for himself in Paris. There were two stories: John Noakes climbing the Eiffel Tower and Valerie Singleton telling the story of Marie Antoinette. A key location was Marie Antoinette's toy village at Versailles, said to be haunted by the tragic queen. During a break, Val, in full costume and make-up, wandered off on her own to sit on the grass and enjoy the tranquillity of the surroundings. A group of tourists came upon her and were convinced that they were staring at a ghost. Val didn't spoil their fun by enlightening them.

1 John Noakes about to 'go for a take' in Norway in 1971. Although shot in colour, for some time films still had to edited in black and white.

2 A royal scoop – Valerie Singleton interviews Lord Louis Mountbatten during her 1975 Special Assignment to the Isle of Wight.

3 Princess Anne appeared in the studio to promote the 'Royal Safari'. She was credited with the presenters on the opening titles.

4 Strolling on a Kenyan beach during the Royal Safari. Val says, 'When I fell off the horse, it was the only time Princess Anne took a picture of me!'

Blue Peter Special Assignments

At the end of that year, exciting plans were under way for a special *Blue Peter* film. This would follow Princess Anne's impending visit to Kenya on behalf of the charity Save The Children. At this time Princess Anne suffered from something of an image problem and this film revealed a different side to her personality. The project was first offered to Richard Cawston, who had made the BBC's highly successful 1969 film *Royal Family* and was now Head of Documentaries. When he told BBC1's Controller, Paul Fox, that he was going to turn it down, Fox suggested offering it to *Blue Peter* as an Easter special instead. Cawston was a big fan of Biddy's and agreed to help, smoothing the way with Buckingham Palace.

The Palace were, of course, well aware of the pulling power of *Blue Peter*. The royal children were fans, which helped. The previous summer, Prince Edward had visited the studio, played with some lion and tiger cubs, enjoyed rides on a model railway and had tea. It had been a great success and Miss Anderson, his nurse, confided that *Blue Peter* was an absolute 'must'. After the first meeting with Princess Anne, Prince Andrew donated a shoe box of old forks and spoons to that year's appeal, which he carried himself to Edward Barnes' car.

Agreement was reached for a *Blue Peter* Royal Safari, presented by Val and directed by Edward Barnes, who recalled: 'Princess Anne was such a delight during the filming, bubbly and not sulky at all on account of the fact that the follow spot was on her!'

The filming had its dramatic moments. During a riding sequence, Princess Anne and Val were asked to gallop towards the camera. As they reached a clump of trees, a tractor suddenly appeared and Val's horse reared up and threw her off. It was a bad fall but luckily she wasn't seriously injured. Edward Barnes recalls filling in the subsequent BBC Accident Report Form with 'Name of non-BBC staff witnessing the accident: HRH The Princess Anne'.

The Royal Safari attracted a huge audience, not only on its first transmission, but also for the subsequent repeats. Its success became the catalyst for the creation of the *Blue Peter Special Assignments* and the gradual phasing out of Valerie Singleton from *Blue Peter* itself.

The premise of *Special Assignments* was that Val would visit famous cities, islands or houses and tell the best stories relating to them. In the first series, there was a notable coup. Edward Barnes had painstakingly negotiated permission to film at a papal audience in Rome. On the day itself, and quite unexpectedly, His Holiness Pope Paul VI approached the *Blue Peter* cameras and gave a direct address to the children of Britain. The crew had been told that no microphones were permitted. Luckily, the sound recordist had had the foresight to conceal one on his person, just in case.

With Val dividing her time between her new role as *Blue Peter*'s roving reporter and her slots on the early evening news programme *Nationwide*, Lesley Judd was introduced as her full-time replacement.

4

BLUE PETER 50th Anniversary

1

2

3

66

1 Time for a carol round the tree. For the production team, making sure that the visiting children knew the words was always a headache.

2 Presents round the tree – but who were they from? This puzzled some presenters and viewers. 'Father Christmas, of course!', explains Biddy Baxter.

3 The carved wooden figures on the crib needed careful placing. Baby Jesus was so small that to get the close-up the camera would often have to switch to a 'times two' lens.

Sometimes all four presenters – Val, Lesley, John and Peter – appeared together, notably at Christmas.

The Christmas show

The format for the *Blue Peter* Christmas show, the last edition before the big day itself, had evolved to such an extent that the same structure was followed, with many of the same words, until the entire tradition was dropped in 2007. As John Noakes put it: 'The script was written one Christmas and every year after that the producers brought out the same one, which meant we didn't have to learn the words again!'

The programme always started with a special arrangement of 'Good King Wencelas' by the Chalk Farm Band of the Salvation Army. The grand finale was the moment that the band led a procession of carol singers into the studio, many of them carrying lanterns, to sing either 'O Come All Ye Faithful' or 'Hark! The Herald Angels Sing'. 'I can hear them coming up the hill and into the studio now...' was the familiar introduction. The two carols were alternated each year, except in 1998 when there was a one-off experiment with 'O Little Town of Bethlehem'.

The only variables were usually a last-minute make, that year's Christmas entertainment or performance and news of the *Blue Peter* appeal. For many years, there was the ritual of presents under the tree, both for pets and presenters. 'That was difficult', according to Peter Purves, 'because we didn't know who the presents were from. How do you say thank you? Who do you say it to?'

Lewis Bronze, the new Editor, finally dispensed with the presenters' presents in 1988, but the pets were still given them and it was always a challenge for the presenters to herd them into position at the critical moment so that the director could get the essential close-ups.

In December 1975, Lesley Judd suddenly contracted measles. There was no way she could be in the studio for the Christmas edition, so Biddy sent a film crew (who wore masks) so that viewers could see her spots for themselves and not be deprived of the sight of Lesley receiving her present. She croaked her thanks for the gift of a music stand.

Organizing the Christmas show was a mammoth undertaking. Every single member of the production team was involved, helping to decorate the studio and marshal the children, many of whom would get over-excited and over-tired, usually in that order. A second studio was booked to corral them between rehearsals. Squabbles would inevitably break out over who got to carry lanterns. Members of staff and senior management would attempt to persuade the floor manager to give their children a favourable position in the final line-up, so that they could be seen by their relatives at home.

In 1978, at the very last minute, the show was 'blacked' by industrial action. Strikes were one of the hazards of the era and there had been other times when they'd meant sharing a studio with another programme or substituting a live edition with a repeat. But having to turn away coachloads of bitterly disappointed children from Television Centre remains a dismal memory for those involved.

1 Moments before the famous bobsleigh run in in 1975 in which Noakes had a nasty accident. Producer John Adcock is still proud of his pioneering use of a 'helmet' camera, which showed Noakes' point of view.

The argument for the Christmas show's resistance to change was that Christmas itself is traditional and that children enjoyed the show's familiar nature. A central moment was always the potted version of the birth of baby Jesus, illustrated by the careful placing of the programme's beautifully carved crib and figures. These were purchased during a 1965 filming trip to the Nuremberg Christmas market. As Britain became more of a multi-faith nation, the script of this section was amended to sound more inclusive. Even so, there has still been criticism about the emphasis on the Christian perspective. Indeed, I was once asked by a senior executive whether the Christmas programme could be 'less Christian' with a non-faith-based seasonal song replacing the carol.

In the 1970s, there were no such doubts. Common sense prevailed over political correctness. This was an era of real confidence and expansion for *Blue Peter*. As well as *Special Assignments*, there were other new or related ventures, such as *Record Breakers*, based on material that had regularly featured on *Blue Peter*.

Noakes's Long Fall

In 1973, an entire programme was devoted to the remarkable story of John Noakes's four-mile free-fall parachute jump. 'The Long Fall', as it was subtitled, gave Edward Barnes the inspiration for another *Blue Peter* spin-off. Originally entitled *Noakes In Action*, it became *Go With Noakes* and ran for five series between 1976 and 1981. Generally shot during the summer months, it meant not only extra money for Noakes but extra work, too. The document that first pitched the idea stated that '…the programme will follow a series of events exploiting John Noakes's ability to have a go at anything and his knack of being accepted by experts as one of the team.' But the real stroke of genius was the inclusion of Shep, who stepped up from his role as John's sidekick dog on *Blue Peter* to become his fully-fledged co-star. Clever cutting made this one of the most charming and enduring small-screen double acts.

There is no doubt that Noakes's schedule was the most demanding of all the presenters. When he was making 'The Long Fall', he remembers: 'I had done some training, which is the hardest bit of parachuting. You wake up full of aches and pains because you've done all this falling and rolling. Then they took me up to 12,000 feet [3,650 metres] and I did three jumps to prepare for the big one from 25,000 feet [7,620 metres]. At the end of the day, I drove back. I was driving my 130 mph car at 30 mph and the production van passed me. When I got to the studio the next day, they said, "Are you all right? You normally drive at a heck of a rate, you were only doing 30." And I suddenly thought, these people have got no idea of what it takes to do this.'

Noakes's stamina was extraordinary, but there was one alarming incident during the live transmission on 17 May 1976, when he was taken ill as a result of exhaustion and actually ended up unconscious on the studio floor. Lesley Judd took over and did such a good job that viewers could hardly have noticed. Noakes missed the next edition to recuperate.

2 John and Shep – one of the best double acts on children's television. The famous catchphrase 'Get down Shep' was, in fact, rarely used.

3 Even so, pop group The Barron Knights released a song called 'Get Down Shep'. It reached number 44 in the charts.

4 Noakes' Long Fall got him into the Guinness Book of Records for the longest delayed drop. He freefalled 22,000 feet (6,700 metres) with the RAF Falcons.

BLUE PETER 50th Anniversary

1

2

3

4

1 On location with long-term director Sarah Hellings. She became a successful drama director, on programmes such as *Dr Who*, *Taggart* and *Midsomer Murders*.

2 Karl Wallenda, whose catchphrase, rather worryingly, was 'break your leg, break your neck', wire-walks at Television Centre in 1971.

3 One of the most moving television interviews ever shown. Lesley Judd talks to Otto Frank about his daughter Anne and the legacy of her diary.

He recalls, 'People would say, "I wish I had your job!" and I'd say, "You can have the blooming job!"'

Breaking news

The programme was often at its very best when it reacted fast to something topical. This was a decade of impressive scoops. In 1971, Noakes reported from the very edge of the erupting Mount Etna, and the following year a nail-biting high-wire walk was staged at Television Centre with the sensational Karl Wallenda. Sadly, Wallenda died undertaking a similar stunt in Puerto Rico just a few years later.

In January 1972, *Blue Peter* transmitted the first colour pictures via satellite of the sinking of the great liner the *Queen Elizabeth*. In 1973, immense efforts secured the first UK television appearance of the fork-bending sensation Uri Geller, while in 1977 there were outside broadcasts from Wimbledon and the deck of the *Ark Royal*, the backdrop to the Royal Jubilee Review of the Fleet.

May 1976 was a remarkable month for *Blue Peter*. On 10 May, there was one of the most historic items ever, repeated many times since. The story of Anne Frank had been told in 1973's Amsterdam *Blue Peter Special Assignment*. Some time afterwards, Edward Barnes had a call from Otto Frank's brother-in-law. Otto, Anne's father and the only member of the family who had survived the Nazi death camps, was paying a visit to Britain and his brother-in-law wondered if it might be possible to arrange a screening of the film. Edward immediately agreed and booked a viewing theatre at Television Centre. Mr Frank loved the film, saying it was the best depiction of Anne's life he had seen. Edward remembers: 'Afterwards, I asked him where the diaries were kept. He told me that they were in a bank in Switzerland. I thought I was pushing my luck, but asked anyway, "Would it be possible to bring them into the studio to show the children of Britain?" He agreed and I was very proud of that.'

The interview, conducted by Lesley Judd, was a masterclass in sensitivity. Lesley triumphed again when *Blue Peter* was offered one seat on the inaugural flight of British Airways' Concorde to Washington's Dulles Airport in America.

The Concorde invitation arrived almost at the last minute, but the team seized the opportunity. The result was ambitious and gripping. '*Blue Peter* Goes Supersonic' was given a specially extended slot on 24 May 1976. The time difference worked almost perfectly to the programme's advantage, although John and Peter had to 'fill' while Lesley struggled to negotiate a jammed door, which was preventing her exit from the plane. In the nick of time, she found her camera and delivered the first words broadcast on *Blue Peter* live by satellite. It was thrilling stuff.

4 '*Blue Peter* Goes Supersonic' happened only because BBC News turned the story down.

'Barnacle Bill' gets a makeover

Ever since Biddy and Edward arrived in 1962, *Blue Peter* had managed to evolve gradually, carefully and without the kind of knee-jerk change that might have alienated children, who can be so wary of such innovation. The set was sometimes refreshed, although it always followed the blueprint of the programme's inspired designer, Darrol Blake. There was one big departure in 1979, when the theme music – the increasingly old-fashioned version of 'Barnacle Bill', used since 1958 – was finally updated. *Tubular Bells* star Mike Oldfield provided the new version, which lasted ten years and became just as iconic as the original. The whole process was filmed with the presenter Simon Groom ostensibly playing the revved-up drum roll that kicked off the arrangement. A single version was marketed by BBC Records and reached number 19 in the pop charts, with the proceeds naturally going to the *Blue Peter* appeal. When it became a hit, the girls from the dance group Legs and Co made an appearance in the studio, doing the routine they'd performed on *Top of the Pops*.

By now, the *Blue Peter* calendar presented a whole series of reliable constants, from putting the tortoise into and out of hibernation, celebrating the pets' birthdays, the annual feature on Crufts dog show, the *Blue Peter* classes at the National Cat Club show, the summer expedition, the garden, the appeal, Christmas and many familiar, cyclical items. Winter wasn't winter without the *Blue Peter* bird-cake recipe. It was safe and cosy, if occasionally worthy and dull. But if you were a loyal viewer, you knew where you were with the programme. The rock-solid presenters were at the heart of this consistency.

In 1978, that consistency started to crumble. Valerie Singleton was long gone. John Noakes and Peter Purves were both over 40, looking their age and in the process of moving on. Lesley Judd's interest and energy was on the wane too. She had fallen in love and married the programme's film editor Terry Gabell. When Gabell was diagnosed with multiple sclerosis, the couple decided to swap the relentless pace of *Blue Peter* for a healthier life in the country. In a few short months, Biddy Baxter lost them all and had to start again with a new, raw team – Simon Groom, Christopher Wenner and Tina Heath. Producer Alex Leger believes that '…she went from presenters who could do exactly what she wanted, who she could orchestrate in tone and delivery, who could change the pace and the style cleverly within seconds, to new presenters who just couldn't. Basically, we went from being a beautifully crafted Stradivarius to a banjo.'

It was hard to warm to these nervy, faltering presenters. Almost every programme contained some hideous fluff or embarrassing moment. The nadir was reached on 26 April 1979 during a mundane item about darts. Simon Groom, looking under sentence of death, completely forgot his words. Despite a very audible prompt from the floor manager, Derek Kibble, he remained lost in his nightmare, unable to recover. It was the apotheosis of car-crash television. Off camera, Tina Heath was frantically trying to get permission to go on and help. At last, after what seemed an eternity, she appeared with script in hand, saying: 'There's so

1 1977 and another *Blue Peter* studio day. During the 1970s, the programme ran from September to June, twice a week, a total of around 80 shows a year. Note the crib card stuck to the camera!

2 Simon and Goldie arrived hot on the heels of John and Shep. Having a dog helped Simon, who at first was completely out of his depth.

3 Mike Oldfield at work. He had been a fan: 'I could identify with John Noakes, who was from Halifax, just over the hill from us in Rochdale. He spoke my kind of language and was a bit like an adventurous elder brother.'

much to remember, but it's terribly crucial.' Which was something of an understatement. The programme finished with Peggy Spencer briskly teaching Simon and Tina a dance to Boney M's 'Holi-holiday'. Not surprisingly, the party atmosphere was distinctly forced.

Tina was the glue between two very green co-presenters: 'I really liked them both. We got on well, but Simon had no television experience. Chris wanted to do it his way, but he was new and who cared what he said? I'd been used to rehearsal and having time to learn the script. To me the script was a sacrosanct thing. I'd be up to three in the morning learning my lines, so I had a degree of flexibility with guests and wasn't just panicking about the words all day. Then there would be the dreaded time after dress rehearsal. A great whack of what Chris had to do would now be given to me.

'I admired Biddy for her standards and I totally wanted to honour them, but it was hard. She later said that I never found my own voice. That's because I was perfecting the voice she gave me! There were moments when I felt I was an unmitigated disaster but, unlike the boys, I'd had ten years' acting experience and could look back at what I'd done and think, "Actually no, I'm not."'

The team struggled on, but the decade, which had started with such bravura, ended with growing concern over this front-of-camera crisis.

Tina Heath recalls, 'John, Val and Pete were the blueprint and they were looking to replicate it' – but the new line-up of Simon, Tina and Chris didn't work out.

Presenter Profile
LESLEY JUDD

JOINED: 15 May 1972

LEFT: 12 April 1979

MEMORABLE MOMENTS: Falling off a racehorse; being hoisted up and down Bishop Rock Lighthouse; lots of dancing including joining *Top of the Pops*' all-girl dance group Pan's People; interviewing Otto Frank, Anne Frank's father; reporting live from the USA after flying there on Concorde; trips to San Francisco, Fiji and Tonga, Thailand, Turkey, Brunei and Brazil

Lesley Judd was just six years old when she was sent to boarding school, where she trained in ballet and made minor appearances in pantomime. On television, she played Clara in the BBC serial *Heidi*. Her career took off when she joined the hip television dance group The Young Generation, then a staple part of Saturday-night TV entertainment. It was a girlfriend who suggested she try for *Blue Peter*, having clocked that auditions were taking place at Television Centre. Lesley had never seen the programme, but left her details in a large envelope on Biddy Baxter's desk. This was just the kind of chutzpah that appealed to Biddy.

Lesley auditioned and got the job, still with only the sketchiest idea about the programme. She admitted: 'Fortunately, I didn't know what I was in for, otherwise I don't think I'd have done it. I had the horrors. I used to get very bad headaches after every programme from nerves.'

When Biddy instructed the Artist Contracts Department to issue a year-long engagement, she was horrified to learn that Lesley was embroiled in a dispute over her abrupt departure from The Young Generation. Light Entertainment was furious to hear that she was now being offered another job at the BBC, but Biddy was unrepentant. She did send a cautionary memo to all concerned: 'I would like Lesley Judd's contract to be completely watertight as regards punctuality and I would be grateful if you would emphasize to Hazel Malone [Lesley's agent] the importance of an artist's total reliability when working on a busy twice-weekly programme. Continuity is a very important factor on *Blue Peter* and I would be unhappy if Lesley did not stay with the programme for at least a year.'

Perhaps surprisingly, her first film centred on her association with The Young Generation. Lesley taught Valerie Singleton, John Noakes and Peter Purves a go-go

It took Lesley a long time to forget 'the panic of "…what do I have to learn?" every Sunday and Wednesday night. It was *Boy's Own* stuff. The art was to make it natural.'

routine to the groovy 'River Deep, Mountain High', and on the next edition, she popped up in the studio helping to demonstrate a new multi-gym.

For Lesley, the initial hurdle was getting the audience to accept her. Val had been on the programme for nearly ten years, and to begin with, wherever Lesley went filming, disappointed children would greet her with a chorus of 'Where's Val?'

Dicing with death

She soon won them over with her combination of enthusiasm, guts and beauty. 'As a dancer, she was brought up on pain', recalls John Adcock, who was in charge of the programme's films. 'She smoked like a chimney and worked through it.' She certainly had more than her share of narrow escapes. She was knocked unconscious when she was thrown from a runaway racehorse. She couldn't swim, which meant that when her raft sank on a jungle survival exercise in Brunei, she very nearly drowned. Her most famous dice with death came on a trip to the Bishop Rock Lighthouse, when she was nearly dashed into a boiling sea while dangling from a rope harness. Her desperate cries of 'Grab me! Grab me!' were

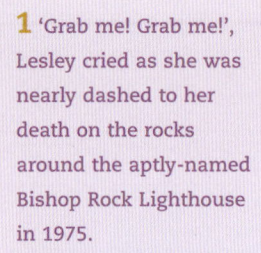

1 'Grab me! Grab me!', Lesley cried as she was nearly dashed to her death on the rocks around the aptly-named Bishop Rock Lighthouse in 1975.

2 In San Francisco for Lesley's first summer expedition, with Assistant Editor Rosemary Gill, who later left to set up *Multi-Coloured Swap Shop*.

3 Lesley on location in Brazil. Producer John Adcock, who had flown ahead to recce the trip, still remembers his surprise when she stepped off the plane with her brand-new perm.

much imitated by heartless children across the land, but, all the same, they loved her for her bravery.

In the summer of 1974, she needed all her stamina and courage for an off-camera ordeal, which nearly brought her *Blue Peter* career to a premature end. Lesley had married the actor Derek Fowlds (a household name as Mr Derek in *The Basil Brush Show*), but it went badly and after a few weeks she left him. Fowlds phoned Biddy, who was on holiday in Cornwall, threatening to go to the newspapers with his side of the story. Biddy did her best to persuade him that this would be in nobody's interests. In the 1970s, divorce still carried a powerful stigma and she was keenly aware that if a presenter was involved in a messy divorce it could be highly damaging.

On 6 September 1974, there was an emotional meeting between Biddy and Lesley, the result of which was that Lesley resigned. Over the next week, a compromise was finally reached and instead she was offered a new three-month extension to her contract. Presenters were normally signed for a year at a time, but Biddy wanted to keep her options open. For some time, Lesley's contract continued to be extended in dribs and drabs. She was also asked and agreed to sign an agreement undertaking that she would not cooperate with '…any newspaper, periodical or any other kind of publication to publish information relating to my relationship'.

Later Lesley commented: 'It was a very bad time for me. I knew I was going to have to fight for my job because of the way the Beeb viewed the divorce of a children's presenter. There was no one else involved in my marriage. It just didn't work. Rightly or wrongly, it was a stain on your character.'

The unhappy situation dragged on into 1975. Between January and March, precautionary auditions for a new female presenter were held, among them Sally James, later to achieve fame on the children's Saturday morning programme *Tiswas*. For Lesley, it must have been horribly difficult to maintain the bright smile and breezy outlook. Her professionalism kept her going and eventually she 'weathered it' and was offered another year-long deal.

Lesley stayed with *Blue Peter* for nearly seven years until Easter 1979, having remarried, this time to one of the programme's film editors, Terry Gabell. She now lives in France and rarely talks about her time on the programme, but in 1997, on an edition of Channel 4's *Light Lunch*, she was reunited with Val and John. Asked if it bothered them that they were still associated with *Blue Peter*, Lesley replied: 'No. We should be so lucky, frankly. Just think of some of the things you could be associated with!'

Presenter Profile LESLEY JUDD

4 In February 1976 Lesley joined *Top of the Pops* dance group Pan's People, just a few weeks before they bowed out for good. They danced together to 'Rodrigo's Guitar Concerto' by Manuel and the Music of the Mountains.

Presenter Profile
SIMON GROOM

JOINED: 15 May 1978

LEFT: 23 June 1986

MEMORABLE MOMENTS: Training Goldie; farming films at Dethick, Derbyshire; taking part in rehearsals for the Royal Tournament Field Gun Race and the Tower Bridge death slide; Boscombe Down RAF test pilot training; trips to the USA, Egypt, Malaysia, Japan, Canada, Sri Lanka, Kenya, Australia, Cambodia and Ethiopia

After a brief spell as a teacher, which he hadn't enjoyed, Simon Groom had gone to London '…with vague ideas of getting into broadcasting'. He worked as a nightclub DJ under the unlikely name of Neil St John. Then, on a visit to his parents' farm at Dethick in Derbyshire, he found a BBC film crew shooting a children's drama called *A Traveller In Time*: 'Make-up and wardrobe had taken over my old bedroom. There were actors cantering on horseback in Tudor costume around the farm. It was magical. For the first time in my life, I thought "I know what I want to do"'.

Simon thought he might get a break if he sent an interesting tape to a radio station. He recorded an interview with Dorothea Brooking, director of *A Traveller In Time*. When she heard *Blue Peter* were looking for someone to replace Peter Purves, she mentioned Simon to Edward Barnes, who recalls, 'She said, "He's a farmer's son, he's been a teacher, he asked some fairly sensible questions, why not have a look at him?"'

Simon had never been inside a television studio before and had no idea what he was doing in the audition: 'I had an embarrassing moment on the trampoline. This world champion trampoline coach said, "Now Simon, I'm going to show you how to do a tuck jump." And I misheard him and said, "What's that? A touch-up?" The crew collapsed and I thought I'd blown it, making innuendo on my audition.'

Once he'd got the job, innuendo became closely associated with Simon. After a film about hedge laying, he quipped, 'You need a good length to make a lay.' Another time, after clanking onto the set in a suit of armour, he came out with, 'Once a king, always a king, but once a knight is enough.' Most famously of all, the camera came to him following an item about a facsimile replacement for Durham Cathedral's historic door knocker: 'What a beautiful pair of knockers', he deadpanned down the lens.

1 Like several other presenters, Simon Groom had a shaky start: 'We persevered because he was a real person', says Biddy Baxter.

Simon comments, 'I think Biddy secretly quite liked all that. Basically as long as you didn't labour it with a nudge, nudge, wink, wink, why not? It's quite harmless, that Kenneth Williams school of humour.'

Simon's good nature was combined with a stubborn, argumentative streak. There were moments of madness, such as the night he was arrested in Japan for drunkenly cavorting in the street with a life-sized inflatable waiter. When producer Alex Leger took him filming to an army base in Germany in 1984, he warned his hosts in the officers' mess that Simon couldn't take his drink: 'They started plying him with alcohol and I thought, "Oh no!". Simon comments: 'I was a bit naïve and fell for it. There was an altercation.'

Leger '…overheard this captain saying, "You point that finger at me one more time and I'll bite it off." Simon carried on gesturing with his finger, so this guy leaned over, bit the top of it and drew blood. Simon looked at his finger, looked at the guy. It took about 20 seconds for the message to infiltrate that he'd been bitten by an officer in the British Army. The next thing I knew they were punching the hell out of one another. I said, "For God's sake, what are you doing?"

'I got Simon out of this mêlée and locked him in his room. But he climbed out of the window, down the drainpipe

2 The tiger who came to tea – a big cat in Tippi Hedren's kitchen. Director Renny Rye went on to direct *The Box of Delights* and Dennis Potter's *Karaoke* and *Cold Lazarus*.

3 The Tower Bridge death slide. Simon recalls, 'This was my first real action challenge. I'm not good with heights but I had to do it a few times and it got better'.

4 In 1984 Simon travelled to Ethiopia to report on the humanitarian crisis as part of the Double Lifesaver Appeal. These films were some of his best work.

and went into town looking for a flight home. He was found by a corporal in the early hours in a bar out of bounds to soldiers. This corporal listened and sympathized, took him back to his quarters and fed him coffee. Next morning, Simon arrived on location looking very sheepish. It was the shoot from hell!'

The incident could have had serious implications for Simon but, fortunately for him, Biddy didn't find out about it until some time later, when the moment had passed.

Pop star

Simon was a huge Elvis fan and leapt at the chance of impersonating his idol with a version of 'Heartbreak Hotel' in 1981. Years after he'd left *Blue Peter*, in 1992, Simon's love of The King led to an ill-advised attempt to release a pop single, a hi-energy disco cover version of 'Can't Help Falling In Love'. Simon persuaded Lewis Bronze to let him perform it on *Blue Peter*, complete with cheesy backing dancers. It was without doubt one of the worst musical performances in the programme's history.

Singing and dancing may not have been his forte, but Simon was always in his element with any item involving animals. One of his most celebrated experiences was the film he made with director Renny Rye at the Los Angeles ranch of movie producer Noel Marshall: 'The ranch was full of big cats. Unbeknown to me, lots of them went in the house too. I was chatting to the film's star Tippi Hedren in the kitchen, and without telling me, the director had set it up so that he could cue this 450-lb [204-kg] Bengal tiger to leap through the window onto the kitchen table. It was extraordinary. You couldn't just stand there like a lemon, you had to react! What's interesting now is that there was a young girl sitting there too, Tippi's daughter, who was about 15 at the time, Melanie Griffith!'

Simon became the programme's Countryside Correspondent for a few months after making his last regular appearance in the summer of 1986. On 1 July he wrote to Biddy: 'My last studio was a remarkable day. Everyone was so kind. It's been a very special eight years. Unforgettable, stimulating, difficult to put into words.'

Simon still farms at Dethick, where his wife runs a successful B and B. He also works as a freelance film maker, recently producing a documentary for the regional BBC series *Inside Out*.

Presenter Profile

CHRISTOPHER WENNER

JOINED: 14 September 1978

LEFT: 23 June 1980

MEMORABLE MOMENTS: Abseiling down the East Tower at Television Centre; working as a steeplejack; hang-gliding; canoeing; playing football in the mud; introducing competition winners to the Queen at Westminster Cathedaral; trips to Egypt and France

1 Chris Wenner was good-looking and well educated. According to Biddy Baxter and Edward Barnes, 'he argued the toss about everything from day one.'

There used to be a tradition on *Blue Peter* that an incoming presenter was always introduced, on film, teaching the others some kind of skill. At the end, the newcomer would say goodbye in a way that made it clear they were about to join the team. John Noakes had started the trend, skiing down the dry slope at Crystal Palace.

Peter Purves first appeared in a swimming pool, instructing John and Valerie Singleton in life-saving techniques. Lesley Judd showed Val, John and Peter how to do a go-go routine, while Simon Groom was unveiled as a DJ in a West End disco. The disco film had to be shot during the day, so the nightclub crowd were actually a motley collection of staff from the *Blue Peter* office.

As Simon Groom was spinning his discs for the last time, Biddy was still looking for a new boy to join him. Peter Duncan had turned her down. The usual parade of actors and presenters were auditioned. Adrian Mills, who later joined the *That's Life!* team, was one. Another who got close was Ray Burdis, a young actor who had made his name in *Scum*, a controversial and searing play exposing the violent realities of life in a borstal, playing the same role in both the banned BBC version and the movie remake. Burdis continued to act and became a highly respected screenwriter and producer on movies such as *The Krays* and series like *Operation Good Guys*.

Both Mills and Burdis might have done well, but the successful candidate was 23-year-old Christopher Wenner. Educated at the elite Catholic public school Stonyhurst, Wenner was the son of a diplomat. He read English Literature at Oxford University and had travelled extensively, claiming to speak '…Spanish, Swedish, German and French'. When it came to picking a subject for his first film, he certainly seemed to have plenty of skills to choose from. Biddy compiled a list of his talents during the casting process: 'Tennis, riding, swimming, rugby, long-distance and cross-country running, water-skiing, sailing, sub aqua. He also plays chess, writes poetry and has learnt to sing. He plays the guitar, trumpet and piano.'

Chris eventually made his debut teaching Lesley and Simon how to water-ski. He was attractive and intelligent but, unfortunately, his early promise soon evaporated. From the very start, Chris liked to argue about the content, which for a *Blue Peter* presenter was difficult enough if you were on top of your game. Producer Alex Leger recalls that it was a '…nightmare. Chris just couldn't remember his words.'

Programme after programme, he would lose his way and flounder. Sometimes the camera even picked up his scarlet face as he tripped and fumbled his way through another script. Once, in the middle of yet another dreadful item, he let slip a heartfelt, 'Oh God'. Immediately, a look of tortured contrition crossed his face. It was painful to watch and it never really got any better.

Attempts were made to capitalize on his apparent sporting prowess, but instead of seeming heroic he often came across as ineffectual. His attempts to master John Travolta's dance-floor moves in an item designed to reflect the then current disco craze remains one of the single most cringe-making sequences in *Blue Peter* history. There were some heinous clothes too, including a beyond-parody pair of dungarees.

Presenter Profile CHRISTOPHER WENNER

2 Chris made his first appearance teaching Lesley and Simon to water-ski, though Lesley, who wasn't a strong swimmer, declined to have a go.

3 Studio work was a problem because Chris found it such a struggle to remember his words.

4 Abseiling down the East Tower at Television Centre, the home of BBC children's programmes, was one of Chris's more impressive moments.

5 The East Tower abseil. During his time on *Blue Peter*, Chris met his future wife, Liz Truebridge, who was working as a production assistant on the show.

A fair cop

Biddy gave him every possible chance, renewing his contract for a second season. Unfortunately, there was little improvement. On 3 March 1980, a lengthy item on videotape broke down. The camera came to Chris frantically going over his words for the next sequence. He did his best to recover, but by now the programme had realized they'd made a mistake – he was very unpopular with the viewers. Chris later recalled Biddy explaining that she couldn't renew his contract because he'd come too low in the recent *Multi-Coloured Swap Shop* Awards: 'She told me that *Blue Peter* presenters should be first.'

Chris thought it was 'a fair cop'. He'd survived two years and left the programme '…still in awe of the way it was made, just like a drama, with every shot and every cut precisely planned.' Viewers were told that Chris was going back to acting, but ultimately he worked more as a television journalist. There were no hard feelings and he was always present at anniversary roll-calls. He made a cameo appearance in the 1998 'Back In Time For Christmas' special, and wrote to Editor Oliver Macfarlane: 'I'm proud to be a small compartment in such a great train, mainlining through the hearts of millions of souls in the broadcasting landscape of Britain. Over the top? Ah well – it wouldn't be the first time!'

With Chris out of the way, Biddy was back to the audition drawing board. She tried out a young actor called Kevin Whately, later to find fame as Sergeant Lewis in the *Morse* detective series and later in his own spin-off. But then she took a call from a certain Peter Duncan. This time he was keen to join.

Presenter Profile
TINA HEATH

JOINED: 5 April 1979

LEFT: 23 June 1980

MEMORABLE MOMENTS: Trips to Egypt and Lake Placid in the USA; gliding; playing Wordsworth's sister; climbing to the roof of Westminster Abbey; having a live scan when pregnant with baby Jemma; making several notable return appearances

Tina Heath was already well known to children as the star of the very successful comedy drama *Lizzie Dripping*. She was engaged for *Blue Peter* at a higher than usual fee of £100 per edition, justified in a memo dated 3 April 1979 by BBC Contracts Manager John Humphries: 'Tina Heath has about ten years' experience as a television performer and will be the most experienced of the presenters. The proposed fees reflect this and in the circumstances seem reasonable.'

When Tina's arrival was announced, there was predictable press interest: 'I was interviewed on Radio 4 and asked, "What made you decide to go for it?" I explained that I didn't apply, I went to see them at their request. They had been looking for ages and wanted someone experienced whom children would recognize. Edward Barnes (the Head of Children's Programmes) told me that he'd been to church and lit a candle, and that as he'd left, it was "as though your name was written in neon lights in front of me". At the time, I was hesitating about doing the job and I laughed and said, "Are you telling me God wants me to do it? Because in that case, I'd have to think carefully about saying no!"'

As a result of this interview, in which she made no secret of her Christianity, she was hauled up by BBC radio executives and sharply reminded that it was the Corporation's rule that presenters must not talk about their faith: 'I said, "Look, I'm sorry, but I can't say that I would never bring up my faith because it's not in a little compartment. I won't start trying to convert people on air, but I do have a faith. Maybe we need to part ways now? I'm happy to step down."

'Biddy was superb. She totally did her nut and got these people together and said, "Here we have a married woman, a moral person – and you're saying we can't

1 Tina Heath had acted in everything from *The Sweeney* to *Jane Eyre*. She'd also presented on *The Sunday Gang*, a religious programme aimed at children.

mention it." She phoned me up and said it was nonsense and that she was going to refer to my faith in the next *Blue Peter* book. As indeed she did.'

In the summer of 1979, the new team of Simon Groom, Christopher Wenner and Tina set off on the summer expedition to Egypt: 'That's where "gyppy" tummy comes from. We were filming in Luxor with these huge columns everywhere. It was baking hot, unbelievably so, and I was feeling a bit dizzy. Then all of a sudden I knew I had to go to the loo. I flagged it up, but there were no loos nearby and no time to go back to the hotel. I said "I'll hang on", but seconds later I piped up, "I have to go now." The director took one look at my face and said to the crew, "Right, form a semicircle around her." They linked arms with their backs to me and I just squatted at the base of one of these columns. Only when it was too late did I realize there was nothing to wipe myself with except the script!'

Baby Jemma

It was on her next overseas trip, to Lake Placid in the USA, that Tina discovered she was pregnant: 'Just before Christmas, I'd gone to buy all the skiing gear I needed for the

2 Tina's ground-breaking scan. She recalls, 'We needed persuading because it was untried technology and no-one was totally sure it wouldn't affect the baby. But it was extraordinary.'

3 As well as a flood of cards and letters, viewers sent Tina and Jemma 43 pairs of bootees, 29 matinee jackets, 7 romper suits, 36 bibs, 10 shawls and a rug.

4 In the 2001 'Rock 'n' Roll Christmas', Tina returned to play Miss E. Dripping, headmistress of Wood Lane High.

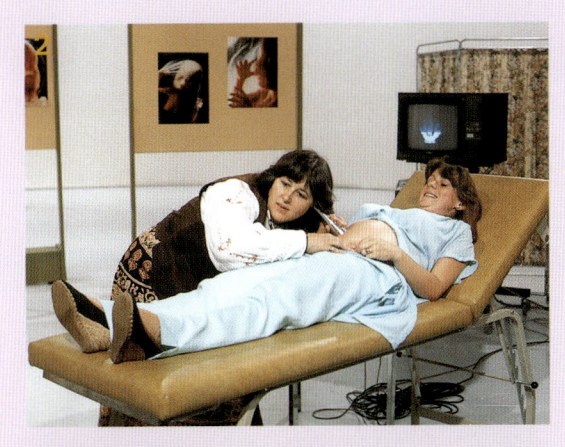

film. It fitted fine. When we arrived, I thought it was the time difference that was making me feel queasy. The next day, I couldn't get the zip up on my suit. I felt grim every morning. At last I realized, "Oh my goodness, I'm pregnant."

'I would definitely have stayed if I'd not got pregnant. Biddy gave me the choice. She was completely on my side – a woman way ahead of her time. But I knew in my heart I didn't have the energy for the fight you needed then to be a working BBC mum. I'd seen what Esther Rantzen had had to go through, with nannies and secretaries and so on. It was a pity but I made the right decision. *Blue Peter* is such a commitment.'

Tina's baby became her defining contribution to *Blue Peter*: 'I think for some people I've been pregnant for 30 years!'

Biddy persuaded her to have a scan live on air so that the audience could hear the baby's heartbeat direct from the womb. It was a revolutionary item and the National Childbirth Trust wrote to say that, in those five minutes, *Blue Peter* had done more to educate children about birth than they'd achieved in ten years of sending out leaflets. Jemma Victoria Cooke, born on 22 September 1980, made regular appearances for the next two years, rather like Daniel before her: 'Most of the time it was good, but I didn't want to push her in any way and in the end said no more before she started at school. I worried about the effect it might have with other children.'

Tina herself had to battle with post-natal depression: 'That first year after leaving was very strange. Like any woman who works, I went from being someone who sparked a lot of interest when asked "What do you do?" to saying you were looking after your first baby and seeing people's eyes glaze over.'

Happily, Tina and her family remained closely connected to *Blue Peter*. Her husband, Dave Cooke, was the talented musical director behind many a Christmas entertainment and song-and-dance item. Jemma grew up to become a superb professional singer and made many contributions to these, ghosting Liz Barker's voice throughout her *Blue Peter* career. Tina herself returned to play character roles in two of the programme's pantomimes in 2001 and 2005. One was a headmistress called Miss E. Dripping, a nod to the role that led her into *Blue Peter* in the first place.

Special Assignment

IN THE GARDEN

In the ceaseless search for bigger, better and more, *Blue Peter* cast a beady eye over every available BBC facility. The horseshoe car park at the front of Television Centre became a useful space for vehicles that wouldn't fit inside the studio. The inner circle of the building, known as the 'doughnut', was also frequently commandeered. The drawback with these areas was that they were in constant use, and securing access to them involved tedious internal bureaucracy.

'You're converting this building into a place of entertainment!' was the acid comment from one lady in charge of 'house services', as she abruptly turned down a request to land a helicopter at the front of Television Centre. The small, secluded green space in front of the BBC restaurant block was more readily available. It had already been pressed into service several times for everything from sunflower growing to show-jumping rabbits before it officially became the *Blue Peter* garden on 21 March 1974.

The idea was 'nicked', as Edward Barnes puts it, from *Blue Peter*'s ITV rival, *Magpie*: 'They did some good things, and I just happened to see that they had a garden at Teddington Lock. I thought, "We could do that." Children would enjoy seeing things grow. Typical of Biddy, she then claimed that land like Captain Cook! We used to get notes from the Editor of Television News asking, "Do you think we might use your garden?", as though we owned it and it was our territorial land!'

'The marvellous thing about the garden was that it was a space you could go to outside without the expense of filming, especially in winter when the days were much shorter. You could do all the items they wouldn't let you do in the studio.'

Enter Percy Thrower

Asking Percy Thrower to become the programme's gardener was Assistant Editor Rosemary Gill's idea. Percy had made a guest appearance in November 1973, talking about planting bulbs, but he hardly needed trying out. He had been a successful television gardener since the 1950s, and was famous enough to be turned into one of Madame Tussaud's waxworks. Percy was undaunted by the considerable discipline needed to fit each garden item into the tightly allocated time slots, and he was enthusiastic about translating his passion for a young audience. Nowadays, older people rarely appear on children's television, and certainly not as regular contributors. But Edward Barnes felt that '…the grandfather figure is a very good thing' and Percy provided that.

His natural authority on screen extended off screen as well. Presenters were dragooned into action. Peter Duncan remembers that whenever he was slapdash or lazy, Percy would tell him off in no uncertain terms: 'If you leave that rake on the ground again, I shall kick your arse!' Eventually, Peter became so keen he used to infuriate the production team by insisting on staying to finish the job in hand, even when recording was complete and he was needed back in the studio.

1 Goldie helps out. Only one pet was ever buried in the garden – George the tortoise. We later moved him to avoid possibility of disturbance by vandals.

2 Thinking of big projects to make a change from planting and pruning was a continuing challenge. 1981's mission was to build the greenhouse. One side lifts out to allow complete access for the cameras.

The sunken garden

The building of the Italian sunken garden in 1978 was a major project. The intention was to refresh the garden items, which were in danger of becoming a rather monotonous parade of planting, weeding and digging. The result, with its pond, benches and the footprints and handprints of the pets and presenters of the day, defined the whole space. Unfortunately, it took several years to secure the area effectively. On 17 April 1978, the programme announced that the garden had been vandalized. The damage was repaired, but vandals returned in 1980 and again in 1983, when security cameras were finally installed. Peter Duncan thought that '…people used to vandalize it so they could see their handiwork on telly the next day. But the intensity with how upset we had to be was a bit difficult to achieve sometimes. The second and third time it's quite hard because you know it just gets put back together again.'

Looking back, it is easy to laugh at the emotive language and earnest tone used each time the garden was vandalized. But Janet Ellis defends the approach: 'It sounds really smug and pompous to say it was very important to a lot of people, but it was.'

As he got older, Percy suffered from periodic bouts of illness and sometimes the gardening slots had to go ahead without him. He made his last appearance in the garden he'd created on 9 November 1987. Before Percy died in 1988, presenter Mark Curry was able to visit him in hospital as part of a touching tribute from the programme and to award Percy his gold badge. A plaque in his honour can be found in the garden to this day.

His successor was a young man called Chris Crowder. Chris had been spotted the previous autumn in a film about the topiary at Levens Hall, the stately home at which he worked. Chris was a good gardener who knew his stuff, but he was a hesitant presenter and always seemed ill at ease. There was another problem. Levens Hall is in Cumbria, hardly round the corner from Television Centre. In January 1991, Chris quietly bowed out.

A new agenda

On 30 May the same year, a special edition broadcast entirely from the garden introduced Clare Bradley. Clare's arrival coincided with the explosion of the green agenda within the programme, and she was used

3 The garden was vandalized three times. This photograph was taken during the clean-up operations after the 1983 incident.

far more widely than her predecessors. As well as the garden slots, Clare became a reporter, travelling all over the world from Cameroon to Namibia and Brazil to Zanzibar in search of ecological and environmental stories. She became a fully integrated member of the team, taking part in pantomimes and studio items as well. Her critics accused her of being 'mumsy', but there is no doubt that she brought real warmth and conviction to the material. Clare was also a fantastic custodian of the garden, spending long hours alone there, ensuring it looked its best, and saving the silver birch tree planted to mark the new millennium from a premature death from disease. She also came up with a scheme to camouflage the camera tower – a necessary eyesore for getting high-angled shots – using timber cladding and creeping plants, so that directors no longer had to hide it.

It's a jungle out there

The growth of the health and safety industry has had huge benefits for everyone working in television, but there have been some drawbacks too. During my tenure, from the 1990s onwards, those responsible would assess the garden and make ever more fanciful and expensive suggestions. The sloping bank was proclaimed a 'slip hazard', and we were asked to find thousands of pounds to put in a set of steps. We pointed out that no one had ever had an accident, that there was a separate hazard assessment each time we used the garden and that the steps would be hideous and probably just as slippery anyway. The request faded away. Similarly, when we were asked to replace all the glass in the greenhouse with Perspex, we pointed to Kew Gardens, which unlike our carefully

Special Assignment IN THE GARDEN

1 Simon Thomas helping Clare Bradley with maintenance. She did much more than garden, travelling the world and reporting on environmental issues.

2 Gardener Chris Crowder followed Percy Thrower. He was young and enthusiastic but never found the knack of being completely himself on camera.

3 The garden contains several generations of foot, hand and paw prints. This 2000 set was destroyed during a (later abandoned) scheme to build a studio for CBBC.

4 In 2007 Chris Collins received the City and Guilds Prince Phillip medal, a deserved reward for the passion and hard work that he invests in his gardening.

supervised space, is open to the public. No one had yet gone down the route of Perspex there. Again, we heard no more.

The worst part for anybody working in the garden was its unique weather system. Whenever we planned to be out there, it always seemed to be freezing cold or pouring with rain, and sometimes both. Most of the items would be pre-recorded on the morning of transmission, which inevitably made the rest of the day horribly tight for time.

By 2000, Clare Bradley's priorities were changing. She'd moved away from London, started her own business and had taken on a huge garden of her own. She was just too busy to remain on *Blue Peter*, and on 6 December we gave her a big send-off. There was now a strong feeling within the programme that a gardener was no longer necessary. The actual gardening items no longer did well with the audience, and increasingly the space was simply used as an extension of the studio.

A proper geezer

This state of affairs persisted until I bumped into Jez Edwards, a CBBC presenter who was friendly with lots of the *Blue Peter* team. Jez was working on Radio 4's children's programme *Go For It!* He strongly recommended a guy called Chris Collins, who had really impressed the Radio 4 team with his ability to enthuse children about gardening without the help of images. He certainly seemed well worth meeting. Like Clare, Chris had worked at Kew Gardens, as well as looking after Westminster Abbey's garden. He always looked as if he had soil under his fingernails and he sounded like a proper 'geezer' – qualities that I thought might be refreshing. He did cover up his tattoos though.

Chris joined on 17 May 2004. He threw himself into all aspects of the job; not just the television work but all the ambassadorial work too – touring schools, giving talks and promoting his craft. He treated children in the completely matter-of-fact way they prefer. Sadly, by the summer of 2007, the amount of gardening was once again in question. Increasing pressure to focus on big action and adventure meant that we had to pull back on the quieter, denser material. Plans for a series of gardening films were dropped and the resources redirected to other projects.

Nobody knows exactly what will happen to the garden when the BBC moves its children's programmes to Manchester and Television Centre is sold. It was one of the first questions asked by the Press to the Director General when the plans for the move were announced in 2004. As no one had considered the issue, it was impossible to answer. It is still a fantastically useful space. One of the last items I booked was a spectacular human cannonball act and the garden was the only practical location within the BBC. Early indications are that the BBC will create an entirely new *Blue Peter* garden in Manchester. This space will include some of the iconic items from the original Television Centre garden, including the statue of Petra. Whatever happens, like the pets, the *Blue Peter* garden really belongs to the viewers, and it is surely one of the most famous and instantly recognizable outdoor spaces in Britain.

Special Assignment

THE BLUE PETER BOOKS

In 1964, Lutterworth Press approached the BBC with the bright idea of a book based on *Blue Peter*. The result cost nine shillings and six pence, and the cover boasted that it was the book 'five million young viewers have been waiting for'. It was a colourful compendium of pictures, stories and puzzles, and it completely sold out. Book number one has since become a rare collector's item, with good-quality copies reaching a selling price of well over £100.

Lutterworth had spotted a lucrative gap in the market, but they were not allowed to enjoy the fruits of their investment. The previously uninterested BBC now stepped in to grab back the goose that had laid the surprise golden egg. From 1965 until 1985, it was BBC Enterprises (now known as BBC Worldwide) who produced the *Blue Peter* annual, although it was never called an annual and always referred to as a book.

The books were written in the first person, as though by the presenters, but they were actually the work of the production team and regular contributors such as Dorothy Smith (Edward Barnes's wife), Bob Broomfield and the artist William Timyn. Biddy ensured that BBC photographers were on hand to capture all the key moments during studios and film shoots. The books were a permanent record of the programme years before the arrival of videos or DVDs. They sold spectacularly well and as the presenters, and later the writers, were on a royalty, they became a substantial source of extra income for them, too. However, Biddy always resisted using the brand for merchandising. 'It'll be the law of diminishing returns,' she said, 'People will be sick of the name *Blue Peter* if it's all over bath mats, mugs and pencil cases.' She also thought such overkill would diminish the value of the badges and team photographs.

Every year there was a competition within the book. The prize was to travel to BBC Television Centre, watch the show go out live and then enjoy a splendid tea with all the pets and presenters. In 1986, one of the lucky children was a ten-year-old girl called Debbie Martin. When Debbie grew up, she joined the BBC and became a successful *Blue Peter* director, filming all over the world from Oman to Bolivia.

There was no book in 1986 because BBC Enterprises withdrew from the 20-year partnership too late for a replacement publisher to be found. The following year, Macmillan stepped into the breach. Although their annual was a colourful effort, it didn't sell and so was a one-off. For the next two years, a small company called Ringpress took over, but they found the costs unrealistic and there followed another gap in 1990 until World Books volunteered to produce the 1991 and 1992 editions. By now, sales were a fraction of the glory days and in 1993, instead of the book, there was an experiment with a magazine format called the *Blue Peter Yearbook*. This failed to make much impact, although from 2001 to 2003 BBC Worldwide did produce a *Blue Peter* magazine, aimed at the younger end of the audience, which had some limited success.

1 The second *Book of Blue Peter*, the title emphasizing that this was not some rubbishy annual, was the first to be published by the BBC.

2 Plugging each new *Blue Peter* book was a regular tradition until the BBC tightened up its policy about the promotion of commercial products.

3 The first *Blue Peter* book is now extremely rare. The artist Bob Broomfield contributed both to this and the 37th book, published in 2007.

There were no annuals released between 1993 and 1997. Their return the following year was prompted by the obvious sales opportunity of the 40th anniversary. Egmont World put a lot of effort into building up the franchise again until their deal expired in 2001 and BBC Worldwide took over – but not for long. After two years, they abruptly pulled out of the arrangement and we were left without a publisher once more.

Most publishers finalize their lists well in advance, so there was little hope of finding a replacement. I wandered into a Waterstones bookshop and looked at the range of annuals on offer. The best seemed to be the work of a company I'd never heard of: Pedigree. We arranged a meeting. Pedigree turned out to be annual specialists and they were delighted to take on the title. They showed their faith by doubling the page count and producing a much glossier product. The sales increased dramatically, proof that quality counts. We did have to compromise in one important detail. The spine still says 'book', as a nod to the collectors, but the cover now owns up to what readers really knew all along, that the *Blue Peter* book is actually an annual, even if it is a cut above the rest!

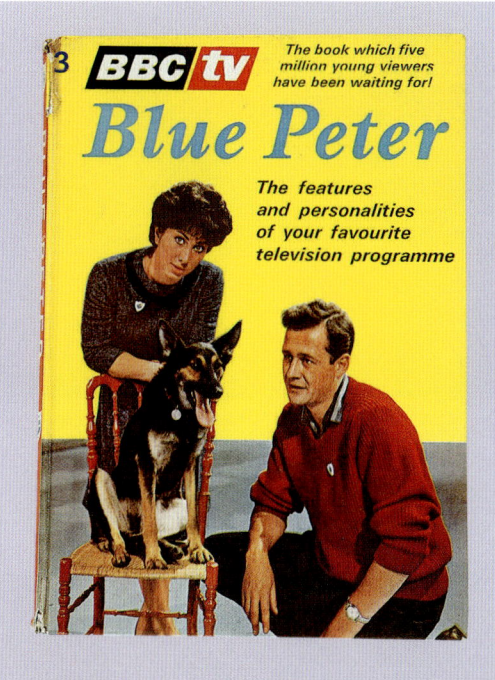

The complete *Blue Peter* bookshelf

1964	Book 1 (Lutterworth)
1965–1985	Book 2 to Book 22 (BBC)
1987	Book 23 (Macmillan)
1988–1989	Book 24 and Book 25 (Ringpress)
1991–1992	Book 26 and Book 27 (World)
1998–2001	Book 28 to Book 31 (Egmont World)
2002–2003	Book 32 and Book 33 (BBC)
2004	Book 34 onwards (Pedigree)
1969–1971	Eight Blue Peter Mini Books (BBC)
1971	Blue Peter Royal Safari (BBC)
1972	The Blue Peter Book of Limericks (Piccolo)
1973–1975	Six Blue Peter Special Assignments (Piccolo/BBC)
1975	The Blue Peter Book of Odd Odes (BBC)
1978	Petra: A Dog for Everyone (Pelham)
1978	The Blue Peter Make, Cook and Look Book (BBC)
1980	The Blue Peter Book of Gorgeous Grub (Piccolo/BBC)
1989	Blue Peter: The Inside Story (Ringpress)
1989	Fit Wit! (Puffin)
1990	The Blue Peter Green Book (BBC/Sainsburys)
1991	Animals Matter (Puffin)
1993	The Blue Peter Action Book (BBC)
1993	Hello, 21st Century (Puffin)
1995	The Blue Peter Book of Things to Make (BBC)
1999	The Day Something Happened (Puffin)
2001–2002	Earth, Ocean, Animal and Food Watch (Dorling Kindersley)
2005	Blue Peter Storytellers (Puffin/BBC)
2008	Dear Blue Peter (Short Books)
	Blue Peter 50th Anniversary (Hamlyn)

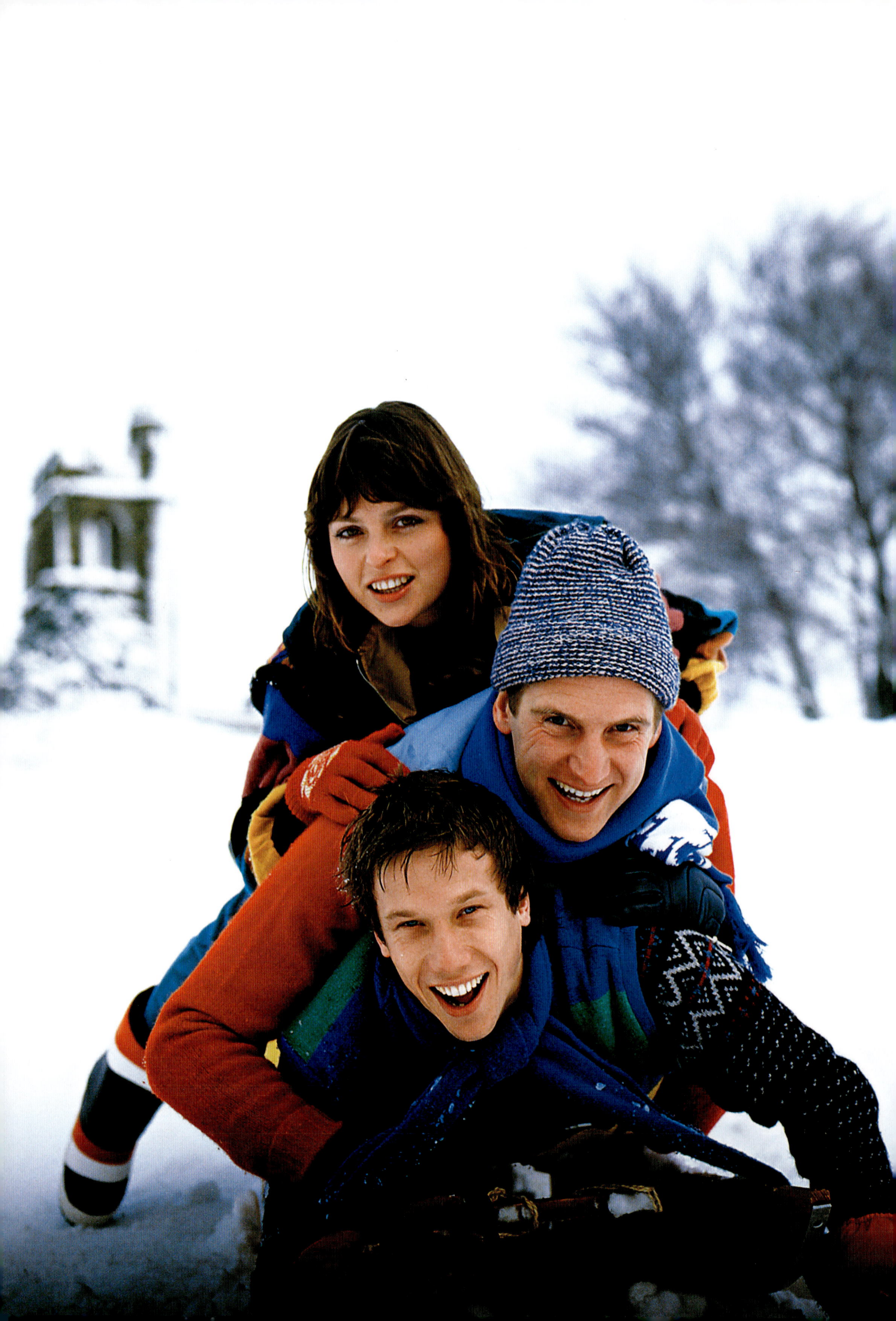

4 Fast Forward
1980–1989

Six months into the new decade it was all change again for *Blue Peter*'s presenting team. In just two years, the line-up had been changed not once, but twice. On 16 July 1980, Biddy Baxter wrote to the recently appointed presenter Sarah Greene: 'Some tremendous news. We've got our new presenter, and in an amazing way, just as extraordinary as finding you. You may have heard of Peter Duncan.'

Trying out the Blue Peter sledge in the snow at Dethick, the Groom family farm which featured many times from 1978 to 1987. Biddy also coined the phrase 'Dethick Time' to refer to Simon's sometimes erratic punctuality.

She continued, 'He's appeared in about 60 "tv's" [television shows] and lots of films and stage shows. Don't worry, he's only 26, not 99. Anyway, to cut a long story short he phoned me quite out of the blue the Tuesday after our last programme saying, "Was there a chance we hadn't found anyone?" Apart from the fact it saved me auditioning the thousands – literally – of people who've been writing and phoning for the job – he really is smashing, and the three of you are going to be absolutely world-beating!'

By Christmas, the programme was no longer a laughing-stock because of its presenters. It was back to doing what it did best. But was this enough for a world in which social and technological change was gathering pace? Not everybody thought so and some of the fiercest critics were within the production team. Peter Salmon, later Controller of BBC1, was a trainee assistant producer on *Blue Peter* in the early 1980s: 'It was moving out of sync with young people. They had the odd black face, even a rock band, but it was still Brownie Britain.' Another assistant producer, Michael Forte, later Head of Children's Programmes at Carlton, claimed that '...my best scripts were spoofs of the programme – "There's a wonderful splash of colour in the garden today."'

Blue Peter has often been accused of being predominantly white, middle class, smug, preachy and remote. Bob Ferguson, a media-studies expert, caused a furore when he suggested a radical departure. His model for a 'Red Peter' would '...campaign against any government that could tolerate poverty, degradation, poor housing or health care. It would be openly anti-royalist, anti-racist and anti-sexist.'

Biddy's robust response always pointed out that there weren't enough middle-class children to account for *Blue Peter*'s massive viewing figures and that middle-class children were responsible for only a proportion of the thousands of letters which flooded weekly into the production office: 'I think it's total rubbish. It makes me so annoyed. It's always the middle classes who criticize it for being middle class. It's inverted snobbery. It's often resurrected by some media analysts who've never made a programme in their lives and don't understand the prepubescent child. They correlate knowledge with being middle class. And there's an awful lot of information on *Blue Peter*, which the audience laps up like blotting paper.'

'I think it's fair to say it *was* white and middle class, which is probably why I fitted in!', was presenter Janet Ellis's observation. 'For instance, in my time, there seemed to be an awful lot of items about the Second World War because they were of great interest to people in the production team and not because they had an enormous amount of relevance to children.'

Edward Barnes used to ask the question, 'Why is *Blue Peter* middle class and what do you think we should do about it?' on interview boards, and he recalls one candidate answering, 'If middle-class values are doing the right thing and being kind to people and animals, I resent it on behalf of the working classes. I think those are working-class values as well!' That man, Roy Thompson, later ended up as the Deputy Head of Children's Programmes.

Edward pointed, in *Blue Peter*'s defence, to presenters such as John Noakes, who offered a regional accent in the days of wall-to-wall received pronunciation, and said the reason for featuring the army films was 'simply a way of getting action cheap'. The royal items were included because they were scoops and British people were always deeply interested in royalty. As he put it: 'The *Mirror* and the *Sun* are not called middle class, but they've got the royals all over them.'

Bronze age

Looking to the programme's future, in 1982, Edward spotted a bright young producer on *Newsround*. His name was Lewis Bronze. After a few months' trial producing on *Blue Peter*, Lewis was fast-tracked to become Biddy's deputy from September 1983. He remembers, 'I hadn't watched *Blue Peter* at all as a child. I went to it knowing nothing about the programme. The first time I had a meeting with Biddy, she was doing some planning for films. I hadn't even realized that not all three presenters went out to make each of the films together. That was the level of my ignorance.'

Lewis was put in charge of all the filming and the running of the appeals. Biddy insisted he directed a few live studios too. Veteran director Alan Russell was brought in to oversee Lewis's efforts. At the end of his first morning, Alan remembers telling him, 'Yes, son, very nice. Only thing is, you spent three hours rehearsing five minutes. You've still got another 20 minutes to get through!'

Lewis was learning all the time: 'Biddy expected the highest standards. She was demanding and unpredictable. I was lucky because she

1 Sarah Greene joined cubs for tea on the Eiffel Tower. By the 1980s there were criticisms of *Blue Peter*'s 'Brownie Britain' culture.

2 *Blue Peter* pushed Television Centre to the limit with items like 1981's fire-bucket chain, which snaked from the studio to the *Blue Peter* garden.

3 Janet Ellis followed in Val's footsteps, dressing up to tell stories like 'Upstairs and Downstairs at Ham House' in 1984.

4 Simon Groom and Peter Duncan gave the programme a strong male double act again. Here they are rehearsing for 1982's Panto Parade.

5 Peter wore the winning green-and-white checked suit, designed by 14-year-old Darren Turner many times.

6 Looking at entries for the competition to design an outfit for Peter Duncan.

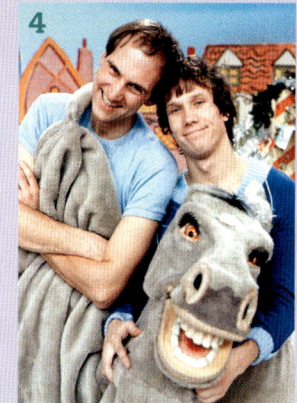

BLUE PETER 50th Anniversary

1

2

3

4

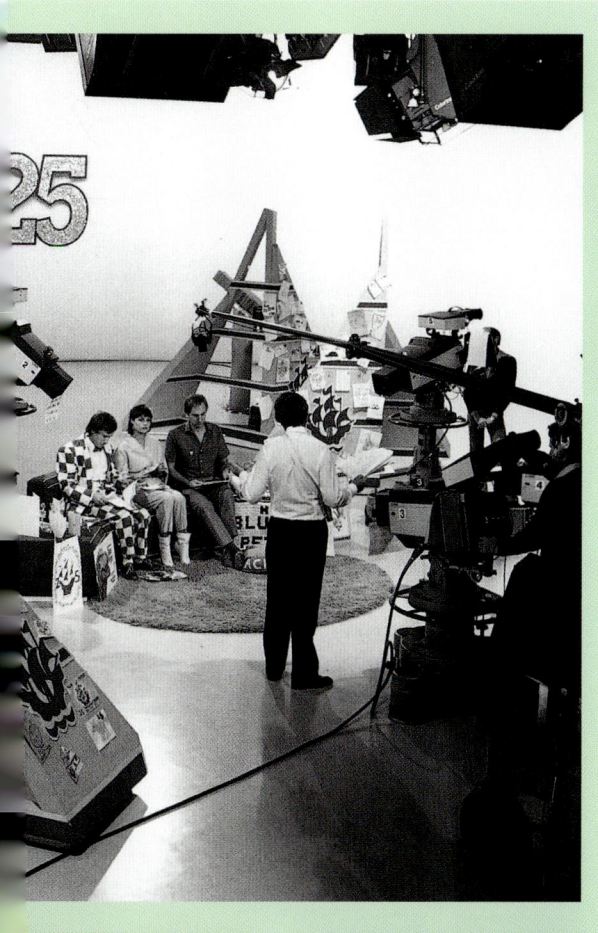

1 Recycling content for an ever-changing audience: this 1985 Roman banquet was first held in 1973 and was remade yet again in 2001.

2 Rehearsals for the 25th-birthday show on 17 October 1983. The day before, BBC1 had screened the first full-length documentary about the programme.

3 Celebrating the corset in 1981. Left to right: Isla St Clair, Tina Heath, Maggie Philbin and Laura and Sarah Greene.

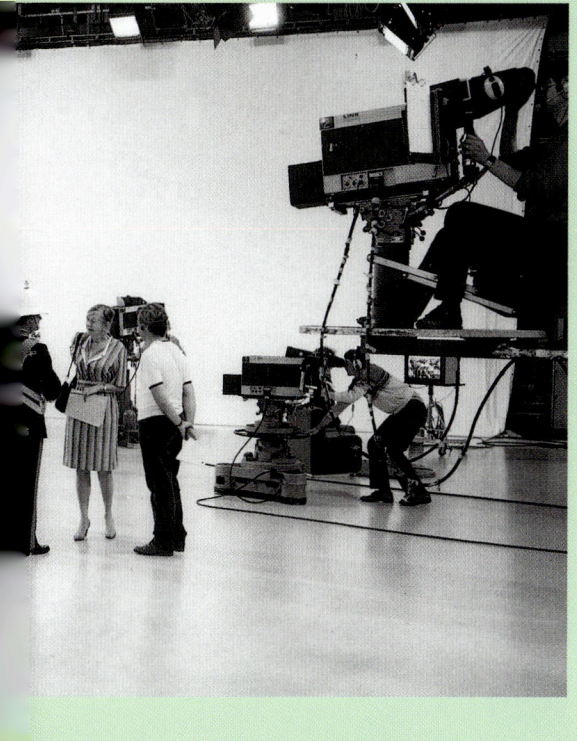

4 Biddy Baxter gave notes to everyone, from presenters to guests, in this case the band of the Royal Marines in 1984.

liked me, which didn't mean we always agreed with one another. I remember a row when I told her I thought a story about St Thérèse of Lisieux, which she wanted to repeat, was just blatant Catholic propaganda. But when I worked for her, the scope of what television can do was revealed to me. I was aware that I was being groomed as the next in line.'

The struggle to keep standards high continued. In 1981 and again in 1984, Biddy had a battle royal to prevent *Blue Peter* being forced to share a studio with *Tomorrow's World*, the BBC's live science magazine programme, which was also broadcast on a Thursday and shared similarities of approach with *Blue Peter*. In a memo to the Controller of BBC1, she commented: 'It will be sheer disaster… the end of our studio spectaculars. There will be no drive-ins or -outs, no appeal or competition displays, none of the panache that keeps the customers on the edge of their seats wondering what will happen next. Nothing but an endless succession of dreary talking heads – anathema to children of all ages.

'You asked me to accept the studio change as a challenge. I am never afraid to grasp the nettle, but I cannot wave a wand. I am aware of *Blue Peter*'s value to BBC1 in helping to build the early-evening viewing figures. This is largely due to the widely ranging content of the programme and its visual impact.'

This disastrous strategy was eventually averted, but ever after similar suggestions were made with monotonous regularity by those charged with saving the BBC money. *Blue Peter* was often resented internally because of its significant resources, but maintaining the flagship mix of big studios, complicated items, dressing up and lots of filming didn't come cheap.

A new look

Throughout the decade, the 'look' of the programme developed faster than ever before. The set became more and more colourful, with a neon *Blue Peter* ship replacing the hanging Perspex version. Lighting became brighter and richer, and the presenters more overtly fashion conscious.

Sarah Greene was the first to be experimental with her outfits and hairstyles. Biddy took a violent dislike to one particular film because Sarah wore 'vulgar' white shoes in it! Janet Ellis enjoyed the chance to try out different looks. Mark Curry opted for loud patterns and primary-coloured glasses, while Caron Keating was *Blue Peter*'s fashion icon.

Generally, Biddy was tolerant of all these forms of self-expression, although on 9 May 1986 she was moved to send a memo to the BBC's Senior Costume Designer, Velma Buckle: 'Very many thanks for sparing the time to come to the gallery to see for yourself how appallingly ghastly Janet Ellis looked. Apart from Janet's hideous outfit, Simon and Peter were wearing almost identical shirts. It's never ideal to ask the presenters to change and particularly awkward asking a girl, as it's not a very good boost to the morale. I would be so grateful if you would make sure that the costume designers give us their expert advice early in the day.'

The arrival of the domestic video recorder meant that audiences now started to have more choice over their viewing. The BBC embraced this revolution by releasing a *Blue Peter Makes* 'videogram' in 1983. After the live transmission on 13 December 1982, Simon, Sarah and Peter stayed on to record the links for this collection of recent makes. It was the first of several *Blue Peter* videos in the years to come. In 1986, the Sunday morning *Blue Peter* omnibus, which compiled the two weekly editions together with a specially recorded link, offered another chance to tune in.

End of an era

Throughout the 1980s, there was a gradual diminishing of *Blue Peter*'s faithful band of long-term contributors – stalwarts such as Percy Thrower, George Cansdale, Peggy Spencer, Derek Freeman and Dorothy Smith. One by one, they retired or died. Then, in 1986, Edward Barnes decided to step down as Head of Children's Programmes and return to active production. His successor was the distinguished children's drama producer Anna Home, who, among her impressive string of credits, had commissioned *Grange Hill*, the first twice-weekly soap for children, set in a London comprehensive school.

Her appointment was a turning point for *Blue Peter*. There had never been any love lost between Biddy and Anna. It was a novel and uncomfortable feeling to have a sceptic at the top of the tree instead of an enthusiastic ally. According to Lewis Bronze, '...the way *Blue Peter* was viewed within the department changed radically overnight. Biddy fell out of favour.' Biddy disagrees: 'What changed was that there was no longer any creative input or enthusiasm from the top. Anna knew she was on to a good thing and didn't want to rock the boat but she was far more interested in the drama output.'

Biddy remained Editor until the summer of 1988. When news of her departure was made public, it was widely reported as the end of an era. In many ways, it was. Biddy had managed a remarkable continuity of treatment and approach for over a quarter of a century. Much has been written and said about her single-minded determination and uncompromising insistence on doing things her way.

Edward Barnes acknowledges that she was '...ruthless on behalf of the audience. She was totally fearless because of this belief that she was doing it for children. If she didn't fight for them, no one else would.'

In the studio gallery, Biddy had a habit of kicking the control desk or pointedly coughing when she wanted the director to cut from one shot to another. Her obsessive attention to detail and frequent commands, 'More fur, less flesh!' (in items featuring animals), 'Keep the feet in!' (during performance items) and 'Where's the close-up?' (in all items), were legacies that lived on for years after she had handed on her responsibilities. Biddy's fierce loyalty to the programme meant she was always willing to offer quotes or interviews for its promotion or in its defence.

Like millions of others, Sarah Greene had '...grown up seeing her name at the end of the programme. When I was introduced to her, there

27 June 1988 – Biddy's last *Blue Peter*. She was given a bigger send-off than many presenters, with a special tribute on the programme and her very own gold badge. A few days later she was a guest on the *Wogan* chat show, where Terry surprised her with a line-up of past presenters.

FAST FORWARD

BLUE PETER 50th Anniversary

1

1 20 April 1989 – will new boy John Leslie, the first presenter cast by incoming Editor Lewis Bronze, measure up?

2 Long-serving producer/director Alex Leger on location with Caron Keating. Alex joined in 1975 and was still on the team in 2008.

3 Yvette Fielding during her 1988 ascent of the spire at Salisbury Cathedral. The youngest-ever presenter, she had a troubled start but became hugely popular.

4 This item about the sculptor Henry Moore marked the beginning of a fresh approach to traditional *Blue Peter* material post-Biddy Baxter.

was this tall, cool, blonde, curvaceous lady who wore proper black stockings. She thought nothing of dipping forward and showing a little too much décolletage, to get the scoutmasters to spend that extra hour in the garden, even if they were freezing to death, just to get the right shots. She taught me so much. *Blue Peter* was like being at the university of television and she was head of department.'

Peter Purves says '…the thing everyone remembers about Biddy is the sound of her. You'd hear the clip-clop of these wonderful, elegant high heels coming down from the gallery into the studio to give notes or to bollock somebody. And we'd think, "Here we go!" Biddy ruled the roost. There was no question about it. While I was shaving in the morning, I'd be imagining what I'd like to say to her. But although she was a control freak, she had a direct line to the imagination of eight-year-olds.'

Simon Groom remembers Biddy's frantic notes given just after the run-through or dress rehearsal: 'She would come down with the script, very often covered with subtle comments like "rubbish" or "mean it" or "not convincing", almost as though she'd been marking a piece of homework. "This is wrong, that's wrong. I'm cutting this and changing that." But looking back, those decisions were vital.'

Janet Ellis felt that Biddy was a '…brilliant Editor. Her loyalty to the viewers was unbelievable. She had absolute tunnel vision about the programme. The things she taught me have stayed with me ever since.'

Peter Duncan '…loved her. I thought she was a one-off. Terribly astute. You knew by the pace of the heels how bad you'd been. She sometimes used to send me a transcript of what I'd said. Often it was absolute gobbledegook!'

The one person who has worked on *Blue Peter* longer than Biddy is producer Alex Leger, who joined in 1975 and is still there today. Alex found her '…fascinating. You'd never know what she'd do next. She wouldn't let anything go until you could categorically say, hand on heart, that it didn't exist, or would cost a fortune to insure or whatever. We did the story of Lowry once and of course she wanted some originals in the studio. Lowry died suddenly as we were planning the item. Trying to get a Lowry out of a gallery when overnight it had gone from being worth £20,000 to £120,000 was a nightmare. But such was the power of the programme that I ended up going to a gallery in Knightsbridge in a black cab, where I picked up three paintings and brought them back to Television Centre, not even protected. Failure was not an option! But I never minded doing whatever she wanted, because if you did, she'd lay down her life to protect you.'

Before Biddy left, Lewis Bronze recalls she said to him, 'In life there are number two people and number one people.' He says, 'I think she was talking about seniority. "You're a number one person and you need to run your own ship."'

When Lewis took over, he told the production team that they were about to experience *Blue Peter*'s version of 'glasnost'. Life wouldn't simply continue as before. But when the programme returned in September 1988, anyone expecting radical change was in for a surprise. Oliver

Macfarlane, a key studio producer and later Editor himself, reasoned: 'We thought the best tactic was for the programme to come back looking exactly the same but then to start gradually changing some of the content.'

This subtle approach was illustrated in the very first show of the season, which included an item about the sculptor Henry Moore. Lewis knew that '…it was typical *Blue Peter* fodder. Biddy would have done it. But what we did that was different was to go out and make a playful film where children ran in and out of Henry Moore sculptures all over London. They felt them and talked about them, and it was very natural. It sounds very ordinary, but it put down a marker that we were going to do those traditional items, but address them in a more modern way.

'The programme had spoken with one voice – Biddy's – and I wanted to make it speak with lots of different voices. I wanted to be more inclusive too. Until then, children had come to the studio and were told what to say. By the time they came on air, they were sometimes stilted and it was awful.'

Standard *Blue Peter* fare, such as the annual fireworks warning, was done in a fresh way, for instance in a quiz format. Others, like the cat show and the rather *Boy's Own*-sounding Outstanding Endeavour Awards were phased out. There was more live music and better representation of Britain's different cultures. Production techniques were changing. Shooting stories on videotape rather than film not only brought a much more immediate and contemporary feel, it brought an end to the tyranny of the 'shooting ratio'.

The biggest impact of the new regime was the introduction of a strongly green agenda. This went further than just reflecting the mood of the times. There was a campaigning feel to the copious amounts of airtime devoted to everything from lead-free petrol and the ozone layer to the greenhouse effect and recycling. In November 1988, the green badge, the first new badge in decades, was introduced. The best-selling *The Blue Peter Green Book* followed.

On 8 June 1989, there was a very significant experiment. The whole programme was transmitted from Carrickfergus Castle in Northern Ireland. Although outside broadcast technology had been used before, this was the first time the show had gone fully 'on the road'. It was a precursor of things to come, but it very nearly didn't happen at all. During rehearsals, a sudden strike was called. It was due to begin that afternoon and would certainly black out the entire outside broadcast. The only option was to record and transmit the dress rehearsal instead. Everybody pulled together and just completed the work before the deadline. Years later, in the so-called summer of 2000, another dress rehearsal, this time of a *Blue Peter* garden special, was transmitted thanks to the onset of something equally non-negotiable – teeming rain. On both occasions, nobody watching at home would have been any the wiser.

Under Lewis's phlegmatic leadership, the programme seemed committed to a policy of evolution rather than revolution. But the next decade would bring *Blue Peter*'s biggest expansion yet.

1 Yvette Fielding and Caron Keating on location for the 1988 summer expedition to west-coast USA. This was a deliberate contrast to the previous year's trip to the Soviet Union.

2 Yvette and Caron in Moscow's Red Square for the 1987 expedition to the Soviet Union.

Presenter Profile
SARAH GREENE

Biddy Baxter once nominated Sarah Greene as her favourite presenter of all, explaining 'she put so much love and energy into the programme'.

JOINED: 19 May 1980

LEFT: 27 June 1983

MEMORABLE MOMENTS: Diving on the *Mary Rose*; helicopter abseiling; barnstorming; hot-air ballooning; playing Jane Austen; trips to Malaysia, Japan and Canada

On 17 April 1980, the cast of the new BBC Sunday teatime drama serial *The Swish of the Curtain* was interviewed by Tina Heath on *Blue Peter*. She was struck by how at home one of them seemed to be in the studio: 'I was so excited. I went to Biddy Baxter and said, "That's your next presenter." She replied, "How extraordinary, I think you're right."'

Biddy then invited a somewhat bemused Sarah Greene to audition: 'At that stage in my life, there was no more thought of me becoming a presenter than becoming a heart surgeon. I talked to a few friends who said, "Go on, do it for a dare and bring us a badge back!" I walked into the studio to audition and there was the crew I'd been working with on *Swish*. They thought it was the funniest thing that here was this girl they were used to getting drunk with after filming!'

Sarah's speedy casting was inspired, but it took some time for her to relax into the role. On 9 May, Biddy wrote reassuringly to her: 'Being "you" may not be easy, but it certainly won't be dull, and all of us on the production team are looking forward to working with you very much indeed.'

Sarah felt '…completely lost. At first, I was playing the part of a *Blue Peter* presenter. A version of Sarah Greene, the perfect elder sister. A sort of virginal princess. And I know what was going on in my personal life at that stage and I certainly wasn't a virginal princess!'

Everyone's favourite big sister

One of Sarah's techniques was to imagine that she was talking to her eight-year-old sister. 'Greeno', as Sarah was known, had genuine warmth and the ability to connect with the material. She also helped to refresh the presenting style on the show: 'It wasn't long before I began to recognize these turns of phrase that would pop up in the script. Biddyisms we used to call them, things like "splash of colour" and "no less than". Handy because you could rattle them off, and while you were rattling them off, it gave you a chance to try to remember what was coming next. Biddy had a whole myriad of adjectives that she'd use and I substituted these with my own words like "brill", which was current at the time. There was a place called Brill and I remember the Brownies from Brill writing to me saying how thrilled they were!'

The success of the Sarah Greene, Simon Groom and Peter Duncan team was rewarded when the programme won a coveted BAFTA award in 1982. Sarah formed a strong bond with her fellow presenters: 'They became like brothers to me. We did play tricks on each other. Pete always did the cooking and I would get down behind the counter and bite his ankles during the transmission to cheer him up!'

All three presenters noticed that the programme's veteran animal handler, Edith Menezes, regularly got through as many as two or three Mills and Boon romances every studio day. Sarah recalls, 'So we found the filthiest, most pornographic novel, glued it inside a Mills and Boon cover and just kept an eye on her all day. "How's the book going, Edith?" "Cor! This is the best one I've ever read, it's marvellous!" I don't think we ever told her!'

BLUE PETER 50th Anniversary

1 Sarah's 1982 dive to the wreck of the *Mary Rose* required months of gruelling training. The whole story was compiled into a *Blue Peter* special, 'A Dive Through Time'.

2 In 1983 Sarah went behind-the-scenes with the Royal Ballet at Covent Garden. She met these rather strange characters along the way.

The joke was on Sarah when she had to deal with an over-excited toy pony: 'This pony was tiny, but the one part of his body that was normal-sized was his willy. And during the live show, it just got bigger and bigger. No matter what the crew did to try to exclude it, it kept flicking into shot. All of them were in hysterics, but I had to keep going, knowing that there was a line coming up in the script where I had to say, "As you can see, he's a very happy little pony." It was one of the most challenging moments in my career!'

It was while she was working on *Blue Peter* that Sarah met the man she eventually married, presenter and DJ Mike Smith: 'He was on the rival programme to *Blue Peter*, a show called CBTV. In those days, it was very much "us and them". When I was learning to dive on the *Mary Rose*, I needed a partner and he was the "mystery blonde" buddy in the background of all my dive training films. We thought that was very funny! Mike absolutely loved *Blue Peter* as a kid, and when he first came to the studio, he wore a suit. Biddy said, "Darling, is that your bank manager?"'

Cat Club queen

Christmas was always a frantically busy time on *Blue Peter*: 'Of course everyone would have flu. On top of all the extra pre-recording of pantos and specials, the girl presenter had to go to the National Cat Club Show. You sat behind this stall and signed autographs all day before doing some judging. You'd got freezing cold sitting there and the smell of cats was quite overwhelming. The second year I got wise. The director stashed a bottle of whisky under the counter. Every so often I'd have a nip and that kept me warm. But by the time I stood up to judge, I was reeling. The third year, I had to wear a fluffy furry cat costume in the panto and I thought, "I'll wear the costume to the cat show. Then not only will I keep warm, but I can hide the alcohol inside the costume!" So that year, I was a warm, happy, drunken cat judging the show!'

Sarah completed three action-packed seasons on *Blue Peter*: 'I left when I still loved it. I look back with great fondness and great affection on three supremely happy years that came at exactly the right time in my life.'

Afterwards, she spent the best part of a decade presenting first *Saturday Superstore* and then its successor *Going Live!* Other TV appearances ranged from *Eureka!*, *Take Two*, *Posh Frocks* and *Holiday* to *This Morning*, *Collector's Lot* and *Dancing On Ice*. She also appeared in television dramas like *Dr Who*, *Ghostwatch* and *Casualty*. She made a memorable return to *Blue Peter* when she played the part of a vampish villainess in the 2002 Quest serial, *The Hunt For The Blue Stone*. As an in-joke, the cameo role of her butler was played by Editor Steve Hocking, who had been one of her directors on *Going Live!*

Presenter Profile SARAH GREENE

3 Sarah with her *Blue Peter* 'brothers', Peter and Simon, during the 1982 expedition to Canada. She once said of her three-year stint: 'The first year was learning, the second consolidating and the third repeating. Then it was time to leave.'

4 Freezing cold but putting a brave face on it, Sarah meets one of her many admirers at the National Cat Club Show.

Presenter Profile
PETER DUNCAN

1 Peter Duncan was one of many presenters who dreaded signing the pile of photo-cards that awaited them in make-up every studio day.

JOINED: 11 September 1980 and 9 September 1985

LEFT: 18 June 1984 and 27 November 1986

MEMORABLE MOMENTS: First *Blue Peter* presenter to run the London Marathon; cleaning the face of Big Ben; puppy-walking guide dog Prince; flying trapeze; speed-skiing; the Royal Marines Endurance Course; helicopter dunking; expeditions to Japan, Canada, Sri Lanka and Peru

In the autumn of 1977, BBC1 screened *King Cinder*, a fast-paced children's thriller set in the world of speedway. It was a big success and its star was an appealing, fresh-faced young actor called Peter Duncan. Duncan had been in show business since birth. Both his parents were performers, regularly putting on summer shows and pantomimes: 'My first memory is lying in a cot in the wings, looking up at the lights.'

Peter auditioned during the search to replace John Noakes: 'I went along as a kind of laugh really, but also partly because it appealed to the variety side in me. I've always regarded *Blue Peter* as a branch of variety.'

Biddy immediately felt that she had found the perfect new boy, but now that the job was on offer, he had doubts. He worried that if he became a TV personality, he might compromise his future as an actor. Keen to get him on board, on 13 February 1978 Biddy invited him to the studio to watch a programme go out. On that day, the star attraction was a variety performer called Linda Grant, who wore a glamorous evening gown with a plunging neckline and whose act involved using household objects as musical instruments. Incidental to the act was the glaringly obvious fact that, at some point, Linda had been a man: 'Nobody seemed aware of this. He/she had all these bathroom objects and was blowing sounds into them. Then I went up into the gallery, where Biddy and the director sat, and there was lots of effing and blinding going on. I thought, "Oh my God, I'm not sure about this." I decided that it wasn't for me really and turned it down. I kind of blame that man/woman with the old bathroom utensils!'

Two years later, he saw that Christopher Wenner was leaving: 'I watched Sarah do one episode and she forgot all her lines. I thought, "Well, that's for me!" I'd always been a sporty person and I knew the role was the Noakes role. Really, the only thing I could do at the start was be butch and climb up something or fall off something because I wasn't very good at the words.'

Over the next four years, Peter resisted attempts to pin him down to the discipline of the *Blue Peter* script: 'I didn't want to become verbose. I wanted to be much more the ad-lib kid and I thought the programme needed that.' There were plenty of mistakes and memory losses, but the audience liked him for being natural and brave. With Peter working with Simon Groom and Sarah Greene, a new 'dream team' emerged.

Blue Peter hero

Peter's first film was cleaning the face of Big Ben. Rather like 'Noakes Up Nelson', the daring film in which John Noakes scaled Nelson's Column, no safety ropes were involved. It wasn't the only demanding assignment. Making a rock-climbing story in the summer of 1983, he was so scared that he cried.

On 29 March 1981, Peter accomplished a major 'first', running the inaugural London Marathon in three hours, 11 minutes and 42 seconds. Other presenters followed, but this time has yet to be bettered: 'I trained very hard for it. At the start we lost the film crew and I had to go back 200 yards

Presenter Profile PETER DUNCAN

2 Training for the Royal Navy Field Gun Race. This assignment, shared with Simon Groom, was incredibly tough. The race has since been discontinued.

3 Peter's daughter Lucy became the third *Blue Peter* baby when she appeared in a series of studio items and films from 1985 to 1986.

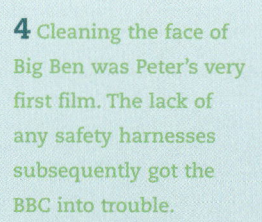

4 Cleaning the face of Big Ben was Peter's very first film. The lack of any safety harnesses subsequently got the BBC into trouble.

[180 metres] and start all over again, which was very frustrating. But to run 26 miles through the streets of London and see that number of people just cheering for you was a wonderful experience.'

Peter's consistently scruffy appearance led to the idea of holding a competition to design him an outfit. The winning entry, chosen by Peter, an offensively loud green and white checked suit that became his trademark, was wheeled out on many occasions thereafter: 'I chose the most extreme outfit I could. If there was a boring item, I wore the suit to brighten it up. I've still got it in the attic!'

After four seasons, Peter left to front his own adventure series, *Duncan Dares*. Named by *Blue Peter* viewers, *Duncan Dares* was on the same lines as *Go With Noakes* but more action-packed, as Peter was younger and fitter. The six challenges included dragon-boat racing, tightrope walking and becoming a stuntman.

Then, following the dismal debacle of his replacement, Michael Sundin, Peter surprised viewers by returning for a second stint. He was the only presenter ever to do so: 'I was a stopgap. I felt fresh again after a year's sabbatical and I said, "Well, I'll stay for a year or 15 months and that'll give you time to find someone else."'

Peter's wife was pregnant when he rejoined the team, and Biddy saw the chance to feature a new *Blue Peter* baby, on the same lines as Daniel in the late 1960s and Jemma in the early 1980s. Peter's daughter Lucy was born on 3 November 1985 and was seen on the programme the very next day: 'We were very keen on showing breast-feeding. I had a long argument about that and said, "We're not doing it unless we show breast-feeding", because that was natural and what we do. You saw a child grow up for its first year, and being the father, on television, was a lovely thing to do.'

Following his second departure, and half a dozen more *Duncan Dares*, Peter continued to pop back for guest appearances, far more than any other presenter. This was a reflection of the fondness felt for him by the production teams and the audiences. In February 2007, when he returned as Chief Scout, Peter was awarded a gold badge for inspiring young people for so long. 'I have great affection for *Blue Peter*. It is a nice feeling to be part of a culture that is very strong.'

Presenter Profile
JANET ELLIS

1 27-year-old Janet Ellis joined *Blue Peter* in April 1983 and had a two-month crossover period with her predecessor, Sarah Greene.

JOINED: 28 April 1983

LEFT: 29 June 1987

MEMORABLE MOMENTS: Free-fall parachute jumping; singing in the Last Night of the Proms; dangling over Derbyshire completing a cable-car rescue (which Simon Groom had refused to do); the Royal Marines Mud Run; trips to Sri Lanka, Bangladesh, Kenya, Malawi and Australia (where she had an asthma attack on Ayers Rock)

Janet Ellis had been working on a children's programme called *Jigsaw* when her agent, Annie Sweetbaum, let her in on the 'absolute secret' that Sarah Greene was leaving *Blue Peter*. Annie looked after many *Blue Peter* presenters and bet Janet five pounds she'd get the job. So, like Lesley Judd before her, Janet left an envelope with all her details in a prominent position on Biddy Baxter's desk. She also made sure that Edward Barnes, Head of Children's Programmes, was aware of her interest. Her agent briefed her on the infamous audition, what to expect and how to prepare.

Annie Sweetbaum won her bet and Janet was introduced to an enthusiastic press. Her big challenge was to follow in John Noakes's footsteps and attempt a record-breaking free-fall parachute jump: 'I had really good training and I enjoyed making the films, but I never enjoyed parachuting. I never got over the fear. There was a crack team of people doing it with me and they were very sweet. I remember saying to them once, "I really feel that you're very concerned for me." They replied, "We just don't want anything to happen to you, Janet. Imagine the paperwork!"'

Unfortunately there were a couple of nasty accidents: 'After one jump, I landed face down and got a large clump of Oxfordshire in my face. I was wearing white gloves, I put my hands up and the gloves were covered in blood. I realized I'd done something quite nasty because these great, strong RAF guys went a very interesting shade of white. One of them said, "Don't look, we'll just get you to the hospital." I'd torn away the skin inside my mouth right down to the gum. It was gruesome. I had nine stitches, but the local anaesthetic I'd been given wore off during my drive back to London, so from Reading onwards I screamed for the rest of the journey.'

When she felt strong enough, Janet phoned Biddy to explain. Biddy persuaded her that she should show the damage on the next programme: 'Everything's an item on *Blue Peter*!'

The next mishap was more serious, and again took place during a practice jump, with no cameras present. Janet fell awkwardly and broke her pelvis. This time she was admitted to hospital and Biddy sent a crew to reassure viewers. 'On the show that day, there was an item about a series called *Tripods*. My father had done the special effects and was going to be a guest. Biddy had got Sarah [Greene] to stand in for me. So I lay in my hospital bed and watched Sarah interview my dad, which was really sad! Luckily, a couple of years later, he was trundled on to do something about *Dr Who*.'

After the accident, Janet explained to Biddy that she now felt a little reluctant to carry on: 'She took me to lunch and said, "Darling, I want you to think of your courage like a ketchup bottle. If there's only a tiny bit of courage left in the bottle, turn it upside down, shake it on the bottom and I'm sure some more will come out!" And it did.' Biddy, however, does not recall giving Janet this advice, adding, 'I've never used the word "ketchup" in my life!'

On 8 October 1986, Janet jumped from 20,000 feet (6,000 metres), a European record for a civilian woman.

2 Following in John Noakes' footsteps, Janet trained to break a civilian freefall parachuting record. It took three years of hard knocks.

3 Janet's first photo call with Goldie and K9 – a reference to the fact that Janet had appeared in the 1979 *Dr Who* story 'The Horns of Nimon'.

4 In September 1987, Janet brought baby Jack to the studio, giving the lie to the story that she was sacked for having a baby out of wedlock.

Janet reflects: 'The hard part of *Blue Peter* was the schedule. You'd be away filming in between studios, often far away. The budget meant that you went on the train or bunched up in a car with the PA. You'd drive for miles and film in the freezing cold until the dying of the light because the director didn't have the studio responsibility and just wanted to get his film in the can. You'd get back late to London and there would be the script waiting for you for the next day's studio. Usually with an item about Chinese mathematics to learn!'

'Quit or wed'

Just before Christmas 1986, Janet discovered she was pregnant. She told Biddy '…who said "Oh good, another viewer!"'. Janet's pregnancy was announced on the programme on 2 February 1987. There was a storm of controversy in the press, in which she was denounced as an unmarried mum, and *Blue Peter* was castigated for 'promoting' such moral laxity. Tory MP Peter Bruinvels demanded she 'quit or wed'.

'Nobody actually minded, viewers or the production team. I was happy. It was like being let off games. The others would have to do all the cold horrible stuff and then it'd come back to me all snug in the studio saying, "That looked uncomfortable. Now let's make some biscuits!"

'The truth was I wasn't offered another contract, so it was interpreted that I was sacked.' Trying to set the record straight, Janet wrote to the *Daily Mail*: 'I was surprised to read that I'd been "axed" from *Blue Peter*. If that's the case, I'm still waiting for my letter of dismissal! I am leaving the show after four very happy years to pursue my career – and have a baby.'

In September 1987, Janet brought baby Jack to the studio to show viewers, but the misrepresentation that she was dropped for having a child out of wedlock persists to this day.

Years later, she made a couple of memorable return visits of her own. In December 2001, she appeared alongside her pop star daughter Sophie Ellis-Bextor. Sophie had been on the show as a child, modelling makes, so this time Janet was able to award her with a silver badge for doing something different – singing her hit single!

The following year, Janet put in a magnificent performance as presenter Liz Barker's ghastly, pushy, stage-struck mother, Enchilada, in the special 'Christmas At The Club *Blue Peter*'. Other TV work has included singing competition *Just The Two of Us*, *When Blue Peter Became ABBA* and regular appearances in *The Wright Stuff*.

Presenter Profile

MICHAEL SUNDIN

JOINED: 13 September 1984

LEFT: 24 June 1985

MEMORABLE MOMENTS: Stunt horse riding; army gymnastics; freestyle water-skiing; looking round Elton John's house; the Royal Marines Mud Run

1 Michael was only on the show for one season. Following his death in July 1989, *Blue Peter* ran a tribute on the first show of the next season.

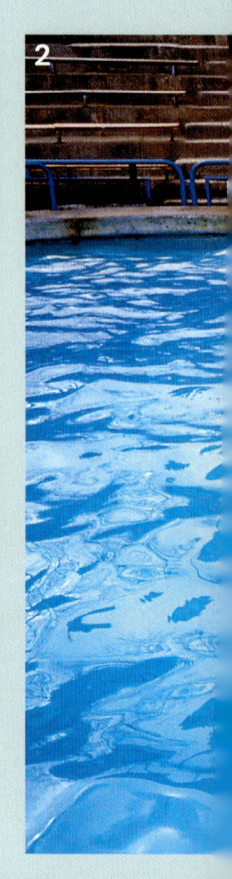

According to Edward Barnes, Head of Children's Programmes at the time, the casting of Michael Sundin was 'our biggest mistake'. It was the summer of 1984. The exceptionally popular Peter Duncan was about to leave and start work on his *Duncan Dares* series. He was a tough act to follow.

On 21 May, an effusive hand-written letter of introduction arrived from an agent called George Garrard: 'It has been suggested in conversation with Mr Edward Barnes's office that we should submit details of our client Michael Sundin.'

The agent enthused about Michael's experience at Gateshead Youth Theatre, his 'trampolining exploits', his enjoyment of 'dangerous stunts', his 'considerable work for charity' and his 'affinity with animals'. Photographs showed a pleasant-looking young man with a wide smile and curly blond hair. On the face of it, this was a textbook CV for an aspiring *Blue Peter* presenter and on 29 May, Biddy Baxter scribbled a succinct note to her secretary Annie: 'Get in this pm'.

Apart from the trampolining, the actual audition wasn't a very competent effort, but Biddy and her deputy, Lewis Bronze, were still keen. They took Sundin's tape to show Edward Barnes, who remembers: 'It was about half past seven on a hot summer's night. The thing that got him the job was the trampolining, but he was a champion for God's sake, he ought to have been good at that. That's not what it was all about. I saw him and I knew he was wrong and I blame myself very much because I didn't say get him out.'

The usual custom was for an incoming presenter to appear hot on the heels of their predecessor. However, Michael's commitments to playing the robot Tik-Tok in the movie *Return To Oz* meant that he wasn't available for the summer trip. Instead, Lewis made a behind-the-scenes film on the movie, screened in Michael's first programme.

A bad start

Almost from the start, it was downhill all the way. Michael's uncertain, stumbling performances became an instant talking point among the audience. He seemed horribly out of place next to his older and more confident co-presenters. His unusual mid-Atlantic/Geordie hybrid accent didn't help. He wasn't the first presenter to start badly, but would he turn out to be a Christopher Wenner, who fell by the wayside, or a John Noakes, who became a star?

The team thought their best chance of star-making was to throw the new boy into the thick of as many action films as they could muster. Michael was strong, capable, brave and determined. But despite the hard work and hard knocks, the audience just didn't warm to him. A decision had to be made. Biddy, Lewis and Edward were unanimous. They felt everything possible had been done. They would only be damaging the programme if they persevered. The contract would not be renewed.

On the final show of the season, Michael put a brave face on his bitter disappointment, saying he was leaving to promote *Return To Oz* and that he'd be making some *Blue Peter* 'specials' in the autumn.

Presenter Profile MICHAEL SUNDIN

2 Michael was one of the bravest *Blue Peter* presenters. Physically, there was nothing he wouldn't tackle – like this ride on the back of a killer whale.

3 Michael's skills as a champion gymnast got him the job on *Blue Peter* and they were showcased during his first photo-call.

While Simon Groom and Janet Ellis set off Down Under, the question of a new presenter had to be faced. No one felt like starting all over again. Instead, Biddy and Edward decided to ask Peter Duncan to return. Duncan turned down the chance to present ITV's Saturday morning offering to accept their invitation.

As for Michael, his relations with the BBC were to be only temporarily cordial. On 2 September he wrote to Biddy: 'With regard to filming with *Blue Peter* in the near future, I have a couple of ideas and would be glad to chat with you about them.' Peter Duncan's return had yet to be made public and he concluded: 'I hope the new presenter has a wonderful time with the team, just as much as I did.'

The filming was never to be. Just two weeks later, Biddy took a call from the *Daily Mirror*. Michael had given the newspaper a scathing interview, claiming that the programme was blinkered and didn't show what the real world was really like. He claimed he had wanted to do items on drugs, smoking and keeping fit, but wasn't allowed. Biddy had told him '…to imagine a five-year-old watching at home'.

Biddy responded: 'He's entitled to his opinion – a shame he didn't tell us when he was with us.'

Worse was to follow. A couple of weeks later, the *Daily Mirror* was back in touch. This time a reporter wanted a comment about a video of an exotic dance act shot at the Hippodrome nightclub in London, featuring Michael Sundin. The BBC stated that they had no knowledge of such a video. Sundin was by now very much an ex-presenter.

Although presenting *Blue Peter* hadn't worked out, his undoubted skill as a gymnast and dancer should have guaranteed him a good living for years to come. But then he was diagnosed with the HIV virus. Treatment for HIV was still in the early stages. Young and fit as he was, Michael could have enjoyed a long life if only he'd had access to the drugs readily available today. He worked on through his illness and, showing his great generosity of spirit, in June 1988 agreed to appear as part of a line-up of *Blue Peter* presenters assembled to surprise Biddy on the Wogan chat show.

Michael died the following summer. According to Janet Ellis, he departed this life '…with incredible grace, charm and bags of humour'.

109

Presenter Profile
MARK CURRY

1 Mark Curry was a highly experienced performer who had started his career as a child on series like ITV's *Junior Showtime*.

2 Despite his fear of heights, in 1988 Mark agreed to be tied to a revolving windmill for a classically bizarre *Blue Peter* action film.

JOINED: 23 June 1986

LEFT: 26 June 1989

MEMORABLE MOMENTS: Facing his vertigo climbing up British Telecom telegraph poles; joining a stunt team; swimming the icy Serpentine in Hyde Park; knocking the head off a Lego man; telling historical stories; his many song-and-dance routines; trips to Malawi and the Soviet Union

When it came to replacing Simon Groom, Biddy was looking for an experienced pair of hands, preferably someone with whom the audience was already familiar. She auditioned a young children's presenter called Howard Stableford, but he turned down his chance and joined the science magazine programme *Tomorrow's World* instead. She tried very hard to persuade Phillip Schofield to sign, after his huge success as the link man on BBC1 afternoons. But he had his sights set on Saturday mornings.

The next suggestion was Mark Curry. Rather like Peter Duncan, Mark had been in 'the business' since he was a child, notably as a performer and host on the ITV talent competition *Junior Showtime*. He'd first come to Biddy's attention as the presenter of *Treasure Houses*, which was, to all intents and purposes, a *Blue Peter* spin-off. In *Treasure Houses*, Mark told the story of historic homes and museums, and the famous people who were associated with them. The scripts were complex and challenging, and his acting skills brought them to life. At the same time, he'd been fronting *The Saturday Picture Show*, which showcased his ability to cope with 'live' – an essential requirement for *Blue Peter* presenters.

Like Tina Heath before him, Mark was offered the job as the new presenter without having to audition, but on 9 March 1986 he rang to say that he didn't want it: 'When it was offered, it came as a real surprise. I never thought of myself as a *Blue Peter* presenter, and as a working-class kid growing up in Leeds, I didn't think *Blue Peter* said anything to me. The presenters always seemed very middle class and well behaved. They always seemed to say things like, "Go into the loft and find some old clothes." We didn't have a loft; we lived in a council house. *Magpie* was the show I used to watch.'

Difficult decisions

Biddy didn't give up and there were more conversations. Mark wrote to her from Manchester: 'It has been the most difficult decision of my career so far. I have a great deal of show business and performer in me, and this I think you would find irritating. The fact that I would need more freedom than *Blue Peter* allows would ultimately mean I was wrong for the job. I would be delighted to step in and help out until you found someone on a more permanent basis, perhaps for six months.'

Then Mark bumped into Sarah Greene: 'She said, "Oh, you're going to have such a laugh. The variety is fantastic, you go to great places, the exposure's good, just enjoy it." And I'd been negative and not thought about it like that. It was after she said that to me that I decided to do it.'

On 10 June, Biddy conceded a contract that allowed Mark the unusual privilege of being able to work elsewhere, whenever his *Blue Peter* schedule allowed. The only ban was on commercials and rival children's programmes. From the start, Mark had more input than most presenters: 'I said, "You've asked me to come in, therefore you must appreciate the way I want to work as well. Let me ad lib a bit more, tell a few jokes, burst into song if I want to, because that's the kind of presenter I am."'

3 Mark was in his element with any musical item. In 1987's 'Hooray For Hollywood' extravaganza he sang 'Have Yourself a Very Merry Christmas'.

4 Wearing a replica of Henry VIII's armour. Mark always managed the difficult task of bringing history to life for a young audience.

5 Mark loved jokes, puns and slapstick humour and he always looked for a chance to include them in *Blue Peter*.

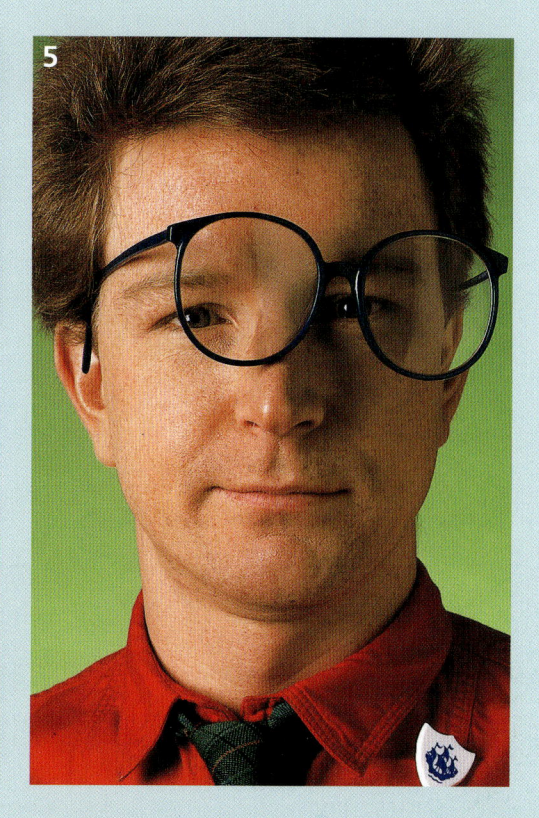

There was still the pressure of learning a demanding script twice a week, then coping with last-minute changes: 'I said to Biddy, "Why don't we have autocue?" She hated the idea, thought it would take the edge off it and make the presenters look a bit automatic. But it was one constant "learn" and you began to hate the script arriving instead of thinking, "Great, I can enjoy this." Biddy really argued against it and I said, "Why don't you move with the times? Please let's just give it a try."

'I think we got an agreement for five shows and I said to Caron [Keating] and Yvette [Fielding], "We can really change things forever!" And we did five really good shows and the autocue stayed. Then we got earpieces, so we were in contact with the gallery like proper presenters should be. Biddy had never worked like that before, but she gave in and it became much more of a team effort.'

Biddy tried to persuade him to take on the new puppy, Bonnie, but '…I just didn't want to be a dog act. I knew if I turned up somewhere without the dog, everyone would be disappointed, I would always have to be "with the dog", like a ventriloquist.'

She also tried her hardest to get him to make at least some of the action films: 'I was the *Blue Peter* wimp! I'm not really that brave. I was strapped to a windmill and that was fine because I wasn't in control. But I'm just terrible on heights. I did a film climbing British Telecom telegraph poles, and halfway up I just froze. My legs were shaking. It was absolutely terrible. And loads of parents wrote in saying, "Thank you for showing that film because my son is terrified of heights and it actually made him more comfortable talking about it."'

Funny moments

Despite his early concerns, Mark was allowed to celebrate his love of show business. There was a whole series of lavish song-and-dance items, especially at Christmas. Meanwhile, his celebrated clumsiness, dropping props, knocking the head off a life-sized Lego man and crashing vehicles into the scenery were sometimes an accident, sometimes a case of 'accidentally on purpose'. A compilation of these 'mistakes' won the vote for viewers' favourite Mark moments when he left after three seasons.

Mark returned to acting and has also continued to present. He took over the central role in *Blue Peter*'s 1998 panto, hurriedly re-written when the original lead, Richard Bacon, was sacked. In a thinly veiled homage to *Dr Who*, Mark played the Keeper of the *Blue Peter* Memory Machine, which had the power to send the presenters back in time.

Presenter Profile
CARON KEATING

JOINED: 13 November 1986

LEFT: 22 January 1990

MEMORABLE MOMENTS: Diving with sharks; North Sea survival training; ice climbing; standing under a freezing Welsh waterfall; the Caron's Clothes competition; interviewing Margaret Thatcher; trips to the Soviet Union, USA and Kampuchea

Caron Keating's first big break was on a regional youth programme called *Channel 1*, in her native Northern Ireland. Her mother was the highly successful radio and television presenter and personality Gloria Hunniford, but Caron used her father's surname, so nepotism was never an issue. Like most ambitious, aspiring presenters, she sent off scores of speculative letters, including one to *Blue Peter*. This wasn't answered for about six months until, out of the blue, Caron was called and offered an interview.

'I was being paid so little at the time, I couldn't really afford to come over. I said, "Will you pay for my flight?" And they said no! I called my mum, who was working on Radio 2 at the time, and the phone was answered by David Jacobs. He said, "Young lady, this is a marvellous opportunity for you. If you have to beg, borrow or steal that money, you must go over and do that interview."'

Caron took the veteran broadcaster's advice and was offered the chance to replace Peter Duncan: 'I was thrilled. I started within about three weeks. Biddy would phone me first thing in the morning after every show. She'd say, "Darling, I thought you did the make beautifully and you were very good on that film piece, but…" And then there'd be this long list of things that I'd done wrong. This went on for months and months. I knew I must be getting better when the calls waned a little. Then one day, she came up to me and said, "I think you've finally got it." That was a real red-letter day.'

As a child, Caron had been a huge fan of *Blue Peter*, badgering her mother for ingredients to try the makes. She completely respected the philosophy of Biddy's approach: 'She was fantastic. She said, "Whatever is going on in children's lives, whether their parents are fighting or getting divorced, or they're having a terrible time at school, I want you three presenters there because you are going to be a really stable influence in their lives."'

1 'Do you have an invisible peg on your nose?', complained one viewer. But Caron's accent softened and she soon became highly popular.

Action girl

Together with Mark Curry, Caron helped to relax and update the entire presenting style. She was a modern young woman, tough, intelligent and questioning, with a genuine sense of 'cool' that was unusual for a *Blue Peter* presenter. It was a definite step forward. She was also the first presenter with a non-English accent: 'They got loads and loads of people complaining. "That girl needs subtitles" and "We don't want our children talking like that". There was nothing I could do about it.'

Soon after Caron arrived, with Janet Ellis pregnant and Mark Curry suffering from vertigo, by default she became the go-anywhere, tackle-anything action girl. She rode horses, abseiled down buildings, swam with sharks, went mountaineering and frequently endured freezing cold water: 'I loved it. You were always doing it with people who were really excellent in their field. You were allowed access to places nobody else would ever have got into. For instance, Yvette [Fielding] and I did a trapeze act with the Moscow State Circus, which was just incredible.'

As Caron's nerves subsided, she stopped gabbling and her accent became less of an issue. But her clothes and hair, so utterly 1980s, caused continual comment: 'I wasn't doing

Presenter Profile CARON KEATING

2 Eleven-year-old Jasmin Nealon designed this dress for Caron. BBC costume designer Tina Waugh had just one week to turn Jasmin's picture into a reality.

3 Ice climbing in 1989. Caron brought a new edge to *Blue Peter*. She was curious, intelligent, tenacious and brave.

4 Caron was *Blue Peter*'s first fashion icon. She had a magpie approach, mixing designer and high street with things she had made or improvised herself.

it for effect or to make a point. It was just the sort of stuff I liked and how people were dressing at the time. The kids just loved it, but a lot of their parents didn't. I used to plot it carefully so I'd get changed too late for Biddy to make me go and get into something else. And she was convinced that whenever she came to give notes that I used my hairspray to keep her away!'

In 1989, the programme made capital from Caron's distinctive sense of style by running a competition to design an outfit for her. It got a staggering 69,928 entries: 'I chose the most beautiful and inventive one I could find.' Peter Duncan cheekily borrowed the winning frock and wore it as a surprise on Caron's last show.

After Caron left *Blue Peter*, professionally she was always in demand. She married her manager, Russ Lindsay, and had two boys, Charlie and Gabriel. When she made a return appearance on *Blue Peter*'s 1998 Christmas special, she looked as radiant as ever. But in fact she was already battling with the cancer that eventually killed her.

She died on 13 April 2004. She had been an immensely popular presenter and we immediately set to work cutting a tribute to show on the programme, with all her best action moments. It finished with a montage cut to one of the song-and-dance routines Caron had performed so well alongside her co-presenters Mark Curry and Yvette Fielding. I phoned the Head of Children's Programmes to let her know what we were planning and was amazed to find she wasn't convinced. 'Should we should do anything? Is it relevant?' she asked. I argued that it was major news and that viewers would expect *Blue Peter*, the show on which Caron had shot to fame, to pay tribute. Children would completely understand.

That afternoon, Simon spoke for all of us when he said: 'Caron will live on in the memories of millions of *Blue Peter* viewers.'

The next day Biddy emailed: 'Just right for the BP audience and ending on the dance routine was a master stroke.'

Gloria Hunniford wrote as well: 'What a wonderful and sensitive tribute you produced in memory of our gorgeous and beautiful Caron. It evoked every emotion possible from joy to huge tears. Great memories for all of us, but in particular for Charlie and Gabriel in years to come. Thank you and all the team for putting the tribute together in such a dignified but fun way.'

Presenter Profile
YVETTE FIELDING

JOINED: 29 June 1987

LEFT: 29 June 1992

MEMORABLE MOMENTS: Painting Jodrell Bank Observatory; screaming throughout the white-knuckle ride Revolution at Blackpool; horse racing; flying a helicopter; singing and dancing; trips to the Soviet Union, USA, Zimbabwe, the Caribbean, Romania and New Zealand

1 The youngest presenter yet, Yvette was planning to become a dental nurse when she got the job on *Blue Peter*.

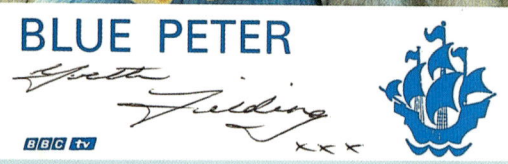

When she was announced to the press, much was made of the fact that, at just 18 years old, Yvette Fielding was the youngest-ever *Blue Peter* presenter. She had been spotted as Sandy in the successful children's comedy series *Seaview*, and Biddy thought that she would appeal to the younger end of the audience. It was typically brave casting, but Yvette's naivety and inexperience caused her huge problems: 'I'd never been away from home before, I'd never been abroad. They moved me into a hotel, and after two weeks there of not knowing anybody, I was flown out to Russia for six weeks. Talk about homesick!'

Yvette's first season began in September 1987, and from the start, she was out of her depth: 'I felt bullied. In the first year, I used to get phone calls from Biddy checking that I was in bed.' Biddy points out: 'I wasn't phoning to check whether Yvette was in bed, but to ensure her script had arrived as I did with all the presenters. They were delivered by bike to save cab fares but they weren't always very reliable.'

The problem was that Yvette was still really a child herself. She did need nannying. Producer Alex Leger took her on a filming trip where she had to sit on a bosun's chair, dangling high above a river. Alex told Biddy that he was worried she'd fall in: 'If she's scared enough, she'll hang on!' came the reply. But in the event, the issue was not falling in. It was Yvette's decision to sunbathe in her time off. She was badly burnt, and although the filming went ahead, she had to cover up the fact that she was in great pain.

Her biggest hurdle was learning her words and delivering them with confidence. Often, she simply didn't understand what she was saying. The fact that Caron Keating and Mark Curry were both on top of their game only highlighted her gauche manner and frequent mistakes.

Yvette has a condition called vitiligo, which affects the pigmentation of the skin. It was this that had made the sunbathing incident so serious. Yvette usually masked her blotchy skin with make-up, but Biddy suggested it would be inspiring to children if Yvette was willing to talk about it. She bravely agreed, but on transmission her nerves and uncertainty meant that, instead of being uplifting and reassuring, the item was awkward and uncomfortable.

'Yvette was having a miserable time', says Lewis Bronze, 'And it was either, "Let's get rid of Yvette or let's get autocue." It seemed ridiculous to blight someone's career and change a presenter for the want of bringing autocue in. We did and Yvette became a much better presenter more or less overnight.'

The children's favourite
Now those early hopes that Yvette would appeal to children were rewarded. She had no 'side' and was completely natural. By 1990, Yvette had become so popular that she was voted favourite lady on television in *Going Live!*'s SOS Star Awards. Yvette was chosen to front that year's extraordinarily successful *Blue Peter* appeal for the orphans of Romania. John Leslie thought it was '…just unbelievable. Yvette volunteered to go out and see what was going on first hand. If I had done it, I'd not have been so emotional

Presenter Profile YVETTE FIELDING

2 About to have another go at water-skiing. Yvette got some good screaming practice for *Most Haunted* during her many action adventures on *Blue Peter*.

3 White-water rafting in 1988 – when she joined, Yvette was thrown in the deep end in more ways than one.

4 A moment of triumph after go-karting on ice in 1992 – just another of the challenges routine to a *Blue Peter* presenter.

5 Yvette's finest hour. Her reports from Romania during the 1990 appeal helped to make it one of the most successful ever.

and you wouldn't have had such good films. She used to get really upset. There'd be these stony silences after we showed them. That appeal raised a phenomenal amount of money.'

Despite her success, Yvette still blew hot and cold about *Blue Peter*. She used to get worn down by the relentless discipline and commitment that the show demanded. Once, she had to be sent home after suffering a panic attack in the studio make-up room. The director was Bridget Caldwell, later to become one of the programme's most prolific directors, who remembers: 'This was my very first show. When Yvette was sent home, I was really worried, but my producer just said, "You can relax now. With all that drama and having to restructure everything for just two presenters, however bad the end result, you'll still be the heroine of the day!"'

Yvette was allowed to miss 1991's expedition to Japan so that she could get married and have a long summer break. The following year, it was decided to ring the changes with the expedition. Two separate trips were planned, to New Zealand and Hungary. The New Zealand trip was to be shot in May 1992, for transmission the following September. Yvette was asked if she was happy to commit to a sixth season. She agreed and the shoot went ahead.

That spring and summer were exceptionally busy. As well as the New Zealand trip, there was a lot of filming in Spain for a live Expo special from Seville. The highlight of this was to be an appearance by the Princess of Wales. Much of this filming involved Yvette, but when she returned from New Zealand, jet-lagged and exhausted, she asked if she could miss the special. As her absence would have made a nonsense of all the planning and pre-filming, permission was denied.

Yvette did as she was told, but handed in her notice at the same time. She was fed up with being owned by *Blue Peter*. As next season's contract had not yet been agreed, there was nothing to be done but accept her decision. By the time the four New Zealand reports were shown at the start of the next series, Yvette was appearing on ITV's Saturday morning children's show *What's Up Doc?* and *Blue Peter* had to dig deep to pay her for the necessary dubbing sessions.

Yvette did return to appear on presenter Diane-Louise Jordan's last programme in 1996, and as a guest presenter in the wake of Richard Bacon's sudden dismissal in 1998. She has since had huge success as the presenter of *Most Haunted!*, a programme exploring ghosts and the paranormal on Living TV, made by the company that she runs with her husband.

Presenter Profile
JOHN LESLIE

1 John Leslie was the first Scottish presenter, and this was often reflected in the content. Once an entire edition came live from John's home city, Edinburgh.

JOINED: 20 April 1989

LEFT: 20 January 1994

MEMORABLE MOMENTS: Bridge-swinging; conducting an orchestra; running the London Marathon; the Royal Marines' Endurance Course; being a Hibs' (Hibernians') goalie; wearing the kilt at every opportunity; trips to Zimbabwe, the Caribbean, Japan and the Falkland Islands

In 1988, having changed his surname from Stott to Leslie, John was working as a VJ or video jockey on the satellite TV show *Music Box*. He was already looking for his next big break, but had been turned down by BBC Children's Presentation, who thought that, with a height of 6 feet 4 inches (1.9 metres), he was too tall. Then he saw an advert in *The Stage*, the show-business newspaper. As it was anonymous, he had no idea what he was applying for, but it sounded interesting: 'It wanted people who were outdoorish and who liked a challenge, so I sent off a tape.'

John went through the famous audition process, but then heard nothing '…for four or five months. But they hadn't put anybody new on the show and I heard whispers that they wanted a fourth presenter. I was just about to sign up for another job, so I phoned Lewis [Bronze], the Editor, to let him know. He said, "Whatever happens, don't sign. Come in and see us." I'd unintentionally forced the issue. Another little interview and that was it. I was the right person at the right time.'

The job of directing John's first film, in which he bungee-jumped from a railway bridge, was given to the highly experienced Alex Leger: 'We knew there was controversy about whether it was a safe sport or not. There was an element of "Should we be doing this or shouldn't we?" It was very carefully set up and tested. You could have hung a London bus off the ropes. But I was very on edge about any press interest. During the lunch break, this man turned up wearing a trench coat. He was very friendly with Mark Curry, who was in the film to introduce John. I gave this man the cold shoulder, and afterwards Mark said, "Who do you think he is?" "A member of the press?", I replied. "It's Philip Madoc, a well-known actor." But that's how sensitive I was.'

John leapt quite literally into *Blue Peter*. For the next five years, he enthusiastically embraced all the physical challenges. They suited him because he was at his best being active: 'Whatever you fancied having a go at, things you missed out on at school, they just let you play. I was very into my music and football, so I did lots about those. They got every ounce of passion out of you.'

Three months of hell

The only major feat with which John struggled was running the London Marathon: 'I'm a team player; I like my football and playing with the lads. To go out by myself was quite hard. It was three months of hell training and four hours of agony doing the actual thing. After all that, I was upstaged by Diane [-Louise Jordan]. She couldn't run and talk at the same time, and kept falling over. Nobody remembered my sweat, toil and heartache. They just remembered Diane falling over!'

Athough he was likeable and never lazy, in the studio, John was easily bored by the painstaking rehearsal process. By nature, he was a wheeler-dealer and it became a tedious and continual chore just to get him off the phone in the make-up room. He'd be cheerfully arranging a deal or a

2 The rigours of the Royal Marines Endurance Course. When the highly competitive John failed by a matter of minutes, he cried.

3 John jumps into *Blue Peter*, trying bridge-swinging. This controversial film had to be vetted by the Head of Children's Programmes.

4 Repeatedly upstaged by co-presenter Diane-Louise Jordan falling over en route, John has mixed memories of the 1991 London Marathon.

personal appearance, or doing an interview. He got away with his cavalier approach because of his sense of humour, his charm and his ability to deliver the goods on transmission. Most of the time, anyway.

'I'd been to the Falklands, an intense, horrendous trip, for the tenth anniversary of the war. I had to link into the film explaining that the Falklands were in the South Atlantic. During the day, in rehearsals, I'd been joking about, singing 'South Pacific' instead. And of course, it just didn't go out of my mind. I said South Pacific on air and had to do an apology. It was lack of concentration, but I did learn from it!'

Gardens and girlfriends

There was only one thing John disliked more than protracted rehearsals: 'I used to hate, with a passion, doing the garden on a Monday morning. I used to get the script and go, "Why me?" You had to get there for 8 o'clock, through the Monday morning traffic. It used to take hours to record. You'd be going over and over it, getting cold. Because I hated it so much, I used to make fun of it. Then it became a real laugh, and as I had such a good relationship with Clare, the gardener, what happened was they ended up giving me all the garden slots!'

John relished the lifestyle that came with the job. He acquired a series of high-profile girlfriends, including the ballet dancer Darcey Bussell and a young actress called Catherine Zeta Jones. One of my most surreal *Blue Peter* memories remains the sight of the beautiful Catherine gyrating on the dance floor at an end-of-series party, oblivious to the fact that she was surrounded by the sweet-faced, grey-haired older ladies who opened letters part time in the Correspondence Unit.

When John decided to move on, it was a wrench, both for the audience and the production team: 'One of the best days of my life was when I left *Blue Peter* for all the right reasons. They gave me a hell of a send-off.' His final programme was packed with as many challenges as possible in 25 minutes, among them abseiling, trampolining and conducting an orchestra.

Professionally, John prospered until 2002, when allegations about his private life brought an abrupt end to his television career. He was later acquitted of the charges brought against him. In 2005, we invited him to a special lunch to celebrate two of the longest-serving members of the team. His famous charm was as strong as ever, but now there was also a noticeable humility and thoughtfulness, too.

Special Assignment

THE BLUE PETER BADGE

Leaving aside the very first programme, 17 June 1963 is probably the most significant date in the entire *Blue Peter* calendar. This was the day that the famous *Blue Peter* badge was launched, each one featuring the ship designed by artist Tony Hart. He explains: 'The opening of *Blue Peter* was a ship plunging about on the sea. I thought of an adventurous ship. The most adventurous ships were those galleons which went off to the Americas. I set to work and showed Biddy a few ships of that character, trying to simplify it and make it as economic as possible, which is what you need in a logo.'

As a child, Biddy had been an ardent fan of Enid Blyton's magazine *Sunny Stories*. One day, she wrote to her heroine and was thrilled to receive a reply. She wrote again and received the same reply. She never forgot the bitter disappointment: 'You can't encourage children to send letters, then throw them in the bin. It's a con trick. So we had to have a team to read them all, a Correspondence Unit. All the badge winners were entered into a card index system so that if they wrote again, as children invariably do, they didn't get the identical letter.'

The ideology was sound, but the investment required was considerable, over £500, at a time when the average edition cost around £180. At first, Biddy followed standard BBC procedure and went to her head of department. He turned her down flat. Children's programmes were already under intense scrutiny for overspending, and this wasn't a good time to ask for any more money.

Biddy returned to the *Blue Peter* office and announced she was going to call the powerful Assistant Controller of Programmes, Donald Baverstock. With neat irony, Baverstock was married to Enid Blyton's daughter. When Biddy called to ask for an appointment, an assistant loftily advised her that the correct procedure was to take up the matter with her head of department. Not for the first time, Biddy wouldn't take no for an answer.

She made her way over to Baverstock's office and confronted him in person. At first, he exploded with outrage at the unauthorized intrusion. It might have been career suicide, but once he'd calmed down, he liked the idea and found the money. What's more, he admired Biddy's guts for taking him on. Years later, when Baverstock was running Yorkshire Television, he tried to persuade her to follow him there as Head of Children's Programmes.

The badges, with the back-up of the dedicated Correspondence Unit, helped to make the programme interactive long before this was a ubiquitous media mantra. Soon there were thousands of letters a week. Today it is emails, and the card-index system is computerized, but the numbers are still huge. As a result there is a real dialogue with the audience and this must remain British television's most comprehensive and consistent audience research.

Badges are never just given away, they are awarded, usually for letters, ideas, poems and pictures – all good programme material. Because they had to be won, badges quickly gained currency. On one occasion,

The full range of *Blue Peter* badges. Famous recipients of the gold badge include David Attenborough, Jonny Wilkinson, Ewan McGregor, Elton John, Quentin Blake, Torvill and Dean, David Beckham, Nick Park, J.K. Rowling, Joe Calzaghe, Tim Henman, Jacqueline Wilson and the Queen.

Blue Peter badges

Blue – awarded for an interesting letter, poem, picture or story, or a good idea for the programme

Silver – the badge you get for doing something different from whatever won you your blue (winning a blue badge is a prerequisite)

Green – for viewers who demonstrate an interest in or commitment to environmental, green or gardening interests

Competition winners' – awarded to all the winners and runners-up of the various *Blue Peter* competitions

Gold – first awarded in February 1964 and the programme's highest award; given in exceptional circumstances, such as saving someone's life, representing your country at a national or international level or showing remarkable bravery

Team player – first awarded in September 2006; awarded to children, selected via the website, who help test new programme and online ideas

Limited edition birthday badges – produced for the 25th- and 45th-anniversary years

Special Assignment THE BLUE PETER BADGE

Competition winners' badge

Blue badge

Silver badge

25th-anniversarsy badge

Gold badge

Competition winners' badge (old design)

Green badge

45th-anniversary badge

Team player badge

Blue badge (old design)

Silver badge (old design)

Green badge (old design)

even the Chairman of the BBC's Board of Governors was firmly refused a badge for his grandson. 'Tell him to write a letter', was Biddy's suggestion.

The appeal of a badge was enhanced by the privileges that came with it. A clever quid-pro-quo system was developed where attractions given publicity on the programme were asked in return to allow free entry for badge winners. Almost all were only too happy to do so. 1999's short-lived Badge Squad featured badge-winning children reviewing attractions on the list. Then, in 2003, I introduced regular Badge Hits, where a presenter surprises a deserving child, usually in their classroom, by awarding them their badge in person. These continue to feature today.

Presenters wear their badges at all times. Lesley Judd called hers 'the mortgage', while John Leslie admitted keeping some handy in his glove compartment as a bribe for traffic wardens. In the 1960s, Christopher Trace's son, Jonathan, used to sell *Blue Peter* badges in the playground for half a crown. In the 1980s, Janet Ellis' daughter, Sophie, enjoyed the same perk. Elsewhere on television, comedian Rik Mayall wore a *Blue Peter* badge throughout *The Young Ones*, and actress Sophie Aldred pinned her own blue and silver badges to her costume as Dr Who's assistant Ace.

A valuable commodity

Their currency has never waned. In 2006, I received calls from some attractions on the badge list, concerned that badges were being marketed on the internet auction site eBay. I had a look for myself. There were pages of them. Many were being aggressively promoted as a way of saving a fortune in entrance fees. Some sellers listed strings of badges, of every colour. These must have been stolen or obtained in dubious circumstances.

1 In 1981, Sarah Greene awarded Morph with his very own *Blue Peter* badge in an animated sequence. The iconic ship logo was designed by Morph's creator, Tony Hart, who asked for a royalty of 1d (one old penny) per badge but instead received a one-off payment of a £100 for the logo.

Special Assignment THE BLUE PETER BADGE

2 The day it all started – Valerie Singleton prepares for the balloon release which launched the *Blue Peter* badge on 17 June 1963.

4 Mr Bean coveted a badge throughout his 2004 appearance. Afterwards Rowan Atkinson wrote: 'I think that what you do and the way you do it are very special.'

3 The gold medallion, specially minted in a limited edition for the 40th birthday, and used as prizes. Gold medallions were also given to all the guests at the big anniversary party held at London's Natural History Museum.

I called in the BBC's Investigations Unit and, with eBay's cooperation, we traced the worst serial offenders. Some badges were tracked to members of staff and disciplinary action followed. Some had been given in bulk to a teacher during a recent filming trip. This teacher was supposed to have distributed them to his class. Instead, he was flogging them online.

By now, journalists were sniffing a good story and it was obvious that, unless we took decisive action, the whole system would collapse. Attractions were not going to allow themselves to be systematically defrauded. I decided to suspend the free-entry perk until we could come up with a solution. We contacted all the 200 attractions on our list to ensure their cooperation and on 27 March we told the audience. A media frenzy followed. Some denounced the amoral greed of the modern world; others attacked the BBC for being so high-handed.

We were always clear that if you win a badge, it's up to you what you subsequently do with it. Our only intention was to prevent the outright thefts and protect genuine winners' rights. There were many ideas about how we might ensure the future security of the scheme. In the end, we decided on a kind of ID card, to be issued alongside the badge. This was also the suggestion of 11-year-old *Blue Peter* viewer Helen Jennings, and we thought it was only fair to give her the credit, especially as she'd even gone to the trouble of designing a prototype!

After a lot of hard work, we were able to reopen the scheme three months after the suspension, a relatively short time for adults, but an eternity for children. The incident made clear that the satisfaction of winning this small, triangular piece of plastic was just as potent for 21st-century children as it had been for their parents and grandparents.

121

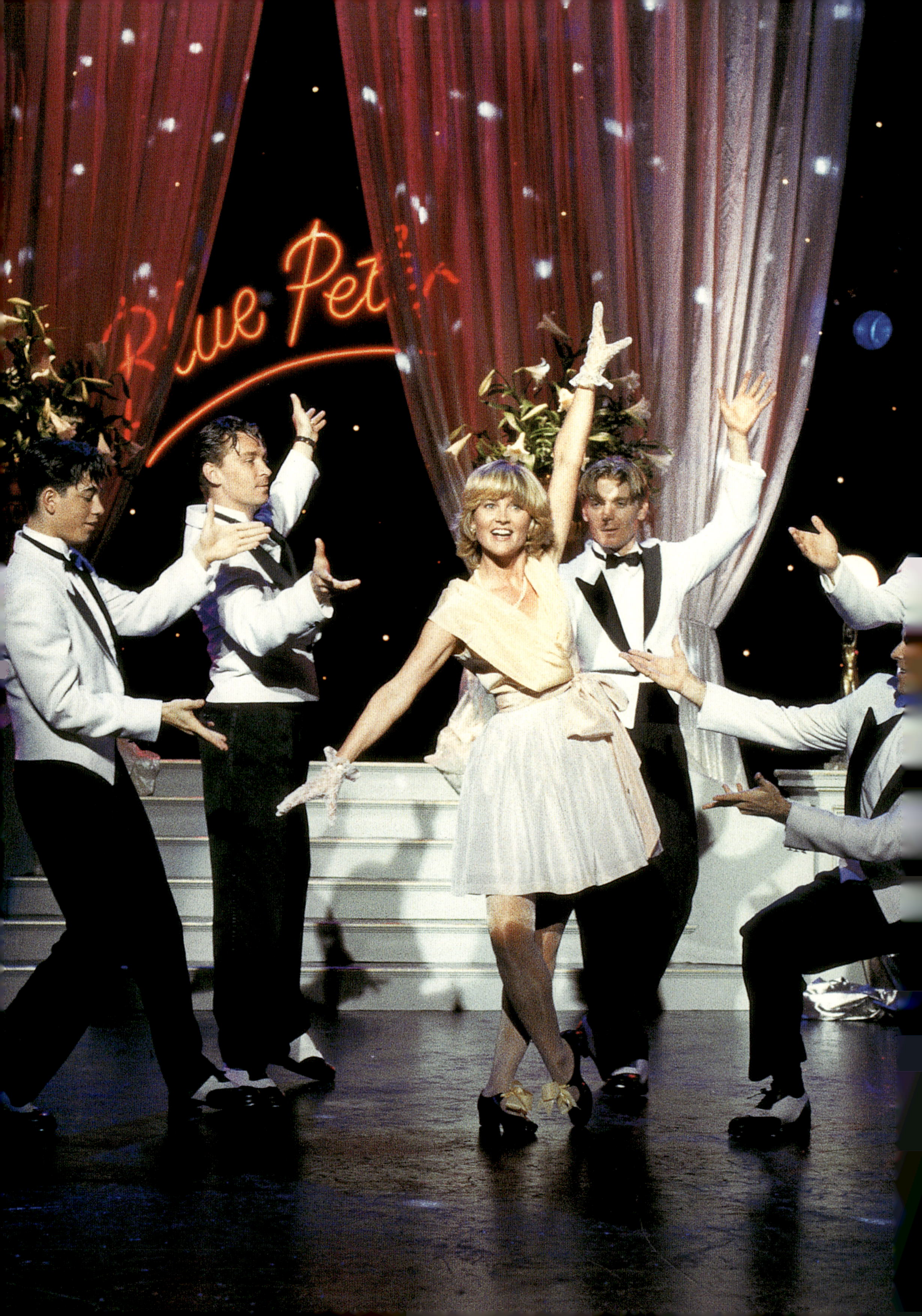

5 Two to Three, Three to Four

1990–1999

On 9 September 1992, the *Blue Peter* team held their annual away day. It was a chance to review progress and look to the challenges ahead. Among those who spoke at length was the man in charge of all the show's filming, producer John Comerford: 'I think there have been far too many programmes in the last series that would have been, putting it kindly, a turn-off. One could go further and say we were trying to drive people to grab the nearest bottle of anti-depressants. We are in danger of worthying out. What with the oldies and the deaf and the swimathon and the fun run, to name but a few, last series I was beginning to long for 'Noakes Up Nelson'. The light and shade in terms of content has failed.'

Anthea Turner gives them a bit of the old razzle dazzle, tap-dancing on her last programme in June 1994. Froth and entertainment were important to counter-balance the more serious factual material.

He had a point. The content of *Blue Peter* has always been as heavily influenced by the people who make it as by viewers' suggestions. Now, reflecting Lewis Bronze's drive to improve standards of journalism on the show, more of the team came from a news and current affairs background. Validation for this approach came when the series won the 1992 BAFTA for best children's factual programme but, as Comerford had warned, the froth and entertainment, the essential counterbalance to the weightier material, sometimes suffered because of the newsier approach.

The desire to push the audience further centre stage resulted in a slew of films presented by children rather than presenters. These sat like oil and water within *Blue Peter*, always so firmly presenter-led, but on the other hand children were now better represented in the studio.

People have always made fun of the programme's choice of pop guests. In the 1970s, *Magpie* would offer up Marc Bolan, whereas *Blue Peter* was more comfortable with novelty groups like The Goodies, The Wurzels and The Wombles. The clip of the group ABBA being interviewed by Lesley Judd has been shown many times, but it is easy to forget that in 1978 ABBA were far from credible. By the 1990s, *Blue Peter* was getting the packaging right – lighting, design and camerawork – but the music bookings were still suspect. At a live transmission from Manchester in 1994, the presenters excitedly trailed the boy band about to perform. Anyone expecting the obvious choice, Take That, would have been disappointed, as the rather less well-known Bad Boys Inc took to the stage instead.

The truth is that *Blue Peter* has never been a fashionable or cool programme and that is certainly one reason it has survived. If you are in fashion one minute, it follows that eventually, and probably before long, you'll be out of it.

Time for change

In September 1989, Lewis commissioned Simon Brint to come up with a new version of the theme music to replace Mike Oldfield's arrangement. The result was certainly contemporary, although today it sounds very much like something knocked up on a home-music system. Brint had another go in 1991, but it wasn't until Luke Cresswell and a group of young musicians called the Yes/No People delivered their radical take on 'Barnacle Bill' that the theme music really made a statement again. Heavy on the drum and bass, there was nothing tinny or cheesy about this signature tune, and it has stood the test of time.

As the Yes/No People music kicked off a new season in September 1994, behind closed doors at Television Centre, big changes were being planned to *Blue Peter*. BBC1 audiences were on the slide and the Controller, Alan Yentob, had suggested that a third weekly *Blue Peter* would be an easy ratings win. The increased number of episodes would have the added benefit of driving down the overall costs too.

At first, worried about overkill and overwork, Lewis was against the idea: 'Then I thought, "Don't be stupid, you've got a fantastic opportunity." I really went for it and had to persuade the production team who were very against it for a long time. There was a lot of boring reorganization to do, but it was a triumph, much to my surprise. The audience figures were fantastic.'

There were some significant changes in approach, including the addition of a fourth presenter. For cost reasons, one of the three weekly editions had to be pre-recorded. At first, Lewis had expected that the new Friday show would simply mean more of the usual mix. The producer he appointed, Joe Godwin, felt differently, arguing that the slot called for more of a 'here comes the weekend' feel. Lewis backed his vision, and Joe and his team created a kind of '*Blue Peter* lite' – nothing heavy; no gardens, cooks or makes. The emphasis was on fun, sparkle and pop music. There was a shiny black floor, and a glittering star cloth enclosed the studio and gave it a sophisticated, show-bizzy atmosphere. The presenters were encouraged to relax their style.

As well as the new-look Fridays, there were far more live outside broadcasts and special programmes shot entirely on location. Fears that the audience wouldn't recognize these or accept them as proper *Blue Peter* soon proved unfounded and they enabled the show to explore a rich new vein of content and use different techniques to do so.

In the first few months alone, these specials included a moving commemoration of VE Day and shows from the Centre For Alternative Technology in Wales, the Moscow State Circus, the seaside at Woolacombe, Universal Studios in America, Warwick Castle in the Midlands and an elephant relocation project in Kenya.

1 Three shows a week devoured material. Presenters were increasingly given long-term projects, shown in series of films, like the 1996 coverage devoted to Katy and Tim learning to dive.

2 The studio make-up room was a haven for presenters. John Leslie was often reluctant to leave it to rehearse, but, when he did, his charm and cheek got him out of trouble.

3 The arrival of Anthea Turner gave *Blue Peter* increased profile. She formed part of a strong presenting team with John Leslie and Diane-Louise Jordan, the first black presenter.

4 Lewis Bronze in charge – the Editor's notes, cuts and changes, given after the 'run-through' in the highly charged interval before transmission, were often the last chance to get a show right.

BLUE PETER 50th Anniversary

2 In the 1990s, specials devoted to one theme, subject or location became a regular part of the schedule. In June 1997, Stuart Miles took on Tim Henman in a Wimbledon special.

3 As part of the 40th-anniversary celebrations, Stuart Miles and Katy Hill took part in the 1998 London to Brighton veteran car run.

1 *Blue Peter* goes *Baywatch* – on location in Acapulco for the 1998 summer expedition to Mexico. When it was first published, after Richard's sacking, he was cut off the picture.

Some of these specials were challenging, as Lewis recalls: 'I remember a live OB [outside broadcast] from an RNLI base, the climax of which was the launch of a new lifeboat, paid for by viewers. During the afternoon, an RNLI official took me to one side and said, 'It's too rough to launch'. I told him it had to, no matter what. And it did – into incredibly rough seas. The boat was virtually standing up in the water and the presenter was terrified but it happened.'

Once he'd ushered in the new three-times-a-week schedule, Lewis dropped a bombshell. He decided to take voluntary redundancy and leave the BBC: 'One of the reasons I left was because three times a week worked and I thought, "It ain't gonna get this good again. Go while you're ahead." I'd turned 40 and been on *Blue Peter* for 12 years. The way the BBC works, children's programmes occupy a ghetto. It's very difficult for senior production personnel in Children's to make a switch to other parts of the BBC, so I felt my career probably didn't lie there.'

On his last programme, presenter Tim Vincent surprised Lewis by awarding him a gold badge on screen. He had accomplished the unenviable job of following Biddy Baxter, retaining her standards but refreshing and updating the show. He was visionary about the emerging internet revolution, and as a result *Blue Peter* had one of the first television websites. Many, including presenter Diane-Louise Jordan, believe that his influence helped to secure its long-term future: 'It's easy to say with hindsight, but I think *Blue Peter* might not have been here today if Lewis hadn't come when he did. I would say that it was just on the verge of becoming a bit twee, and with Lewis it had more of an edge to it. I think it took the viewer more seriously and he knew that young viewers could think about other things beyond the dolls' house or the nice summer trip.'

The programme's third Editor was Oliver Macfarlane. A graduate of the Royal College of Music, Oliver had joined the BBC and arrived at *Blue Peter* as a director in 1987. He was brilliant at the job and good at passing on his knowledge. Clever, cultured and always calm and considerate, Oliver had been made Assistant Editor at the start of the three-times-a-week schedule: 'Being Editor was not something I'd ever set my heart on. I really wasn't sure whether to apply or not. After thinking about it, I decided it was an opportunity too good to miss. I was very much aware of the huge responsibility and somewhat daunted at the prospect. I made the decision that I would be Editor for three to five years, after which I would pursue my long-held ambition to work in TV music.'

There were changes at the top too. Lorraine Heggessey had replaced Anna Home as the Head of Children's Programmes and although she was delighted that *Blue Peter* was still performing so well, she wanted more of a say in its direction. Oliver adopted a strategy of passive resistance. She was keen to make her mark with a children's docu-soap, at a point when this genre was still fresh and interesting. When the right idea wasn't forthcoming, she suggested that *Blue Peter* should devote one of its three editions to a docu-soap format, preferably without presenters. Oliver nodded and listened, but did nothing about it.

40 years of Blue Peter

In 1998, the programme celebrated the milestone of its 40th anniversary. To mark the occasion, Lorraine secured an entire *Blue Peter* night on BBC2. A lavish party with all the key names from four decades of presenters and production teams was held at the Natural History Museum in London. A limited-edition gold medallion was issued as a competition prize and BAFTA conferred the honour of a special award in recognition of the programme's many achievements over four decades.

It was against this backdrop that the Richard Bacon saga exploded in the tabloid press. Richard had gone to warn his Editor about the impending story the morning after the Natural History Museum party: 'On the way, something he had said to me the night before was ringing in my ears. "I have made a good choice in picking you. Don't ever let me down."'

Richard knew that he would have to go, and his dismissal was announced within hours of the story breaking. Behind the scenes, it was the old adage of the show must go on. Then Oliver Macfarlane announced his own imminent departure. For most of the team, this came as a complete surprise. For Oliver, it was the chance of a lifetime: 'Ironically, it was the *Blue Peter* 40th-birthday Prom which facilitated my move. To get that recorded and aired, we had to work closely with the TV Proms team. The head of TV classical music told me that he

3 Floating in the Dead Sea – Katy and Simon in Israel. In the 1990s the programme started to travel the world throughout the year and not just for the summer expedition or appeal.

1 16 October 1998 – the 40th-anniversary party at the Natural History Museum in London. A night of celebrations and reunions, with a bitter aftertaste as the paparazzi lay in wait for Richard Bacon.

2 As the decade drew to a close, the new team of Katy, Matt, Konnie and Simon settled in during the 1999 summer expedition to Australia.

was looking for a new executive producer and I just couldn't let the opportunity pass. Here was a job that had always been my ambition – my 15 years in the children's department, 11½ of them on *Blue Peter*, just happened to be a wonderful diversion!'

Most people on the programme felt that the succession was assured. John Comerford, now the Deputy Editor, was the obvious choice. He was highly experienced, talented, popular and devoted to *Blue Peter*. He'd recently put in an immense amount of work for Lorraine on a strategy paper dedicated to projecting how the programme should develop beyond the year 2000. His competition came from two former *Blue Peter* producers, Joe Godwin and Steve Hocking.

Nobody paid enough attention to the fact that the latter had spent the last year working in development for Lorraine, and when the email went out with the news that Steve was the successful candidate, it caused shock waves throughout the department. John was swiftly found a new position elsewhere, although he generously stayed long enough to ensure some kind of hand-over.

To many of those working on the *Blue Peter* team, the start of 1999 felt grim indeed. They were still reeling from the trauma of losing a presenter, the Editor and the Deputy Editor in short order. The milestone birthday had become a hollow joke.

Consequently, Steve Hocking walked in to face a demoralized, suspicious and uncertain production team. The budget was overspent, and for several depressing weeks, the Wednesday programme had to be recorded in an evening session of just three hours, after a long day working on the live Monday show. This was stressful and exhausting for everyone. Although the results weren't bad, it was not sustainable.

From the start, Steve made it clear that, in his opinion, the programme was strictly for pre-teens. This was a direct challenge to growing pressure from some of the children's department who felt that *Blue Peter* should now be cool, sexy and aimed at teenagers. Steve banned the use of the abbreviation 'BP' on air, pointing out that BP was not our brand but belonged to a very well-known commercial company. Makes, which the presenters had started to send up, were now to be done straight. They were reminded that, if you don't believe in your own material, why should your audience?

Steve was a skilful 'player' in the internal staffing process. Until his arrival, *Blue Peter* was becoming something of a dumping ground for deadwood and time-servers. A natural politician, Steve was carefully predatory in his choices, and this made a huge difference to mindset and morale.

He negotiated an increase in the budget and brought to an end the dreaded Monday night recordings. Instead, the programme saved money by using new lightweight outside broadcast equipment to mount live transmissions from locations around the UK. These led to the *Blue Peter* road shows, a series of live summer specials, usually from seaside resorts, which drew huge crowds and raised the programme's profile.

Within a year of Steve's arrival, instead of looking fearfully over its shoulder, *Blue Peter* was striding ahead towards its future.

Presenter Profile
DIANE-LOUISE JORDAN

JOINED: 25 January 1990

LEFT: 26 February 1996

MEMORABLE MOMENTS: Rally driving; The Well Water Appeal; Norway icy dip; trips to the Caribbean, Japan, Argentina, USA and South Africa

1 Diane is still proud of the fact that 'I was the only presenter in my era who could toss the pancake on Pancake Day!'

2 Messing around during rehearsals. It was all smiles for the camera but this team didn't have much in common and there was tension behind the scenes.

Although *Blue Peter* had auditioned black presenters in the past, Diane-Louise Jordan was the first to actually get the job, as a result of a concerted effort by the production team. Diane was originally spotted by *Blue Peter* producer Oliver Macfarlane, who was watching the BBC's internal ring-main system, which gives production offices a direct feed into the studios' rehearsals and recordings, and saw her in rehearsals as a presenter on a children's programme called *Corners*. This was Diane's first presenting job. All her training and experience was as an actress, but Oliver saw her star quality and suggested she come in for a chat.

The studio audition that followed was a disaster, but Lewis Bronze offered her an unprecedented 18-month contract on the basis of her potential. At the same time, Diane was offered a nine-month contract with *Coronation Street*. She turned her back on Britain's biggest soap and chose Britain's biggest children's programme instead.

The first few months were painful. Diane would cope during rehearsals, but as the run-through loomed she'd get more and more nervous. The last-minute notes and the actual transmission often passed in a blur of fear and fluffs. She recalls: 'Because *Blue Peter* is so scripted, it wasn't even like I was speaking my own words. It was an absolute nightmare. Now I think he was the best teacher any presenter could wish to have, but then I was petrified of Lewis. He would say, "That was rubbish, what were you doing there? Absolutely awful – do it better." Then you had to pick up all the pieces and do the show.'

It didn't help that there wasn't much rapport between Diane and her co-presenters, with whom she had little in common. Diane was effusive, easily distracted and found it hard to concentrate, but there were flashes of hope, glimpses of magic and no question about her motives for being there. She really understood and believed in *Blue Peter*. She cared passionately about the audience. In 1991, a whole programme was devoted to a lavish celebration of the 18th-century composer Mozart. It was lauded within the production team as blue-chip *Blue Peter*, but Diane spoke up, arguing that, although it had been beautifully made, it wasn't very relevant and that most children must have been bored to tears by it.

Both programme and presenter persevered until June 1992, when she was summoned to a meeting with Lewis and Oliver. They explained that, in their opinion, she hadn't fulfilled her potential, and as a result they would only be contracting her until the following February. Then she would have to leave. Diane was sad but stoical and as a small palliative was allowed the unusual and lucrative privilege of appearing in pantomime that Christmas.

Diane finds her feet

At the same time, she learnt that her new co-presenter was to be the already established Anthea Turner. 'I thought it was probably the worst decision that the Editor had ever made. I didn't believe that she wanted to be on *Blue Peter* for the right reasons. I couldn't have been more wrong. She turned out to be absolutely brilliant, a real team player, who just pulled everything together.'

Presenter Profile DIANE-LOUISE JORDAN

3 Getting stuck in – recycling the Trafalgar Square Christmas tree and putting a brave face on the early start and freezing temperature.

4 In January 1992, Diane renamed the vintage loco 532 *Blue Peter*, for the second time in the programme's history.

5 Diane's boys – Tim Vincent and Stuart Miles. Diane got on so well with Tim that one newspaper reported their 'romance', although, as the saying goes, they were just good friends.

In Lewis Bronze's opinion: 'Anthea really rescued Diane's career. Suddenly there were two women there of roughly the same age and outlook. Overnight Diane became a good presenter because she had the confidence behind the scenes that I couldn't give her.' Just before Christmas, delighted with her dramatic turnaround, Lewis offered Diane a new, year-long contract. From this point on, she just got better and better.

In 1994, Diane opened her water bill and read an enclosed flyer from the charity WaterAid, who provide clean water and sanitation to people in developing countries. Diane took it to work with her and became the first presenter to suggest an idea for a *Blue Peter* appeal. She subsequently travelled to India to film for The Well Water Appeal, as it was named. By its close, over one-and-a-half million pounds had been raised by viewers through bring-and-buy sales.

Diane never felt defined by her colour on *Blue Peter*, but did recognize that it enabled the programme to tell some important stories with a different and highly personal perspective: 'My first trip was to the Caribbean, which is where my family came from, so that had obvious significance. We did a piece on slavery with me saying, "If I was standing here a couple of hundred years ago, it would have been as a slave girl." And no other presenter could have done that. My final trip was to South Africa. That's probably the best thing that's happened to me in my life. I never felt in my lifetime that I would be allowed in as a black person. You just weren't welcome. You've got to be mad if you discriminate to the extent they did in South Africa. Not just because of skin colour, but the shade of their skin colour.

'I interviewed a white Afrikaans who was saying, "These blacks are so disgusting, you just don't understand." And I kept looking over my shoulder to see if there was somebody else he was talking to. There were often moments during that trip where I thought, "Gosh, this is so surreal."'

Diane left *Blue Peter* having completed an epic six-year stint. She's remained a powerhouse of energy, constantly embarking on new projects and ideas, by no means only within the media. Two stand-out jobs have been presenting on *Songs of Praise*, the long-running Sunday worship programme, and being chosen to sit on the Princess Diana Memorial Committee. Her slow burn from shaky beginnings to becoming one of the definitive *Blue Peter* presenters is one of the programme's happiest success stories.

Today she looks back with '…fantastic memories. *Blue Peter* is not a trendy programme, it's got its own identity and I think we should be really proud of what it is.'

Presenter Profile

ANTHEA TURNER

JOINED: 14 September 1992

LEFT: 27 June 1994

MEMORABLE MOMENTS: Making Thunderbirds' Tracy Island; being rescued from a Ferris wheel; learning to drive a Channel Tunnel train; bonding with Bonnie and starring together in Dog Agility at Olympia; trips to Hungary, Romania, the Cook Islands and Argentina

1 Some presenters found it a drag having to wear the *Blue Peter* badge. Not Anthea. 'I was very proud to wear my badge.'

Anthea Turner broke the *Blue Peter* mould. She was 32 years old when she got the job, already a seasoned presenter who'd appeared on everything from live Saturday morning shows to *Top of the Pops*: 'I actually believed that time had passed me by for *Blue Peter*. Younger people were getting it and there was no way anybody would look at me.'

But Anthea was much better connected than most. At the time, her husband and manager was Peter Powell, a former Radio 1 DJ who had turned his back on the limelight to establish a highly successful agency. This represented most of the big names then starring on children's television, from Phillip Schofield to Andi Peters. Powell's partner was a man called Russ Lindsay, who was married to another of their star names, Caron Keating. They'd recently signed John Leslie too. It was a small world and made it easy to suggest to Lewis Bronze that he might consider Anthea in the wake of Yvette Fielding's abrupt departure.

Anthea had been a dedicated fan: 'I still had my original annuals and even the pictures of Petra I used to have on my wall. I got my first badge when I was seven by collecting shells and making them into animals. I thought, "This is a marvellous idea and I must let Valerie know about it", so I sent in my shell mouse and dog and a diagram of how I'd actually made them. They probably arrived in millions of little pieces!' Anthea pinned this very same badge inside her back pocket as a good-luck charm for her audition. Unfortunately: '…Lewis told me that I did the worst audition for a successful applicant.'

He realized that it might be difficult to 'sell' Anthea to the Head of Children's Programmes, Anna Home. He decided to edit the audition tape to present her in the best light possible. Home still wasn't convinced and remained so throughout Anthea's subsequent *Blue Peter* career, branding her 'insincere' and feeling that she always came across as though she were 'performing'. However, once she had expressed her reservations, she left the final decision to Lewis. A few days later, Anthea was introduced to the press, bouncing up and down on a trampoline in the *Blue Peter* garden: 'It was my proudest moment in television, getting *Blue Peter*. I was walking on hallowed ground. I've often said that *Blue Peter* was like the University of Televsion because I learnt about everything. It's all well and good doing what I refer to as 'freefall TV' – screamy, shouty, children's telly. That's great fun but actually to be able to be good at your job, to make it look easy, that's what *Blue Peter* taught me. The art of TV is to be natural in unnatural circumstances.'

Lewis felt that it was '…a marvellous stroke of luck that this person fell into our laps. She'd done glamorous shows, had the clothing allowance and the cars, and she wanted to do something serious that she really cared about rather than being this flouncy blonde playing second fiddle. Anthea and *Blue Peter* matched each other perfectly. She needed to be heavily produced, and when you gave her that help, she rewarded you with the most fantastic, radiant performance. It was her best work.'

Team bonds

The team of John Leslie, Diane-Louise Jordan and Anthea Turner worked so well together that real friendship was

2 Editor Lewis Bronze with Anthea and the most successful of all the makes, which she demonstrated – Thunderbirds' Tracy Island. Over 100,000 requests poured in for the factsheet and a special BBC video was released.

3 Bouncing away on the trampoline at her photo-call in the *Blue Peter* garden: 'I was nervous, but very, very happy to be there'.

established between them. Even though autocue was now in use on every programme, Anthea's mild dyslexia still meant that she arrived every morning having thoroughly prepared her script. She was enthusiastic and keen to learn. 'I actually never let on about my dyslexia until after I left. I didn't have the confidence. Because I knew I had a problem I would work twice as hard as the next person to get it right and rely a bit more on my memory because I had to. But I didn't find it disabling at all, in fact because I worked harder at it, it's actually done me some favours.'

Her positive attitude, fresh focus and professionalism spread to the others, qualities they'd been sorely lacking in previous months. 'She was such a Pollyanna', remembers Diane. 'Just like a good girl at school, she wanted to wear the badge the whole time. But we really got on and it didn't even feel like work, it was such good fun.'

Slip of the tongue

Anthea did get herself into trouble with one careless ad lib: 'Tim [Vincent] was mentioning where Bonnie the dog was going to be that weekend. He said, as an aside, "And Bonnie, who's just sitting between my legs at the moment..." and I just went, "That's a nice place to be."'

Seconds later, the show went off air and Lewis Bronze came flying down the steps from the gallery. The comment had been off camera and he thought it had been made by Diane. The latter recalls: 'He was absolutely furious. He came marching straight up to me and said, "Why did you say that? Have you lost it completely?" And Anthea said, "It wasn't her, it was me." He was so shocked because I was the naughty one and she was Miss Goody Two-Shoes. It was the first time I'd seen him lost for words! He was mortified. He just did not see the funny side, especially when it was in the papers the next day.'

It was Anthea's only lapse. She threw herself into the life of a *Blue Peter* presenter, from the action films and the travelling to looking after Bonnie and fronting the makes. In fact, she is probably best known for making the most popular *Blue Peter* make of all, Thunderbirds' Tracy Island: 'I practised for hours and hours to get it right and it worked very well. I don't think we realized how big it was going to be. It was the talking point of the nation for a few weeks. We were inundated with people wanting the fact sheet and in the end we produced a video so that people could watch it and slow it down.'

Anthea left *Blue Peter* after her second season. She'd intended to stay three or four years, but when she was asked to present the breakfast show on GMTV, it was too good an opportunity to miss: 'In TV terms it was a lifeline, as we all know how difficult it is to go from children's TV to adult TV. But I left before I wanted to and I can honestly say that my happiest times on television will always be with *Blue Peter*.'

Presenter Profile
TIM VINCENT

JOINED: 16 December 1993

LEFT: 24 January 1997

MEMORABLE MOMENTS: Motor racing at Silverstone; flying with the Frecce Tricolori, the Italian Airforce aerobatic team; training with the England rugby team; the Parachute Regiment's log race; helping paint the Blackpool Tower; running the New York Marathon; trips to the USA, South Africa, Hong Kong and China

Tim Vincent made his name as a juvenile star on ITV's *Children's Ward*, although Vincent is actually his grandad's name. He grew up Tim Walker but had to change this when he joined actor's union Equity, as there was already an actor with the same name. When *Blue Peter* started the search for someone to replace John Leslie, Tim auditioned alongside the current crop of eligible young presenters. These included Mark Franklin from *Top of the Pops* and Chris Rogers, who went on to present *Newsround*. It came down to a choice between Tim and Stuart Miles, who was working on *Saturday Disney*. Both were recalled for a second audition and Tim's film-star looks gave him the edge.

'Lewis asked to see me again. I thought he can't be such a nasty person that he'd ask me to come down to London just to tell me that I hadn't got it. I was sitting in his office and he was asking me, could I drive, could I move down to London, do I want the job? And I didn't realize that he was actually offering me the job. The following Monday was my first show.'

Diane-Louise Jordan had been told about this 'gorgeous babe', but when she first met him, she thought, 'Oh, what a sweet little boy. I only found out later that he was the babe they were all talking about! Before he was on *Blue Peter*, he did some modelling and a newspaper printed this topless photo of him. Anthea and I photocopied it, blew it up and stuck it to the bottom of every camera in the studio so that everybody could see this "heart-throb". He was really embarrassed!'

Tim was soon accepted into the team. There was a brief hand-over with John Leslie, who became a good friend and mentor. He wasn't the only one: 'Anthea knew everything. She used to say, "Be nice to lighting because they'll make you look good, be nice to make-up because they'll make you look good too."'

1 As the show's pin-up, Tim got lots of mail: 'The ones that raised my eyebrow usually came from ex-sergeant majors, asking for a signed photo "possibly in the shower"'.

A reluctant hero

Tim inherited the traditional 'action-man' role, although this was never something he especially enjoyed. There were problems because, perhaps curiously for an actor, he didn't enjoy dressing up, feeling it made him look silly. He was self-conscious about anything where he felt he was seen to fail and would ask directors to cut these moments out, whether it was falling off water-skis or being sick in a plane. They never did, trying to explain that these so-called 'failings' helped the audience to empathize, and that constant success would be dull and uninspiring, as well as unrealistic.

Any problem areas were simply caused by Tim's youth and lack of experience. But the audience liked him and he was a consistent, hard-working performer:

'Everyone used to say, "You've done rock climbing and speed boats and everything." But the most difficult and dangerous thing I did on *Blue Peter* was make a cake. You've got six minutes. You've got to make it informative and fun and there's somebody talking in your ear at the same time. You have to remember when to bring things out, what the temperatures are and which cameras to look at and show

Presenter Profile **TIM VINCENT**

2 During one of his two auditions, Tim had to try this bucking bronco machine. It was also how he was introduced to viewers.

3 Formation water-skiing in America. Tim made a convincing action man, although he didn't always enjoy this aspect of the job.

4 Filming the super-tough Paras log race in 1994. Says Tim, 'A year on *Blue Peter* is like a dog year because you pack so many experiences into it.'

things to. That was much worse than throwing yourself out of a plane.'

Running the New York Marathon was probably Tim's finest hour: 'Everybody kept saying, "You're tall, you've got long limbs, it's easier to run." Absolute codswallop; there were people dressed as Mr Blobby lapping me. You're either good at it or you're not. I would never do one again.

'On the morning it was freezing. I had a tracksuit on. Somebody had said, "Take some chocolate bars with you for energy on the way round." After about two or three miles, I was hot and thought, "I've got to take this top off." I threw it into the crowd and there was a big cheer. The camera caught it and I was doing the slo-mo action in my mind. Four or five miles later, I was peckish and thought, "I'll have one of those chocolate bars." But I'd thrown them all away.

'Eventually, we'd run through most of New York and got to the Bronx. The director was running beside me and I said, "I'm not going to be able to finish this unless you get me some chocolate." So he ran off to this really dodgy store in the middle of the Bronx, handed the money through some bars and they handed the chocolate back.

'My enduring memory is when I saw the finishing line. I was at my wits' end. Diane and Stuart were cheering me on, the camera crew was there and I thought, "It's all over." I crossed over the line and raised my arms. My glory moment. Somebody took a photo. A month later when the photos came back, there was a guy dressed as a rabbit alongside me and it just looked like a walk in the park.'

Tim was too ambitious to stay on *Blue Peter* for long. He was signed up by Peter Powell, one of the best managers in the business, who had steered Anthea Turner's lucrative move from *Blue Peter* to GMTV. Powell shrewdly negotiated an unusual perk for Tim during his final year on the programme, allowing him to take a regular role in *Dangerfield*, as well as a slot presenting on *The Clothes Show*. Predictably, these commitments caused tension among the other presenters and the production team. After a few months, an amicable separation was agreed and Tim moved on.

Since then he has combined acting, including a stint on *Emmerdale*, with presenting. Recently, he has worked extensively in America, returning to try his luck as one of the stars of *Dancing On Ice*.

Presenter Profile
STUART MILES

JOINED: 27 June 1994

LEFT: 21 June 1999

MEMORABLE MOMENTS: Parachuting with the RAF Falcons; the River Avon death slide; learning to talk 'chimp'; trips to the USA, South Africa, Hong Kong, China, Kenya, Canada, Mexico and Uganda

Stuart Miles had been runner-up in the auditions, losing out to Tim Vincent. However, six months later, when Anthea Turner left, Lewis offered him the job. Stuart was thrilled, although his pleasure was dissipated when Lewis made it clear that the end-of-season party was Anthea's moment and that Stuart should stay away. He recalls, 'It was horrible. I did my first show and then just went home.'

Stuart was chosen as the next in line to carry on *Blue Peter*'s long parachuting tradition. During his training he had a narrow escape: 'I'd jumped out of the plane and pulled my parachute. There was a cameraman filming me with a camera mounted on his helmet. I was steering into land when suddenly we collided in mid-air, while descending at 40 mph. It was no one's fault, but the impact was enough to knock me out and I started falling in and out of consciousness. The other parachutists saw what was going on and kept shouting at me, which was enough to bring me round.'

Stuart had severe concussion, but carried on jumping until he was able to take part in a public display as one of the famous RAF Falcons. Throughout his five years on the programme, he was the most rock-steady and reliable presenter. He rarely made mistakes and had a total understanding of the technical side of television. He became the first *Blue Peter* presenter to direct a film himself and the word the production team would invariably use to describe him was 'professional'.

But there was a problem. Stuart was a very closed person. His best friend on the show was Katy Hill and yet even she felt she didn't really know him. Because he didn't appear relaxed about himself or who he really was, most of the time you felt that what you were getting was a polished performance. The audience sensed this and it affected Stuart's popularity. In the summer of 1998, when he'd been there four years and should have been high up in any viewer poll, broadcast research revealed that children thought he tried too hard to be funny and that he was thought to be boring. Some believed he would sit in front of a television after he'd finished work and gone home.

That summer, Stuart began to plan his future away from *Blue Peter*. It was the year of the 40th anniversary and he was looking forward to enjoying a final season, starting with the kudos of being the linchpin presenter for the programme's big birthday.

1 Stuart Miles was a highly reliable presenter known for his professionalism, but he sometimes had mixed feelings about *Blue Peter*.

Growing discontent

The sacking of Richard Bacon changed all that. Now what should have been a time for confidence and celebration became a time of doubts, upset and worry. All the presenters faced an immediate increase in their already considerable workloads. Although they were given extra payment as a result, they were constantly tired and stressed. Stuart seemed to feel it the most. He correctly predicted that Richard's newfound notoriety would only propel his career forward. Stuart, always the 'good boy', understandably resented the injustice of this.

From my point of view as producer in charge of all *Blue Peter*'s filming at the time, a wearisome side-effect of Richard's departure was the need to reshoot certain films. One of these was a historical epic about the First World War, which had involved Stuart and Richard in some elaborate dramatized sequences. These now had to be made all over again. In the interval since we'd completed the filming,

2 Mid-freefall with the RAF Falcons. Stuart later nominated taking part in one of their public displays as his favourite *Blue Peter* moment.

3 Stuart was on location playing the doomed Charles I when the *Guardian* published his controversial interview. There were lots of 'off with his head' jokes.

4 A still from the First World War film that had to be re-shot in the aftermath of Richard Bacon's abrupt departure.

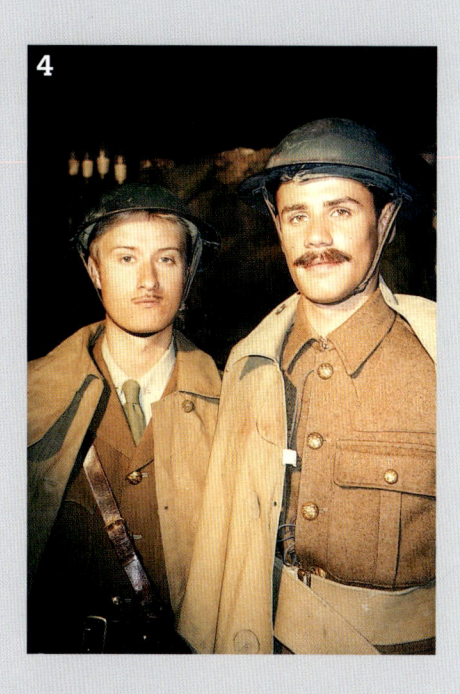

Stuart had cultivated a fashionable goatee. When I broke the news that he'd have to shave this off for continuity, he exploded and threw his bag across the make-up room, shouting, 'Everybody wants a piece of me!', before storming off. Katy looked up and said, 'Don't worry, he'll be back. He's just upset.'

Sure enough, Stuart, the steady, safe pair of hands, soon returned, looking rather sheepish. He apologized, shaved and did the reshoot brilliantly and in good humour.

By Christmas, there was a new presenter (Simon Thomas) and a new Editor on the horizon. Steve Hocking took up his job on the morning of 8 February 1999. As he waited for his train, he took a call from the BBC Press Office, warning him that there was a big story in the *Guardian*.

Burning his boats

Stuart had given the paper an incendiary interview. He told the reporter that '…we've got to make *Blue Peter* more relevant to modern-thinking children. Less twee, more hard-hitting.' He suggested that the programme should tackle subjects like 'divorce, bullying, eating disorders or drugs'. His comment on Richard's exit was that '…it could have been handled better. I think the department should have made a drugs education special.'

As well as the *Guardian*, Stuart appeared in the glossy pages of *OK!* magazine, proclaiming that '1999 will be my year'. There was a moody photograph of him, clutching a smouldering cigarette, although he didn't actually smoke.

It was a very obviously orchestrated campaign, designed to give Stuart profile in the wake of the Richard Bacon fallout. But Stuart had been badly advised and the campaign backfired. Leader columns and letter pages turned on him for his disloyalty and defended *Blue Peter*.

Stuart saw out the series and was given a generous send-off, including a special 'chocolate friendship' cake, although during rehearsals some wag on the studio floor rearranged the Smarties on it so that instead of reading 'Bye Stuart' they read 'Die Stuart'!

In leaving *Blue Peter* in such a self-consciously dramatic way, Stuart had created a splash, but burnt his boats. No high-profile television jobs followed, although he did return to *Blue Peter* for Katy Hill's last show. But Stuart seemed much happier away from the pressures and scrutiny of children's television. He has since proved that he didn't need to appear on TV to enjoy a successful life. He has made several forays into the comedy scene, appearing at the Edinburgh Festival and performing, in drag, as a satirical comic character he created and christened Stella Ratner. He was also in good form when he (and his dog Nellie) took part in Channel 4's 'When *Blue Peter* Became ABBA' in 2005.

In 2007, he was back in the news when he joined Gaydar Radio as a DJ. Stuart told *Time Out* magazine: '*Blue Peter* was fantastic. It was a great launching pad. But I started in [college and hospital] radio, so when the job at Gaydar came along, it seemed like the perfect opportunity to get back to doing what I love'.

Presenter Profile
KATY HILL

JOINED: 23 June 1995

LEFT: 19 June 2000

MEMORABLE MOMENTS: Flying with the Red Arrows; being dunked in an underwater Royal Navy helicopter escape exercise; horse riding; interviewing the Spice Girls; trips to South Africa, Hong Kong, China, Canada, Mexico and Australia

Katy Hill wanted to be a *Blue Peter* presenter from the age of five: 'I'd pretend to wallpaper the bath with my flannel and talk through the whole process.' What made Katy different from the millions of other children who shared her ambition was her single-minded pursuit of it. Instead of taking up the offer of a place at Hull University, she learnt to type and joined the BBC as a production secretary.

This was her 'in', and she persuaded and pestered until she won her own slot on BBC Radio Essex. It was called Katy's Kapers: 'I presented, edited and packaged up the whole lot, but the programme organizer told me I'd never make it because I have a soft 'r' like Jonathan Ross.'

Katy eventually became PA to the Head of Children's Programmes, Anna Home. Although now on the doorstep of her dream job, this was in itself a precarious position. Television's junior ranks are crammed with 'wannabe' presenters. Usually, as soon as their ambition is declared, it has an immediate and detrimental effect on their credibility.

False modesty was never Katy's problem. She worked weekends presenting for the children's channel Nickelodeon, while bombarding *Blue Peter* Editor Lewis Bronze with letters, photographs, ideas for items and showreels – short tapes giving an idea of how an aspiring presenter looks, walks and talks. She was offered an audition partly to shut her up and partly to make up the numbers. Katy remembers: 'I practised making my Christmas card millions of times and interviewed my younger sister Naomi while I jumped up and down on my bed. As soon as I got to the studio, I was shaking.'

Girl power
A few days later, Lewis called her with the news she had waited to hear for so many years. Katy brought immediate sparkle and energy to the show. This was the era of the Spice Girls, and in many ways, Katy was *Blue Peter*'s very own version of a Spice Girl. She was pretty and fashionable, but tomboyish and fearless too. There was no faking her enthusiasm. She added a sense of cool to the most traditional items. The audience just loved her and she scored some of the highest-recorded appreciation figures for a *Blue Peter* presenter. Unusually, boys liked her as much as girls.

Everybody who worked with her encountered the same winning combination of glitter and attack. You couldn't be half-hearted about Katy. She demanded attention and repaid it by being enormous fun. She brought a whole new slang to work – anything twee and old-fashioned was 'jolly', and anything that didn't work was 'oogie' and left 'oeuf sur le visage'. Bad acting by her or one of the other presenters was pronounced 'jambon'. But the most overused word, to describe anything from a freezing morning in the garden to a dreary stamp item, was 'heinous'.

It wasn't long before Katy was the queen of all she surveyed. In fact, I nicknamed her 'Queen Mother' and she liked this joke enough to start ending her emails to me with the initials 'QM'. She wasn't always the most generous of presenters. Her ambition to be the best meant that she wanted the best material too. She campaigned vigorously for all the juicy trips and the action films, especially anything with fast cars or planes. And because she was fun and delivered every time, she usually got her way.

1 A *Blue Peter* fan from childhood, Katy was one of the most popular presenters of all – not many could light up a room like she did.

2 On the Great Wall of China during the 1996 summer expedition. Katy brought a new freshness and sincerity to *Blue Peter*.

3 This 1998 day-in-the-life of gamekeeper Jake Fiennes (brother of actors Ralph and Joseph) gave a realistic view of some of the harsher aspects of country life.

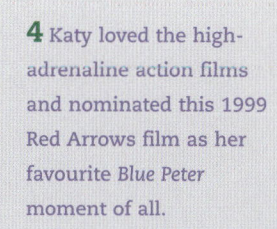

4 Katy loved the high-adrenaline action films and nominated this 1999 Red Arrows film as her favourite *Blue Peter* moment of all.

Although Katy always made her feelings clear, she never crossed the line. So when she acquired a black eye playing rugby and was told to take a few days off to spare viewers the sight of her battle scar, she thought this was craven and hypocritical, and said so. But having said so, she did as she was told. Her heartfelt Christian beliefs sometimes put her in an awkward situation. When she was rather insensitively scheduled to present a film telling the story of Charles Darwin and the theory of evolution, she had a moan but didn't shirk it.

Similarly, Katy wasn't a fan of period costume, aware that wigs, bonnets, crinolines and bustles rarely suited her. I once asked for her to be dressed as Edwardian beauty Lily Langtry in order to model thousands of pounds worth of Cartier gems. When I arrived in the studio, I was greeted by a wail from Katy in wardrobe, 'Is that you, Marson? Not a good way to start! Making me wear a ginger wig and a fat suit!'

During the 1996 summer expedition, Katy spent a week living with a Mongolian family. The result of this assignment marked a departure from *Blue Peter*'s characteristic storytelling approach. Almost nothing was pre-planned. It was just Katy's off-the-cuff reactions to the colossal contrasts between her life and theirs. The film was intimate and moving, with Katy in tears as she said goodbye to the family.

Eventually, pressure from friends and other colleagues in the industry and the lure of an even brighter future began to take the bloom off Katy's *Blue Peter* idyll. Aware of her popularity, she not unnaturally began to think where this might take her next. But when she had to announce the news of her departure live on air, she could barely get through the words. Her whole body shook with sobs. She knew that she was turning her back on her dream.

For a while after she left, Katy seemed to lose sight of who she really was. She slimmed down and joined the revamped Saturday morning show *Live and Kicking* with a head of long nylon extensions and lots of lip gloss, but this supposedly sexier Katy just confused her fan base. It didn't work and she only completed one season on the show, although it was where she met her husband, co-presenter Trey Farley.

About two years after she left, Katy popped back into the *Blue Peter* studio on a nostalgic flying visit. I found her in make-up, deep in conversation with the presenters. Essentially, she told them it was a cold, hard world out there and that they were lucky to have one of the best jobs going. She said she wished she'd stayed longer herself. It had a powerful effect on those listening and I still think Katy's influence was one reason that that team stayed so long.

She has since made a new life for herself, her husband and their daughter Maia in America. Katy still treasures her *Blue Peter* memories and has the satisfaction of knowing that not only did she achieve her childhood dream, she did so with style and immense success.

Presenter Profile

ROMANA D'ANNUNZIO

JOINED: **1 March 1996**

LEFT: **20 February 1998**

MEMORABLE MOMENTS: Tracing her roots in Edinburgh and Rome; rock climbing; wing walking; dressing up and acting with aplomb in a variety of films and studio items; trips to Hong Kong, China and Canada

Romana d'Annunzio always wanted to act and perform. As a young delegate at the Edinburgh Television Festival, she presented a film about the event: 'After it was shown, I was given Lewis Bronze's card two or three times in a row and got the message that he wanted to meet me.' In Romana, Lewis had identified 'something very much on the lines of the charm and engagement I saw in both Caron and Diane.'

Romana was invited to audition. Her chief competition was another Scottish girl, Gail Porter, who later became the darling of the lads' mags. The production team thought it was no contest. Romana had done respectably well, considering her lack of experience, but according to Oliver Macfarlane, Assistant Editor at the time, Gail's audition was '…brilliant. I was underwhelmed with Romana rather than anti. Lewis was very keen, saying she was a lovely girl with a nice personality, which was true, but many of us couldn't see great potential as a successful *Blue Peter* presenter. I did voice my opinion strongly that Romana was not the right choice, but Lewis, as Editor, rightly had the casting vote.'

The problem was that Lewis left the programme just four months after Romana arrived and so her 'star maker' couldn't nurture his protégée's potential: 'I would say that I carried the production team as long as I was there, but once I left nobody was prepared to invest the time in bringing her on. When a presenter is not an experienced performer, it can take one to two years before you begin to see the talent emerge. Diane is a case in point. Romana was given about nine months. I think that in time she would have been good.'

Oliver Macfarlane, who followed Lewis as Editor, felt her 'heart was never really in it. She didn't have the hunger and drive you need to be a strong *Blue Peter* presenter.'

Romana acknowledges she 'had a major confidence crisis with Oliver. I wish he'd been more upfront with me, rather than giving notes to Stuart, Katy and Richard and then ignoring me. I didn't really stand up for myself. I knew I had a lot to learn. I'm not a very narcissistic person so I wasn't a born presenter. I need to be bolstered and believed in. I never did as well with the directors who screamed and shouted. Often I felt I was falling and there was no one to catch me. I really took it to heart. My mum said, "Fight it – show them what you're capable of", but I was very insecure and that had a knock-on effect on my performance.'

Romana didn't stand a chance against the take-no-prisoners dazzle of Katy Hill. She often gave the impression of running to keep up with her co-presenters. They liked her, perhaps partly because they could sense that she was no competition.

The relationship between presenters and production has always been complex. They need each other but there can be resentment on both sides. Presenters sometimes kick against the 'infantilizing' of their lives, every minute of which is defined by the job. The hard-working production team get frustrated when presenters seem unwilling or unable to bring a positive attitude to the work. Romana became an acute example of the divide between the two.

Production felt that she wasn't really listening or trying. Once Romana turned up for a rock-climbing item wearing platform shoes. Another time, she had a radical new haircut without consulting the team, making that year's summer trip films look out of date before they were

1 Romana was spotted in a film made for the Edinburgh Television Festival: 'Another girl in our group wanted to do it and I wasn't fussed so it nearly didn't happen'.

2 Romana with her co-presenters at Niagara Falls on the 1997 summer expedition to Canada. They were fond of her and called her 'Roma'.

3 Romana gets stuck into promoting the 1998 *Blue Peter Stamp Annual*, which turned out to be a one-off.

even shown. She was taken wing-walking, an expensive action film that involved her standing upright, attached to the front of a flying biplane. The pictures were spectacular, but the all-important commentary, which action films need to bring the experience alive for the viewer, was uninspired. 'It's so cold' was the principal lament.

Viewers weren't convinced and the problems got worse during the 1997 expedition to Canada. The trip was masterminded by the new Assistant Editor John Comerford. When Romana refused to be filmed on a white-knuckle ride with the other presenters, he intercut them with shots of her on a rollercoaster designed for infants. It summed up the division of enthusiasm in the presenting team.

When Comerford returned, he discussed the situation with Oliver Macfarlane, who spoke to Romana: 'I said she needed a more positive attitude, and I wanted to see a vast improvement in the autumn and for her to engage more with the activities both in the studio and on film.'

On 31 October 1997, there was a Hallowe'en special. For Oliver, it turned out to be the '…straw that broke the camel's back. Of course I can forgive people not wanting to be thrown out of aeroplanes – after all, Mark Curry didn't have a head for heights and he was an excellent presenter. But in this programme there was an apple-bobbing game with the presenters competing. Romana just faked it, not putting her head in the water and giving me the excuse later that she didn't want to ruin her make-up. For me that was the end. If a presenter can't even take part properly in a simple party game, there's no point in them being there. When the inevitable request came for Romana to take part in a pantomime, something we usually refused, I let her go, suggesting she pursue acting instead.'

For the audience, at least, this was logical as acting was the area in which Romana had shone, playing a variety of parts from Grace Darling to an upper-class suffragette. She was given a fantastic send-off, with novelty band The Mike Flowers Pops performing a special song in her honour: 'I was sad to leave because I felt I could have done so much more but on the other hand I felt a relief I could be me again. There's nothing like that show. Even though I had some bad experiences, I did love doing it. There were so many facets to it. I loved the storytelling and educational aspect. The show taught me how to conduct myself with people too. I don't have a 'woe is me' attitude and it's all been great since.'

In 2005 Romana appeared, along with fellow former presenters Peter Duncan, Janet Ellis and Stuart Miles, on the Channel 4 *Faking It* special 'When *Blue Peter* Became ABBA'. In the summer of 2008, she completed a four-year English Literature and Italian degree at Edinburgh University: 'I hope to become a secondary-school teacher. I've done some teaching and I absolutely love it. I drew upon my *Blue Peter* experiences, knowing that if kids smell fear, you've had it!'

Presenter Profile

RICHARD BACON

JOINED: 21 February 1997

LEFT: 16 October 1998

MEMORABLE MOMENTS: Officer cadet training at Sandhurst; barefoot water-skiing; dragon-boat racing; trips to Canada and Mexico

Richard Bacon joined the programme ahead of competition that included future DJ and presenter Tim Lovejoy and *The Bill* actor Matthew Crompton. His *Blue Peter* career has naturally been eclipsed by its dramatic conclusion, but when he first appeared, he was the epitome of the fresh-faced boy next door. Richard was charming and intelligent, but also gauche and immature. He still had the teenager's love of an argument for argument's sake, boring crews to death at the end of a long day's shoot with pointless debates like whether having coffee after dinner was 'offensively middle class' or not.

To begin with, he hero-worshipped co-presenter Stuart Miles (whom he nicknamed LED, short for 'light-emitting diode') and he constantly tried to banter with *Blue Peter*'s queen bee Katy Hill, only to be slapped down like a slightly annoying cheeky younger brother. To Konnie Huq, with whom he later had a seven-year relationship, he was at first relatively indifferent.

Richard was obsessively interested in the media and had an ability to retain all kinds of obscure trivia. *Blue Peter* was transmitted from any one of six big studios at Television Centre. Weeks after a show, Richard could tell you exactly which show came from which studio. He was never wrong. He loved the cult status of being on *Blue Peter*, especially in its 40th-anniversary year. When Simon Groom arrived for the birthday show, he was pleased but slightly bemused by Richard's effusive greeting: 'One of the greats', he proclaimed, 'I've got the annual with you wearing that brilliant Seventies brown leather jacket…'

There was no doubting Richard's ability. He was shaping up as a likeable and self-deprecating presenter. We took him to the Royal Military Academy at Sandhurst to make a two-part film about their arduous officer cadet training. He turned this into a comedy classic with his understated humorous reactions to the relentless drill and giving of commands. 'And while you're about it, Bacon, get those sideburns shaved off!' barked one fearsome NCO.

1 Before joining *Blue Peter*, Richard had been working at infamous L!VE TV, reporting, interviewing and dressing up as the News Bunny.

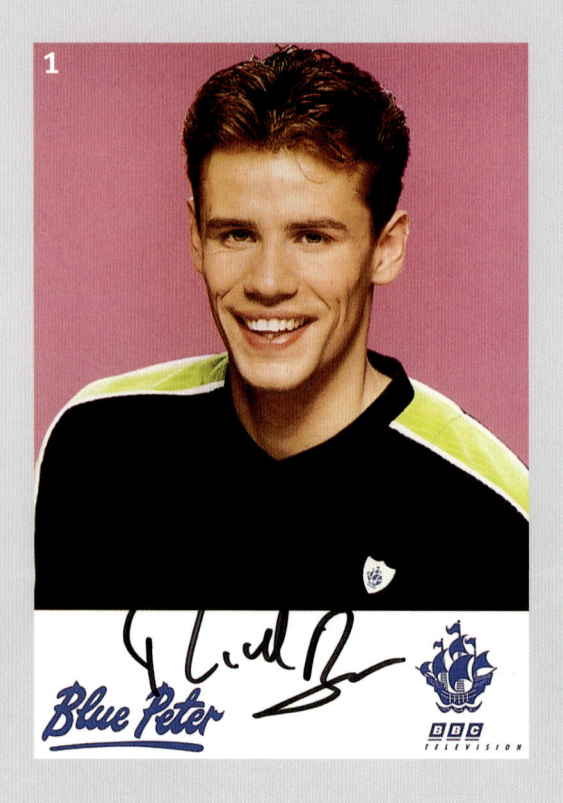

A slight, perfectly timed beat and Richard piped up, 'With the greatest possible respect, Colour Sergeant Harvey…' He didn't get to finish his sentence, of course.

The *Blue Peter* posse

Richard wasn't the only children's presenter who craved to be 'cool'. Some, like Jamie Theakston and Zöe Ball on Saturday morning's *Live and Kicking*, actually were. Stuart Miles, Katy Hill and Richard began to be seen 'out and about'. Richard in particular threw himself into the exciting but empty social life available to any television presenter. The tabloids weren't slow to notice and make fun of the *Blue Peter* party posse. With hindsight, these regular reports – small but snide – were a warning sign. At the time, as Richard's work was unaffected, they didn't seem much more than red-top nonsense.

The revelation that Richard had taken a class A drug was unleashed to the world at the end of a week of highly publicized celebrations for the 40th anniversary. On Sunday, 18 October 1998, the *News of the World* screamed, '*Blue Peter* goody-goody is a cocaine-snorting sneak.' They'd sat on the scandal for three weeks so that it would have maximum impact. The story had been sold to them for thousands of pounds by Richard's best friend, who'd tricked him into talking about the incident on the phone. The conversation

2 Richard salutes the Adjutant at the Royal Military Academy, Sandhurst. 'Who's the smartest man on parade?', the Adjutant asked him. 'I am, sir' was the answer that he was looking for, and eventually got.

3 Richard played 'Capability' Brown in a film presented by Clare Bradley. It was shown just before he left but several others had to be junked or re-shot.

was recorded as proof. This betrayal remained the most bitter aspect of what followed for Richard and his family.

Richard's fate was sealed later that morning in a meeting at Television Centre between him, Editor Oliver Macfarlane, Lorraine Heggessy, the Head of Children's Programmes, and Personnel Controller Sandra Horne. Lorraine told him that she had no alternative but to terminate his contract. He handed in his BBC pass and left the building. Oliver set off to receive a special BAFTA award marking *Blue Peter*'s four decades of achievement. It was supposed to be the crowning glory of all the celebrations, but all of us there felt self-conscious and funereal.

On the Monday morning, I had been due to shoot a story with Richard as a junior reporter on a teenage magazine. Stuart Miles replaced him, and as we set up the first shots on Shaftesbury Avenue in the heart of London, cabbie after cabbie slowed down to comment cheerily about Richard's sacking.

That afternoon's programme was a special, following Stuart tracking gorillas in Uganda. It was decided that Lorraine would precede the transmission with a direct message to the audience. Dressed in black, she read a carefully prepared statement: 'I believe that Richard has not only let himself and the team on *Blue Peter* down, but he's also let all of you down badly.' She told viewers that Richard had been sacked for taking 'an illegal drug' and that

he agreed with the decision. John Leslie felt that she made '…a bad situation worse. She broke the golden rule of children's television presenting, and that is, if you want to get through to children, you never, ever talk to them like they're children.'

Getting the message across was a real headache. We had hundreds of emails, including one from a seven-year-old that summed up the problem: 'I don't know why Richard's been sacked because my teacher lets me drink Coke at school all the time.' What do you say to that?

On the next live *Blue Peter*, the remaining presenters worked hard within the considerable confines to say something meaningful. They closed the show holding hands as a sign of solidarity.

Meanwhile, Richard made his own statement to the press: 'I fully accept and agree with the decision. I regret what I did, but it was in my personal time and I therefore hope that it does not reflect on the show. I am very sorry that I have let everybody down.'

Richard has stood by those views, but acknowledges the unavoidable irony that his sudden notoriety actually helped rather than hindered his subsequent career. He went on to present a wide range of television shows, including *The Big Breakfast* and *Top of the Pops*, as well as having his own show on London's Capital Radio and the BBC's Radio 5 Live.

Presenter Profile
KONNIE HUQ

JOINED: 1 December 1997

LEFT: 22 January 2008

MEMORABLE MOMENTS: Rally driving; walking on hot coals; powerboat racing; being the production assistant on a live *Top of the Pops*; Bollywood dancing; interviewing Tony Blair; trips to Bangladesh, Mozambique, Sweden, Bolivia, Mexico, USA, Spain, Vietnam, Morocco, India, Japan, Brazil, Oman, Australia, Hawaii and the Bahamas

Konnie Huq made her first appearance on *Blue Peter* on 7 December 1989 as part of the cast of the National Youth Music Theatre production of *The Ragged Child*. She had been a 'telly junkie' as a child and grew up determined to make a career in the industry. While still reading economics at Robinson College, Cambridge, she was also presenting Channel 5's children's strand, *Milkshake*. Then she sent in a showreel to *Blue Peter*: 'It was terrible quality, just a tape-to-tape thing, but it got me an interview. I know it sounds awful, but I just thought, "I'm brown and they'll definitely go for me." I was a contrast and after the audition I knew I'd got it.'

She had impressed Editor Oliver Macfarlane: 'I was immediately struck by her sharp mind and lively personality, and her undeniable enthusiasm for *Blue Peter*.'

Konnie joined the team of Stuart Miles, Katy Hill and Richard Bacon, and recalls: 'They were very cliquey and I couldn't be bothered to compete. Katy was the star. I always remember when Katy received death threats, she was put into a safe house and given 24-hour guards. When the same thing happened to me, I was sent on the ferry to the Isle of Wight to make a film about a Victorian photographer!'

Nobody could have predicted Konnie's marathon run. She was tiny and slightly off the wall, qualities that children liked. But like many intelligent people, she was easily bored and sometimes lost focus, using her considerable charm to get out of trouble. When she was late, which was fairly often, there was always an excuse, effusively given. Sometimes it was even plausible. I once had a surreal conversation with her in which she argued, with all apparent seriousness, that it was just too far from the make-up room to the studio floor for her to be expected to tell the floor manager when she'd returned from lunch. She seemed to believe it too!

1 Konnie is *Blue Peter*'s longest-running female presenter. When she left, she wasn't replaced. The team reverted to three presenters, for the first time since 1995.

Best of Huq
For all her 'naughtiness', when she was on form, Konnie brought a unique 'kooky' quality to *Blue Peter*. She was always better 'off script', because unless she had to use her wits, she'd switch off and the words would sound droning and monotonal. Given the choice, she happily deviated from standard *Blue Peter* 'speak', especially during makes, when she'd substitute her own phrases, such as 'Here's one I made a little bit previous to now' instead of 'earlier'. Sometimes these ad libs went too far. She once suggested going to look for some crêpe paper 'in your father's study'. We teased her for a long time about that one.

On another occasion when the actor Ewan McGregor was a studio guest, the twinkle in his eye put her off and she started giggling during her link into the next item. Unfortunately, she was still convulsed when we came out of the item. She just couldn't pull herself together.

Konnie was the envy of other presenters who would rehearse diligently all day and still make mistakes on transmission, while Konnie would breeze in, distract everybody with amusing gossip, seem to pay little attention and then turn in a fabulously energized performance. When we introduced 'video blogs' on the website, she loved the freedom of this trivial, intimate form of confessional.

2 About to board the Orient Express, in the last film I directed for *Blue Peter*. Konnie played the part of a wealthy but eccentric passenger with great skill and timing

3 Konnie hated this mini-skirt which she was asked to wear for her first photo-call. She wasn't too keen on sharing the limelight with a dog either!

4 The lady in red – Konnie looking stunning during the 'Uptown Girl' number, part of the 2001 musical extravaganza, 'A Rock 'n' Roll Christmas'.

She was great fun to be with, but her carefree manner didn't stop her going fiercely into battle on her own behalf whenever necessary. She would erupt into angry eloquence if pushed too far. She once phoned up from a film shoot in Belgium to abuse me roundly for insisting she return from a holiday a day early to watch Matt Baker perform in *Chitty Chitty Bang Bang*. I explained that children would think it was odd if only Simon Thomas and Liz Barker were there. 'I could be ill that day! You couldn't stop me!' she threatened. But I knew that once she had let off steam, she would do the filming with a good grace, and sure enough she did.

Unlike many presenters, she wasn't preoccupied with what she wore on television. She valued a bargain and would take you to one side and confide, 'What do you think of this jacket? A tenner from New Look'. She hated what she called the 'try hard' brigade and resisted attempts by stylists to 'sex up' her image.

In 2000, she very nearly left in a protracted dispute over her fee. She had discovered that the BBC was paying her proportionately less than the boys. She carefully worked out the figures to show exactly how she had been short-changed and won equality just in time for the new season.

As the years went by, jokes about when Konnie was going to leave started to gain momentum. When she had been there six years, we surprised her with a special show devoted to celebrating this landmark. 'But people will think I'm leaving!' she protested afterwards. Every so often, we would sit down and talk about the right timing. Konnie would 'um' and 'ah', and so would we. One controller once wisely advised, 'If the talent is doing a good job for you, why change just for change's sake?'

Increasingly, Konnie liked the idea of becoming *Blue Peter*'s longest-running female presenter. In today's internet age, it is much harder to keep anything confidential. In the summer of 2007, press leaks accurately predicted that she was finally going to leave, having achieved her record-breaking goal. When the speculation spread to the *Blue Peter* message boards, we decided we had to let the audience know. Konnie announced her departure some seven months ahead of time, while admitting that she still didn't really want to go: 'It is the best job in the world. I just love it. The live studios. Doing the makes. The people. What other show takes you away for a month abroad with your friends? All those experiences. It is so cult and so cool. I'll really miss it.'

On her last programme, she was awarded her own gold badge and there was a sequence of tributes, including a message from the Prime Minister Gordon Brown, thanking her for her long service.

Presenter Profile
SIMON THOMAS

JOINED: 8 January 1999

LEFT: 25 April 2005

MEMORABLE MOMENTS: Climbing Mount Kilimanjaro and Mont Blanc; scaling the spire of Salisbury Cathedral; running the London Marathon and in the Indoor Athletics Championships; undergoing the Parachute Regiment's 'P' Company fitness tests; submarine escape training; escapology; free-fall parachuting; trips to Australia, USA, Vietnam, Morocco, Brazil, India, Belize and the Solomon Islands

Simon Thomas had already applied twice before when he finally achieved his ambition to become a *Blue Peter* presenter. At the very beginning, his enthusiasm wasn't obvious. As producer and then Editor I was making a film about the auditions, which I'm not sure in retrospect was very fair. The selection process is hard enough without the knowledge that, even if you are unsuccessful, your efforts will still be seen by millions.

1 We made a film about Simon's audition. His competition – Michael Underwood, Jonas Hurst and Jake Humphrey – all became successful presenters elsewhere.

Under this pressure and realizing that, at 27, it was probably his last chance, Simon was understandably tense and standoffish. Lots of us took this the wrong way. Was it a sign of a bad attitude in waiting? Assistant Editor John Comerford saw beyond Simon's surface cool and backed him vehemently. He did us all a favour.

Simon arrived, utterly focused from the first. There was a lot to learn. To begin with, he found it very hard to walk naturally on camera. He tried all kinds of different approaches. Hands behind his back, he looked like Prince Charles touring a factory. Hands by his side, he looked like a robot. Hands in his pockets just looked odd. Simon is the epitome of perfectionism and he got very frustrated. I told him he just had to keep doing it and eventually it would click. Likewise, he started with a strange, slightly fake London accent. Over the next few months, the strangled vowels subsided and he relaxed into being himself.

Very early on in his *Blue Peter* career, just before we recorded an item about famous diarists, I walked into make-up where Simon was being bewigged as Samuel Pepys. One of the more established presenters was giving him 'advice': 'Don't be any good or they'll make you dress up all the time.' I wasn't best pleased, but Simon was never going to contribute anything less than his best. He turned out to be a gifted natural actor. Given that these were never his favourite items, he was patient and did them very well. The only real explosion came during a busy filming schedule for *The Quest* serial, which made him miss most of that year's World Cup.

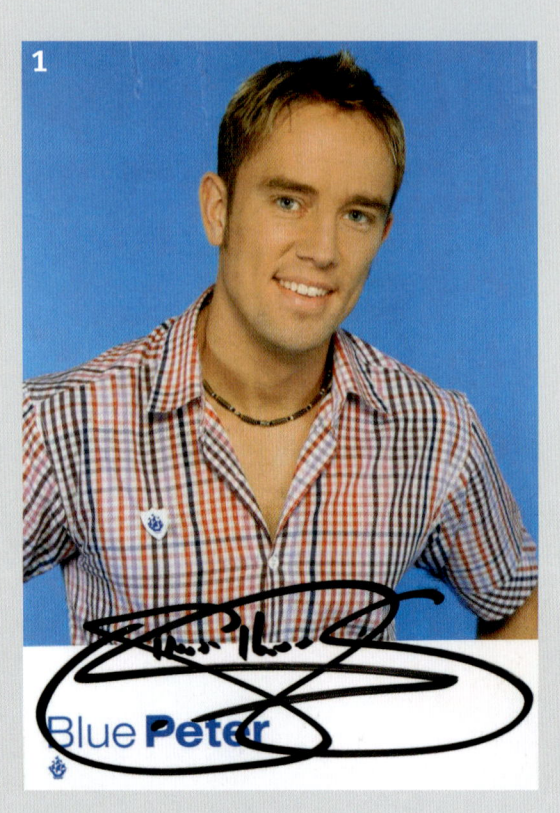

A role model for all

A run of stories required Simon to wear drag. He went along with this for a while, but after the third or fourth occasion, he did begin to wonder if we were simply trying to wind him up. The trouble was that, unlike Matt Baker, he made quite a convincing woman. The drag wasn't just for laughs. After one historical film in which he played the cross-dressing 18th-century courtier and secret agent Chevalier, we were sent a magazine for transgender people. Under the title, 'What did *Blue Peter* ever do for you?', there was a rave review of Simon's performance: 'In over 35 years as a media monitor I have never seen anything like it on any programme and never expected to on *Blue Peter*. It may just ease those burdensome years slightly for young trans.'

If it wasn't drag, it was lederhosen. These were admittedly more tongue in cheek. They started when we featured traditional Austrian dancing, which had, somewhat bizarrely, been taken up by a school in Leicestershire. Simon

2 Two lads in lederhosen. During this shoot, while we were filming a high-angled shot of Simon in the streets of Munich wearing his lederhosen, he was disconcerted to be stopped and congratulated in German for being a 'true nationalist'!

3 Life's a drag. Simon and Matt sang 'I Enjoy Being A Girl' in 2000's 'East End Christmas'. Note the *Blue Peter* badge earrings!

4 Telling both sides of the story. In this 2002 film about the 1914 Christmas Truce, Simon played a German soldier in the trenches.

and Matt resignedly agreed to wear lederhosen and join in. It was a busy live programme and there was no time for them to change before introducing the next guests, the Royal Scots Dragoon Guards. The whole regiment had flown in from Germany to make a special Burns Night appearance. In a carefully rehearsed piece of theatre, Simon and Matt had to walk to the huge studio doors and open them to allow the guards to pipe in. Unfortunately, between the dress rehearsal and the transmission, somebody had locked the doors. The sight of the boys, in their incongruous lederhosen, struggling to open the massive doors while the guards can just be heard on the outside, piping and drumming for all they were worth, became a clip shown many times on out-take programmes.

The lederhosen item inspired a bizarre follow-up filming trip to Germany and Austria, in which the highlight was the boys performing a bottom-smacking dance alongside the locals with gusto and barely contained hilarity. Only on *Blue Peter*.

Simon's Christianity was important to him, but he was never the pious type. He was a realist with a quick wit and easy sarcasm. His passion was sport and action, and with these films he was in his element. He was always ready to push himself. At a time when many other male children's presenters were spiky-haired and rather camp, Simon and Matt scored by being real role models for little boys. Simon had pin-up potential too, and we were always teasing him about his fine cheekbones. He used to counter by claiming that we took every opportunity to show off his bare chest, but then again, he never seemed that reluctant to show off his hard-won muscles!

You could always rely on Simon. He was the big brother of the team – loyal, self-disciplined and ultra-professional. Typically, he gave me 18 months' notice of his intention to leave. For a few weeks, as the time approached, he suddenly became morose and difficult to work with. I talked to him and he quickly got his act together, but he later explained: 'I think you have to make yourself fall out of love with *Blue Peter* to make it possible to leave.'

When Simon took centre stage for his final show, he was choked with emotion. In the gallery and on the studio floor, many of us were also in tears. It was hard to say goodbye to such a superb colleague and brilliant presenter.

A few weeks later, recognizing Simon's professional skill as well as his passion for their subject matter, Sky Sports signed him up. He has been there ever since, though he did make a memorable return to *Blue Peter* in 2006, in heavy disguise, as part of an elaborate practical joke on his former presenting colleagues.

Presenter Profile
MATT BAKER

JOINED: 25 June 1999

LEFT: 26 June 2006

MEMORABLE MOMENTS: Looking after the Border Collie Meg; passing the Royal Marines potential recruits' course; achieving a world tandem hang-gliding record; lots of dancing including backing the pop group Steps on stage and appearing in *Chitty Chitty Bang Bang*; writing a Christmas song for the boy band Phixx; many trips, including Tanzania, Cambodia, Russia, Australia, Sweden and Iceland

When Matt Baker saw *Blue Peter* as a child, he would watch the action films and then immediately go out and re-enact them. His hero was Peter Duncan. Years later, when Matt was in the second year of a drama course in Edinburgh, his girlfriend's aunt tipped him off that Stuart Miles was leaving the programme.

Seeing Steve Hocking's name at the end of the credits, Matt phoned the BBC to speak to him. He recalls: 'His secretary told me he was in a meeting. I phoned back about ten minutes later. He was still in the meeting. The third time I called, I said "I'm not going to get to speak to him, am I?", and she said, "No", but suggested I make a showreel.'

The tape he sent in, shot by his dad on the family farm, glowed with potential. Matt was called for an interview and then an audition, explaining his absences from drama school with a series of imaginary dental appointments. At this point, the favourite contender was established presenter Rhodri Owen. Matt's audition changed all that. He recounts, 'It was just amazing to go into the *Blue Peter* studio. I felt petrified. But it went like the clappers, and afterwards, Steve Hocking shook my hand and said, "You couldn't have done any better."' When he was told that he'd got the job, he '…rang home and just went crazy!'

Matt was plunged straight into his bizarre new life. There were some serious difficulties. He struggled with words that he didn't understand. He was a superb natural mimic, but unfortunately this meant that to begin with he had a tendency to exactly copy the director's intonation. The biggest hurdle, however, was the wrench of moving to London: 'I entered into a world that I knew nothing about. I didn't think I was going to last six months. It was horrible because I was so lonely. I used to wait around in the office until everyone went because I didn't have a reason to go back home. I would ride up and down Chiswick High Road on my bike, just to have something to do.'

Characteristically, Matt got on with it. He was always willing to get his hands dirty. During a trip to St Petersburg in Russia, we were scheduled to film at a naval dockyard where Matt was to join a crew hard at work on a magnificent replica of Peter the Great's royal yacht. I had arranged with our fixer, Valery, for Matt to be given a sailor's uniform, so that he would look the part. When we arrived, the sailors were very friendly, but there was no sign of the spare uniform. Ever aware of time ticking by, I prompted Valery. He had a hurried conversation with the nearest sailor, who smiled broadly and stripped off, handing over his own clothes to the bemused Matt. The smell was atrocious – they had obviously been worn for days if not weeks. Matt just followed the sailor's lead and changed into them in front of everybody, laughing and chatting as though this was all perfectly normal. A while later, he needed the loo. One of his cheerful new workmates pointed in the direction of a solitary wooden hut on the horizon.

It was the worst toilet in the world. You could smell it from far away. Inside, someone had thoughtfully provided a fur toilet seat cover. The fur was now in an indescribable state. Poor Matt was desperate and had no choice. Trying not to retch, he faced the inevitable – and the fact that there was

1 Matt had several favourite phrases – 'Hello there!', 'Dear me!', and (said in terms of exaggerated wonder), 'I cannot believe what I've just done!'

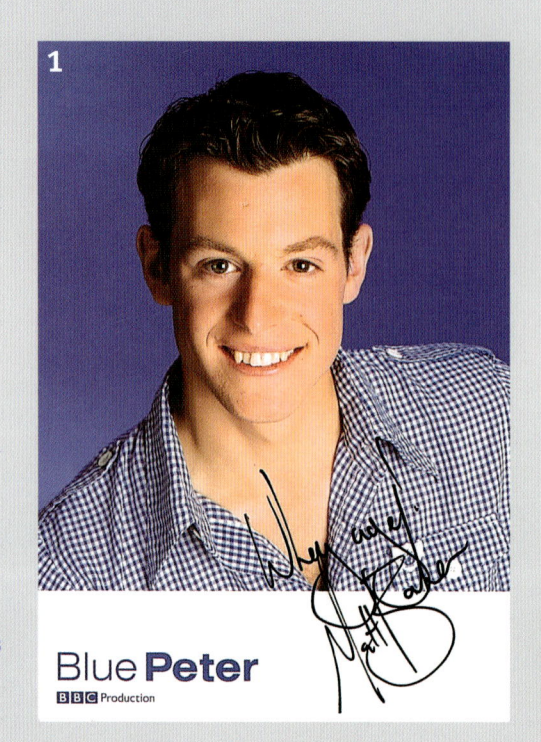

2 Matt threw himself into everything. He even agreed to an authentic Royal Marine haircut, though he worried what his mum was going to say!

4 It was cold when we first arrived in St Petersburg in Russia. Matt chose to wear this warm fleece. Then the sun came out and stayed out. Continuity meant he was trapped, constantly sweating for the rest of the trip.

3 Acting, singing or dancing and Matt was your man. In 2001's 'Rock 'n' Roll Christmas', Matt had to transform from school nerd into heartthrob hero.

nowhere to wash his hands afterwards. His acute sense of the ridiculous got him through and he always laughed at the hapless situations we sometimes landed him in.

Directors clamoured to work with Matt because of his invention and commitment. Bad directors relied on him to save their story. He was a perfectionist, whose high standards derived from a childhood of dedicated gymnastics training. 'Is there anything that Matt can't do?' became the running joke within the team. He could be stubborn and argumentative, but his humour and warmth usually offset his more aggressive moments. He was a brilliant *Blue Peter* presenter and his triumphs piled up.

Seven action-packed years

In addition to achieving a world record in tandem hang-gliding, he passed the daunting Royal Marines potential recruits course, setting a first for a presenter by agreeing to take part in every aspect of the experience, even the bits we didn't film. It was an intense physical and emotional undertaking, but his attitude earned him huge respect from the Marines. He reflects, 'I was frightened, but I loved the camaraderie and I learnt a lot about myself. That you can just keep going. It was such a sense of achievement.

'The worst thing I ever did was the Paras log race. I just couldn't carry on and a Para said, "You sacked yourself there. You'll regret that for the rest of your life." And I have done. I look back and think, "It was only a few more hundred metres. I could have got there and it would have been the best feeling of my life, instead of the worst."'

He was a superb athlete and dancer, a natural with any animals and wonderful with children. In short, there was no other presenter like Matt, and the industry recognized this by awarding him with two of the coveted BAFTA awards for Best Children's Presenter.

He was also part of a highly successful team: 'It amazes me that four people could be put together and get on so well. We all believed in *Blue Peter*. We were in it together. It was never forced. We had a major understanding of each other and our roles. Looking back, it was magic.'

For a while, Matt claimed he would beat John Noakes's record. In the end, he stayed for seven action-packed years. He concludes: 'My period on *Blue Peter* was my journey from boy to man. My biggest regret is that I took on so much. I put myself under a ridiculous amount of pressure. It was an obsessive disorder. I cared about it more than I cared about myself. I was taking on everybody's job and I was at breaking point. I think that's eventually what drove me to leave. Zöe and Gethin arrived, there was a re-formation of the team and I couldn't handle it. But for me, *Blue Peter* is and always will be something that is so special and precious. It was just the most important thing in the world to me.'

Special Assignment

WE NEVER ASK FOR MONEY

For millions of children, taking part in a *Blue Peter* appeal is their introduction to altruism. The appeals started in a simple way, soon after Biddy Baxter first arrived on the programme: 'There'd been a tradition that every Christmas the studio would be piled high with toys. The presenters did a commentary on them and the whole atmosphere was "What's in it for me? What am I going to grab?"

'Edward Barnes and I agreed it was really pretty nauseating and we finished it. Edward said, "Why can't we have something for children who aren't going to have toys at Christmas?" So we asked children to send in toys, not clapped-out, broken old things, but nice toys they would like to have themselves. We had a huge response. They all got distributed and we did the same the following year.'

There has been an appeal every year ever since. The style and treatment have changed, but the psychology behind the scheduling remains the same. Christmas is a time for giving and for thinking about others. In purely practical terms too, the audience is always at its peak during the cold, dark winter months.

Unlike other television appeals, *Blue Peter* never asked for money. Converting rubbish into cash made the appeal as accessible as possible to all children, no matter how poor their background. The only cost was the price of a stamp.

Charity doesn't begin at home

The famous 'totaliser', the method used to chart an appeal's progress, was Rosemary Gill's idea, inspired by her childhood memory of the Second World War Spitfire Fund, through which communities contributed to the cost of building fighter planes. In 1965, the scope of the appeal expanded beyond Britain. This established an important principle. On *Blue Peter*, charity doesn't begin at home. During the first few months of the famine in Ethiopia in 1984, *Blue Peter* was on the ground delivering aid via its charity partner, Oxfam, before Band Aid had made any impact there. According to Paul Sherlock, the senior humanitarian representative from Oxfam, 'In the first six to 12 months of the crisis, it was *Blue Peter* money, and others that came in, not the Band Aid money that saved people.'

Bring-and-buy sales were popular because they made the appeal a community activity. They were such a good way of raising funds that schools increasingly used them for their own causes. When bring-and-buys were rolled out three years in a row from 2001 to 2003, they became dangerously over-exposed. It was the law of diminishing returns. We went back to recycling, but these campaigns present their own challenges. In some cases, *Blue Peter* has been the victim of its own success.

After *Blue Peter* organized the first big aluminium-can collection and the first junk-mail collection, both became routinely recycled. It is the same with many other commodities. This is great for the environment, but it does limit the programme's choices. All recycling

1 The first recycling initiative was to collect silver paper. On New Year's Eve 1964, Chris and Val rolled a giant silver ball of the stuff into the studio.

2 For many years, it was a tradition that the appeal target was reached on the first programme of the New Year. 1969 was no exception.

3 When bring-and-buy sales were introduced, the bringers were always as important as the buyers. This photo-card was sent out to viewers taking part in 1980.

Special Assignment **WE NEVER ASK FOR MONEY**

projects generate lower revenue and take longer to process. But the audience really values them, so that's why they have endured.

One of the hallmarks of the appeals is that they are long-term propositions. *Blue Peter* has regularly returned to and revisited the stories, sometimes many years later. This is unique in television, where the pressure is generally to provide instant results and a quick feel-good fix.

Children often see the world in black and white. The appeals are a chance to show shades of grey. Over the years, there has been some hard-hitting material. An effective barometer was often the reaction of the presenters: Simon Groom cradling a dying baby in Ethiopia; Yvette Fielding overcome at the desolate nature of a Romanian orphanage; Matt Baker faced with the reality of children forced to drink polluted water every day; Zöe Salmon living for a week with Malawian AIDS orphans, coping themselves with HIV. Peter Purves is still haunted by the tragedy of a herd of oxen bought by *Blue Peter* for the people of Ethiopia: 'We were going to cattle-drive this wonderful herd to this desperate area and give them to the people there. And we couldn't go near them because the entire herd had got foot-and-mouth. You say, "Is there a God?" It broke my heart.'

Blue Peter appeals don't claim to solve all the problems and are never designed to raise the maximum amount of money. They encourage children to think. They empower them, no matter how badly off they may be themselves, to do something, no matter how small, to help others less fortunate than themselves. They are what the programme is all about.

Special Assignment WE NEVER ASK FOR MONEY

1 Jumping for joy at the result of the 1983 Weather Beater Appeal. Unveiling each year's totaliser design was always a special moment on *Blue Peter*.

2 Two appeals have been named Treasure Hunt. A third was called The Treasure Trail. 'Treasure' is a word guaranteed to appeal to children.

Blue Peter appeals

1962 1963	Hundreds of sacks of toys, for children who would otherwise have no Christmas presents
1964	**Guide Dogs Appeal** Seven-and-a-half tons of silver paper and milk-bottle tops paying for two-and-a-half guide dogs and providing funds to maintain a brood bitch
1965	**Tractor For Uganda Appeal** 45,000 parcels of wool buying equipment for the Bugosa Farm School in Uganda
1966	**Lifeboat Appeal** 240,000 paperback books buying four Royal National Lifeboat Institute inshore lifeboats. Renewed and expanded in 1972
1967	**Houses for the Homeless Appeal** 750 million stamps buying four *Blue Peter* houses to provide homes for eight homeless families
1968	**Nigerian/Biafran Appeal** Two million parcels of wool and cotton buying three hospital trucks, six emergency doctor's cars, two jet injectors and six rehabilitation trucks for the children of the Nigerian/Biafran civil war
1969	**Old People's Buses Appeal** 500,000 parcels of old electric plugs and old model cars buying four buses to take elderly people to day centres plus many aids for the handicapped and housebound
1970	**Holiday Caravans Appeal** 2,250,000 parcels of spoons and forks buying three holiday caravans and a log cabin to give 3,000 children a week's holiday every year
1971	**Dormitory Appeal** Six million parcels of socks and pillowcases buying two dormitories for the Starehe Boys' Centre in Kenya
1972	**Treasure Hunt Appeal** Over 225 tons of old metal 'treasure' buying two centres for the elderly, eight hot-dinner vans and holidays each spring and autumn for 100 elderly people
1973	**The *Blue Peter* Stampede** Six million envelopes of stamps buying oxen, ploughs, seed and an irrigation scheme for the victims of the Ethiopian drought and famine
1974	**The 3 B's Appeal** Over six million envelopes of buttons, buckles and badges buying 11 guide dogs and new buildings and equipment for the Guide Dog Association
1975	**The Clothes Horse Race** Over 800 tons of old wool and cotton buying 21 ponies, including Rags, an indoor riding school and equipment for the Riding for the Disabled Association
1976	**The Lifeline Lebanon Appeal** Five million envelopes of stamps and postcards buying staff, medicine, food, equipment, a training centre and a nursery for injured and homeless babies and children, victims of the civil war in Lebanon
1977	**The Key Note Appeal** 2,500,000 parcels of old keys and toy cars buying the four mobile classrooms and video equipment for deaf children
1978	**The Medi-Bike Appeal** Parcels of used stamps and pre-decimal coins to buy over 1,000 medi-bikes and medicines for health workers in Tanzania
1979	**The Great *Blue Peter* Bring & Buy Sale for Cambodia** £4,000,000 raised buying 57 lorries, food, fuel, medicine, equipment and a ferry across the Mekong river to help three million Cambodians
1980	**The Great *Blue Peter* Bring & Buy Sale for the Disabled** Over £1 million raised buying six bungalows, one *Blue Peter* flat (opened by the Queen) and equipment for many schools and hospitals
1981	**Operation Pipeline** Five-and-a-quarter million envelopes of stamps and coins providing 150 pure-water systems and health care for villages in Java

| 1982 | **The Treasure Hunt Appeal**
Five million parcels of 'treasure' buying equipment and covering running costs for hospitals to help babies and children suffering from acute and chronic kidney failure |

| 1983 | **The Weatherbeater Appeal**
£1,610,000 raised through bring-and-buy sales, providing aid for 150,000 families in 21 of the world's poorest countries suffering the effects of droughts and floods |

| 1984 | **The Double Lifesaver Appeal**
Over 800,000 envelopes of buttons and postcards, replacing all four *Blue Peter* lifeboats and providing two extra boats. Over 3,200,000 envelopes of stamps funding irrigation schemes and equipment in Ethiopia |

| 1985 | **Lend an Ear Appeal**
3,500,000 envelopes of coins, keys and scrap metal providing a *Blue Peter* hearing aid library plus 70 radio hearing aids for profoundly deaf children and babies |

| 1986 | **Sightsaver Appeal**
Over £2 million raised through bring-and-buy sales, saving the sight of two million people in Malawi, Mozambique, Nigeria and Tanzania. Another result of the appeal was that the charity Royal Commonwealth Society for the Blind changed its name to Sightsavers! |

| 1987 | **The Rags Appeal**
2,308 tons of old wool and cotton, buying Jet, a replacement for Rags, plus ten other ponies and equipment for the Riding for the Disabled Association |

| 1988 | **The Great *Blue Peter* Bring & Buy Sale for Kampuchea (Cambodia)**
Over £1 million raised funding repairs to the 1979 ferry, 200 pumps, a maintenance workshop and a school to train electricians and welders |

| 1989 | **The Babylife Appeal**
Over 40 million cans recycled to provide vital equipment in 65 baby-care units across Britain |

| 1990 | **The Great *Blue Peter* Bring & Buy Sale for Romania**
£6,582,534 paying for the refurbishment of 25 orphanages, 12 houses, a nursery-nurse training course and a foster-parent scheme |

| 1991 | **The Golden Age Appeal**
19 million aluminium cans collected, funding services for old people across Britain |

| 1992 | **The I-Care Appeal**
£1,289,172 raised through bring-and-buy sales, funding eye units fighting river blindness in Mali and Ghana |

| 1993 | **The Pieces of Eight Appeal**
Enough 'booty' collected, including broken jewellery, watches and postcards, to replace the six Royal National Lifeboat Institute *Blue Peter* lifeboats and provide an additional ocean-going lifeboat |

1 1984 was the only year a double target has been set, raising money for the people of Ethiopia and for the RNLI. By March 2008, *Blue Peter* lifeboats had saved the lives of 1058 people.

2 The Great Bring & Buy Sale for Romania was, in cash terms, the most successful of all *Blue Peter*'s appeals and funded work for years afterwards.

Special Assignment WE NEVER ASK FOR MONEY

3 February 2007 and the exciting moment the Shoebiz Appeal totaliser exploded. The 2007–2008 appeal featured a 'virtual' totaliser created by computer graphics.

1994	**The Well Water Appeal** £1,568,806 raised through bring-and-buy sales providing clean drinking water and sanitation to rural communities in India, Pakistan and Bangladesh	
1995	**The Paperchain Appeal** 8,500 tonnes of junk mail collected providing mobility for 385 disabled children across Britain	
1996	**The Great Bring & Buy Sale for Leprosy** £2,635,405 raised to fund work for curing leprosy in Brazil and India	
1997	**The *Blue Peter* Appeal for Cystic Fibrosis** £2,045,000 raised through bring-and-buy sales for day-care centres, staff and equipment for children with cystic fibrosis	
1998	**The New Future Appeal** Collecting 500 tonnes of aluminium foil and cans to build and equip schools in Mozambique	
1999	**The New Life Appeal** £2,303,683 raised through bring-and-buy sales for three specialist baby ambulances and neo-natal equipment for 115 hospitals	
2000	**The Stamp Aid Appeal** Over 350,000 envelopes of stamps collected to fund health care in Peru	
2001	**The Wheel Help Appeal** £1,013,104 raised through bring-and-buy sales funding equipment and social groups for the elderly	
2002	**The Waterworks Appeal** £1,431,000 raised through bring-and-buy sales funding clean-water schemes in Tanzania and Uganda	
2003	**The Get Together Appeal** Nearly three-quarters of a million pounds raised through bring-and-buy sales funding training of volunteers helping children with learning disabilities in out-of-school clubs	
2004	**The Welcome Home Appeal** 102,537 bags of old clothes collected and sold or recycled to raise funds to reunite hundreds of families torn apart by civil war in Angola	
2005	**The Treasure Trail Appeal** Enough 'treasure' – old coins and mobile phones – collected to pay for 151,000 calls to Childline	
2006	**The Shoebiz Appeal** 1.3 million pairs of shoes collected to fund UNICEF children's corners in Malawi for children dealing with the consequences of HIV/AIDS	
2007	**The Disc Drive Appeal** Over 500,000 unwanted discs – CDs, DVDs and computer games – donated to sell in Barnardo's shops to fund support for hundreds of young carers across the UK	

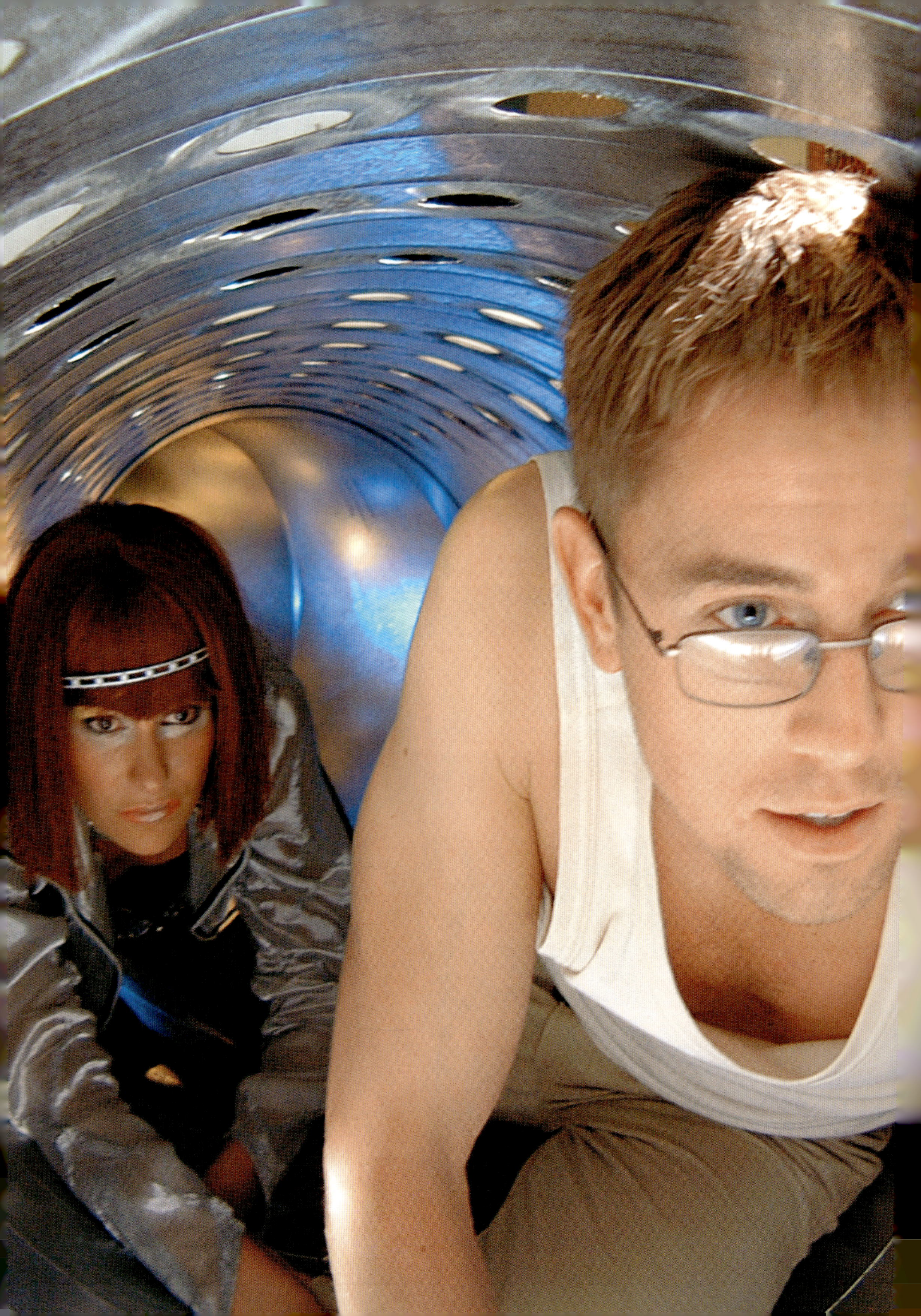

6 Flagship
2000–2008

At the dawn of the new millennium, while the rest of the world may have been worrying about the threat of computer meltdown, up in the *Blue Peter* office thoughts were more focused on the complexities of organizing the digging up of the 1971 and 1984 time capsules.

Liz as the alien Princess Banana and Simon Thomas as Dr Sam Bennett in the third Quest. *It was Nigel Pickard's idea to have a weekly cliffhanging serial. The audience could help to solve the mystery and win a prize.*

As with so many classic *Blue Peter* items, the original idea was the result of another item falling through, leaving a yawning hole in the running order. That's why, on 7 June 1971, Valerie Singleton announced:

'Now we're going to look forward into the future, to the year 2000. If you're, say, eight today, in the year 2000, you'd be 37 years old and you could well be watching *Blue Peter* with your children…'

Edward Barnes had remembered an article he'd seen, urging people to plant a tree for the year 2000. *Blue Peter*'s contribution was planted in a prime position at the front of Television Centre, while near by a box was buried too, full of 'souvenirs of what we were like and what the programme was like here in 1971'.

The item caught the imagination of the audience. Children loved the notion of working out how old they would be in the year 2000 and wondering whether they might have children of their own. In the 1970s and '80s, it still seemed such a long way off. As entries in the programme's 1974 Year 2000 competition revealed, many of them clearly expected us all to be living a silver-suited, super-futuristic, science-fiction life by the time the magic date came around.

Opening the capsules

In 1978, the box and tree were joined by William Timyn's statue in honour of Petra. Six years later, building work at Television Centre meant that they all had to be moved out of the way. A lot of airtime was devoted to the complicated process of moving the statue, the tree and the box to their new location in the *Blue Peter* garden. At the same time, presenters Simon Groom, Peter Duncan and Janet Ellis got in on the act by burying their own time capsule for the year 1984. This was perhaps not such a good idea. The millennium was no longer quite such a distant prospect and the contents of the 1984 box too markedly similar to be of tremendous additional interest to the audience.

Nevertheless, over the years, the *Blue Peter* time capsules had achieved cult status, and while I was thrilled that the job of disinterring them fell to me, I knew too that we had to satisfy viewers' expectations that this would feel like a major television moment.

The first challenge was to get the ex-presenters on board. Not easy when we were only able to offer them a modest flat fee. As producer I wrote to Valerie Singleton, John Noakes and Peter Purves: 'You could say that this letter has been in the post for 29 years!' In the event, all of them, along with Simon Groom and Janet Ellis, agreed to appear. Only Peter Duncan was absent, as he was filming abroad. I felt strongly that the programme shouldn't be live. We had no idea how long it would take to find the boxes or what state they would be in. I remembered too the hell, on the 40th-anniversary programme, of trying to focus a set of presenters alternately excited and bored by the proceedings. It was one of those rare occasions when pre-recording could only make the end result better.

The tree had been saved a premature death from disease by our gardener Clare Bradley, but it wasn't quite the towering beauty predicted back in 1971. At least we knew where it was. Despite an artistic map, the exact location of the boxes was pretty sketchy. We filmed this as a kind of treasure hunt, but those few minutes on screen took a whole freezing cold day of back-breaking digging to achieve.

Back to the '70s

In the studio, we built a 1971 house, full of the toys, food, comics and entertainment of the time. Simon Thomas, in flares Peter Purves would be proud of, and Katy Hill, in satin hot pants of the type made by Val but never worn by her, acted as our time-travel tour guides, allowing a rush of nostalgia for the adults and explaining the context to the current audience.

Finally, we assembled all the presenters in the garden for the grand opening ceremony. The 1984 box was first and a taste of what was to follow – once open, the lid revealed that the contents were mired in a thick, evil-smelling green slime. As ever, we made the best of it – at least Goldie's collar was still in one piece!

The 1971 box was in an even worse condition. It was obvious that when it had been moved in 1984, someone had opened it up to check the state of everything inside. The inadequacy of the waterproofing must have been obvious then, as the contents we unearthed were all wrapped up in layers of tape and plastic. Some items had clearly been replaced at the same time – presumably the originals had perished in the ooze. Despite the plastic, they were still pretty badly damaged. The packaging meant that the clip of the original item didn't exactly match what we were unearthing. In the end, we simply kept the clip short and no one seemed bothered by the discrepancy. It was more fun watching the presenters' hilarious attempts at finding something worth saying about the sticky, stinking remains in front of them.

1 7 June 1971 – burying the box. Other *Blue Peter* time capsules include one beneath TV Centre's car park (1982), the Millennium capsule (1998) under the O2 Dome (to be opened 2050) and the 2029 capsule in the garden, buried the week after the unearthing of the '71 and '84 boxes.

2 When the BBC started work on their Stage Five expansion of TV Centre in 1984, both tree and box had to be relocated in the *Blue Peter* garden.

3 In a letter to Editor Steve Hocking, Biddy Baxter noted: 'The "oldies" were very touched by the attitude of the "currents" – Val said, "They're so nice to us!".'

4 We sent Simon and Katy back to 1971 to bring the context of the occasion alive for the children of 2000.

5 Both boxes and a full line-up of presenters (except Peter Duncan, who was abroad). After we'd taped the big moment, there was a celebratory lunch in the BBC canteen.

BLUE PETER 50th Anniversary

1

1 Simon, Konnie, Matt and Liz – the programme's new dream team, dressed in black to raid the BBC archives for the 2000 review of the year. This team stayed together for five years and were the focus for another 'golden age'.

2 Simon and Matt formed an excellent double act. Their homage to spaghetti Westerns was part of the 2000 expedition to Spain.

3 Playing baseball with the San Francisco Giants. Both Simon and Matt loved sport and action, and competed hard.

4 Sarah Greene was one of several past presenters to play memorable cameos in *The Quest*. We stopped making it after three series because of budget cuts.

Val was wearing her gold badge, which she'd been awarded some years earlier. We decided to surprise John Noakes and Peter Purves with gold badges too. I felt that, despite their various quarrels with the programme, both deserved the accolade, and it gave us a wonderfully feel-good ending.

Dream team

Blue Peter was now entering a new era of confidence and expansion. The programme had another 'dream team' of presenters in the line-up of Konnie Huq, Simon Thomas, Matt Baker and Liz Barker. Just like the best of their predecessors, their personalities and skills complemented and contrasted with each other, which gave the production team a huge range of options in choosing the best content. The often contrary Victor Lewis-Smith wrote in the *London Evening Standard*: 'When I last watched *Blue Peter* about five years ago, the dumbest animals in the studio were the two-legged presenters, so I was agreeably surprised by how much smarter the current bunch seem to be. The present crop all look like members of girl and boy bands, but their "wicked" appearance didn't prevent them from hosting a programme that was both authoritative and educational.'

Crucially, perhaps, this team stayed together for five years and that gave the show a secure base from which to explore new territories while staying true to the core content and values. Instead of being a text-heavy add-on, the website began to become an entity in its own right. The annual *Blue Peter* Book Awards were established. The Friday programmes, with their strong entertainment bias, included games and quizzes, among them a revamped Double or Drop, once the mainstay of *Crackerjack*, the children's variety show. They also featured the thrilling and expensive weekly adventure serial *The Quest*, with which the audience could play along and which, coincidentally, allowed us to use lots of former presenters in cameo roles – a neat nod to the adult audience that was never self-indulgent because they were all actors and there for a reason. And for a time, another veteran entertainer, Basil Brush, joined the team to be in charge of the postbag.

In 2000, Nigel Pickard arrived as the new Controller. Previously regarded as an ITV 'lifer', Nigel was a passionate champion of children's programmes. Happily, he was a fan of *Blue Peter*. Indeed, shortly after his BBC appointment, he described walking onto the *Blue Peter* set as a 'hair-on-the-back-of-the-neck moment'.

Nigel asked Editor Steve Hocking whether *Blue Peter* could transmit 52 weeks a year. It was a rhetorical question, but it meant an increase in budget and was clearly not an opportunity to turn down. But could it be achieved with just four presenters?

The answer came in juggling the schedule. From October to March, the programme would remain three times a week. From April to September, it would revert to two weekly shows. By a convoluted process of pre-recording, enough material could be 'banked up' so that the summer expedition could remain intact and allow the presenters a holiday as well.

1 Simon presents the Queen with a gold *Blue Peter* badge during her visit to the studio on 28 November 2001.

A royal visit

It was in the first weeks of running this new schedule that Buckingham Palace got in touch. They were planning a day in which Her Majesty the Queen and the Duke of Edinburgh would tour some of Britain's key broadcasting institutions and they wanted *Blue Peter* to be one of them. It was an honour, but a huge undertaking too. By now, I'd been promoted to become Steve's deputy, and while Steve had the nerve-racking task of acting as the royal tour guide on the day, it fell to me to organize the actual programme, devise a guest list of suitable people for Her Majesty to meet and liaise with the Palace, on a seemingly constant basis, on everything including timing, security and press coverage. The plan was for the Queen to arrive during rehearsals. She would walk through the production gallery into the studio, where she would be introduced to a line of key *Blue Peter* people, from the young gymnasts on that afternoon's show to Margaret Parnell, our 'queen of makes'. As well as the current presenting team, I suggested inviting one classic presenter from each era, so we had Valerie Singleton representing the '60s, Peter Purves the '70s, Peter Duncan the '80s and John Leslie the '90s.

All was finally in place when I had a call from the Palace on the afternoon before the big day, asking for 'the biographies'. I countered with 'What biographies?' and was told in no uncertain terms that Her Majesty required a page of useful detail about each person she was to be introduced to. What's more, she needed it by 10 pm at the latest. It was time to stop asking questions and get on with it. When I'd finally

2 After the Queen left, Peter Purves claimed Val stole the anecdote he had planned to tell Her Majesty about Prince Edward's childhood visit to the studio!

3 Meeting my monarch – I wittered on about all the royal locations in which I'd be filming during the forthcoming Golden Jubilee year.

finished and emailed them off, I spoke once more to my Palace contact and said, 'This is procedure, I assume? She isn't really going to read them, is she?' I felt an instant freeze down the phone line. "Of course she will. I'm going to take them to her now. Myself!"'

It is a curious thing, the presence of royalty. More than mere celebrity, it has the power to impress and induce nerves, and it did so even among the supposed republicans on our team. Everything went according to the infinitely precise plans. Perhaps predictably, Her Majesty spent most time with the dogs, Mabel and Lucy, and their handler, the garrulous Leonie Pocock. There was a sticky moment when Steve introduced Liz Barker: briefed to say something interesting (and related to the painstakingly written biography I had prepared), she blurted out 'I've been to Auschwitz', which could have been the conversation-stopper of all time. Luckily, the Queen has obviously dealt with potentially awkward moments a million times before, and Liz was able to relax and explain that she'd been there to make a film for *Blue Peter*. Simon, ever reliable, raised a royal smile when he presented the monarch with a gold badge and cheekily informed her that this meant she could now get into the Tower of London free of charge!

Christmas spectacular

Something I always championed was spending money on an all-singing, all-dancing Christmas spectacular. They were a chance to show off the presenters doing something surprising and fun, and as most children are involved in some kind of show at Christmas, I thought them completely relevant. Also, I'd grown up with the long tradition of BBC Christmases with their seasons of Hollywood musicals and glitzy specials ranging from *Morecambe and Wise* to the *All Star Record Breakers*, as well, of course, as *Blue Peter*'s own contributions. In 2001, I'd written and directed a 'Rock 'n' Roll Christmas', a happy homage to the late 1970s retro musical *Grease*, which transplanted the action of a 1950s high school to the unlikely location of Wood Lane in West London. The presenters were superb. There were lots of highly complimentary letters and emails too, including one from former children's presenter Timmy Mallet, who wrote: 'Very funny lines… great songs… lovely production values and brilliant performances. It's one of *Blue Peter*'s great skills to develop its talents like this and I want to congratulate you on a top show – hope you get to make some more…'

In the New Year, I bumped into Nigel Pickard. He told me he'd thought Liz's performance in particular had been 'a revelation'. He said that the Children's Entertainment Department was pitching for a Christmas special for 2002. He had the money, but didn't like their idea. Would I like to come up with something, using *Blue Peter* and the presenters as the key talent, with cameos from lots of other CBBC stars? It was another rhetorical question. The result was 'Christmas At The Club *Blue Peter*', set in a 1920s night club, a heady mix of *Singin' In The Rain*, *Bugsy Malone* and *Moulin Rouge*. Liz would star as the foxy but evil Venus Chartreuse. An hour long and with a budget close on £350,000, it was without doubt the most glossy and lavish production *Blue Peter* had ever mounted. It also had fantastic viewing figures. There were, it is true, complaints about some of the costumes – but

1

2

1 The big-budget 'Christmas at the Club *Blue Peter*'. Liz played Venus Chartreuse.

2 The Talented Mr Baker – Matt played two roles. As Big Daddy he had to endure hours in make-up.

3 Konnie and Liz in the 2001 'Rock 'n' Roll Christmas'. Liz's performance led to the commission for the 'Club *Blue Peter*'.

4 The costume that caused complaints, designed by Robert Hawcutt, one of 20,986 viewers who entered a competition to create an outfit for Liz's character.

ironically, the costume that caused the most controversy was based on a design by an 12-year-old *Blue Peter* viewer. It seemed a lot of parents got very hot under the collar at the sight of suspenders!

New Editor, new energy

By the start of 2003, it was obvious that Steve was becoming less and less interested in the day-to-day running of *Blue Peter*. He'd always been a brilliant ambassador for the programme, but for some time had left the actual content to me. Just before he moved on, he wrote to the Controller in charge of appointing his successor, Dorothy Prior: 'As you know, the show celebrated its 40th birthday looking 40. Attention then seemed to be focused on making *Blue Peter* hip and trendy. Eyes were taken off the ball. There was an impression that making, cooking and celebrating the achievements of under 11s were all lacking in "cool" and were a bit naff. This is wrong. Any Editor has to recognize that the *most* popular things are the makes, cooks and pets.

'The Editorship is a horribly responsible position. You are as exposed as the presenters when it comes to misdemeanours and held to account by every letter writer in the country. This is a time for reinvigoration. A new Editor has to bring that. New ideas and, above all, new energy. That said, I firmly believe that there should be no shift from the fundamentals. We have to recognize that it's hard work sticking to principles. There will always be siren voices suggesting that the programme is tired, needs a change of format, is middle class, is too comfortable. *Blue Peter* is a comfortable programme. We shouldn't make excuses for that. It's a programme which aspires to be excellent and which sticks to its guns.'

I was appointed Editor in June 2003 with a big challenge on the horizon. The previous year, the BBC had launched its two digital channels aimed at children, CBBC and CBEEBIES. On the CBBC channel, *Blue Peter*'s presence was weak. Repeats of the current shows were bolstered with a couple of specially produced spin-offs, *Blue Peter Unleashed*, where the focus was on compiling the best of our sport films, and a long run of *Blue Peter Flies the World*! It all felt very secondhand.

Blue Peter needed to enter the digital arena with conviction. This meant offering a five-times-a-week schedule and the planning was eye-wateringly complex. The strategy evolved so that Monday would be live; Tuesday live on the CBBC channel, with that show repeating on Wednesday on BBC1 while the channel screened a compilation; Thursday was a channel-only show, recorded in the mornings on Mondays and Tuesdays; and Friday was a special shot entirely on location. There was a new set, graphics and theme music. With regret, I dropped the 'bubble' logo, the alternative ship designed by Kevin Hill in 1999, because I felt there was only room for one logo. Clever though Hill's design was, the Tony Hart original was always going to have more impact with the public.

I drastically cut back on our booking of pop acts too, which rarely added anything distinctive to the mix and often caused problems with

1 Versailles 2005. On a *Blue Peter* shoot, everybody mucks in – even Marie Antoinette!

2 In 2000, we were given special permission to film at midnight in the basilica at Assisi, for the story of St Francis, as told by Simon.

overt lyrics or unsuitable performances. Exceptions were made for the really big names. But when James Blunt made his appearance on *Blue Peter*, he wasn't in the public eye at all. He was Captain James Blount of the Army's elite Household Cavalry regiment. I was filming a special about the regiment's Norfolk camp where Matt was trying all kinds of equestrian stunts. There was the ritual of tea in the officers' mess. It was all very posh and Matt found it hard not to get the giggles when he was told things like 'Don't bloody fall off, will you? That'd be a prep schoolboy error.' 'What's a prep school?' he whispered. He couldn't get over the sight of these young officers, all immaculate in their uniforms, enjoying tea and polite conversation, served by ordinary troopers from silver trays.

We were introduced to Captain Blount. 'He's a bit of a muso', we were told. The Captain himself couldn't have been friendlier. 'Yes, it's true – I'm planning to leave the Army and concentrate on my music.' We took his photo – 'just in case I make it big', he smiled.

Blue Peter often works like a magic charm, opening doors and inviting collaboration, whether from pop stars or the Prime Minister. Some of our competitions offered truly life-changing prizes, like the chance to design a Fabergé egg. There were nearly 30,000 entries and Natalie Learmouth, the 15-year-old winner, had her idea turned into reality by the descendants of the great Carl Fabergé himself. As well as being given her own copy of the egg, she was flown out to Russia to take part in a grand ceremony in which the original egg was presented to the Mayor of St Petersburg for permanent exhibition there.

It was a pleasure to be able to think and plan in such ambitious terms. We were constantly inspired by our audience. A series of films called 'Me On TV' focused on children leading interesting or unusual lives. The subjects included an asylum seeker, a girl at boarding school and a young traveller called Martin with a passion for poetry – and boxing.

I had used a dilapidated West London boxing gym as a location in one of our Christmas specials. Towards the end of the day a group of boys, all regulars, arrived and watched us from the sidelines, laughing and exchanging sarcastic remarks. During a break in filming, I went over to talk to them. 'Hey mister,' challenged one of them, 'Why don't you do something about boxing then?'. 'Cos it's the BBC,' said another, 'they don't agree with it.' I thought about it and could see their point. We ended up making a programme all about the sport. It was challenging and contentious, but in its way just as ambitious as the Fabergé competition.

When we went five times a week, I was determined to keep standards as high as ever. As CBBC's Head of Presentation put it: 'Most digital TV is pick 'n' mix but *Blue Peter* is like a box of Belgian chocolates.'

Nobody was surprised it was gruelling. It was a case of proving that we could do it, though all of us worried about the wallpaper effect of being on all the time. I had negotiated a return to having a two-month break over the summer, which helped. On the whole, I think the two live programmes and the Friday specials succeeded but the channel programme always suffered by being crammed into a few hours'

3 This was the anonymous advert placed in newspapers during the 2004 search for new presenters. We thought the questions made it fairly obvious!

4 In 2001, artist Quentin Blake gave a live masterclass and sketched this superb caricature of presenters Simon Thomas, Liz Barker and Matt Baker.

5 In 2005 there was a special 'Editors' dinner'. Left to right: Steve Hocking, Oliver Macfarlane, Biddy Baxter, Richard Marson, Edward Barnes and Lewis Bronze.

pre-recording. It was like the awful Monday night scenario in reverse. After a pre-record, the presenters and studio crew had to steel themselves to deliver that day's live transmission. There were a few disasters with exhausted presenters, notably the day Liz completely dried during an interview with Emma Thompson and the cast of *Nanny McPhee*. It was so bad that we persuaded our guests to stay on afterwards so we could re-record it for the repeat.

In the 26 years that Biddy ran *Blue Peter*, she reported to five Heads of Department. Over my four years as Editor, there were four different people at the top. Inevitably, each had their own ideas, prejudices, preferences and ambitions. The biggest impact was in the scheduling. Over the last few years the programme has been placed on Monday, Wednesday, Friday; Monday to Friday; Monday to Thursday; Monday to Wednesday; Tuesday to Thursday; Tuesday and Wednesday. And that's just the BBC1 five o'clock slot. The repeats have similarly followed the whims, necessities and fashions of scheduling. In my time, the key five o'clock slot became ever more competitive as commercial channels realized the potential for reaching audiences at home at teatime. Indeed, in February 2008 *Blue Peter*, along with all the other five o'clock BBC1 shows, was moved to a new time of 16.35.

During my final season, the Whose Shoes? competition took place with its seismic aftermath. The plan was to run six of these during the run-up to Christmas. Viewers would be shown a pair of mystery shoes and given clues as to whom they might belong. They could call in during the programme, and we'd announce the winner at the end. Calls cost ten pence with the proceeds going to the appeal, less operating costs.

The day we launched the competition was fraught even by *Blue Peter* standards. It was a truly dreadful programme. When it came to the Whose Shoes? section, all of us in the gallery were aware only of a delay in patching through a caller. If no caller had been there, the presenters would have coped easily – it would have been the best moment of the show, in fact, as viewers love it when things go wrong. Minutes after we were off air, I learnt what had really happened. There was a fault with the telephone system, meaning that the member of the team responsible hadn't been able to retrieve any callers. Thinking that the lines had failed and that no-one was getting through, this individual asked a child visiting the studio to stand in.

Back in the office, the Deputy Editor and I held an immediate, angry and emotional post-mortem. The person concerned was in floods of tears. The next day, we asked the telephone company to donate all their costs to the appeal and I cancelled the remaining five slots. We weren't told that the genuine calls had been recorded or it would have been only too easy to do what we eventually did and re-run the competition off air. At the time we felt it had simply been a terrible mistake, an error of judgement but not one we could do much more about. It was a dark time for the Corporation and for all of us on *Blue Peter*, a programme where the audience does and always did really matter to the production team.

1 21st-century presenters often have to film their own material, blog online and strive to hold the attention of an audience with many alternative choices.

2 Another gathering of the clan in 2005. Back row, left to right: Simon Thomas, John Leslie, Gethin Jones. Middle row: series producer Kez Margrie, Biddy Baxter, producers Anne Dixon and Alex Leger, Katy Hill, Edward Barnes and Lewis Bronze. Front row: producer Bridget Caldwell and Richard Marson

Over the next couple of days, the junior member of staff remained distraught. Concerned, two of the producers came to see me. Across the board, morale was at rock bottom. At our next team meeting, I pointed out that the person involved had acted in good faith, in trying to keep the show on the road. This was not about commending or congratulating but simply acknowledging that while a serious mistake had been made, the intention was not cynical or malicious. Official reports followed. There were plenty of 'if only' moments where what happened might have been averted or the impact lessened. Both *Blue Peter* and the BBC apologized and work began to ensure mistakes like this could never happen again.

Throughout the crisis, I continued to edit three weekly programmes but as the end of the season drew near, it was time to move on, to draw a line under what had happened for both *Blue Peter* and myself. Vowing not to cry, I broke the news to the team and did pretty well till one by one, they all stood and gave me a standing ovation. Then I couldn't stop the tears.

So what did *Blue Peter* mean to me? Something I always believed in – giving children the very best you can. A constant creative challenge. Lasting lessons in compassion and understanding. Laughing myself silly on many, many occasions. Some wonderful friendships which will last a lifetime. A whole pendulum of experiences. Take a few at random:

Meeting one of the last survivors of the *Titanic*... filming on board Concorde... getting covered in mud with the Royal Marines... vomiting from a RNLI rescue boat... choosing songs and writing for each year's Christmas special... directing the magical Christmas show... making pizzas and ice cream in Rome, *apfelstrudel* in Vienna, croissants in Paris and gingerbread in Nurenberg... paragliding over the Austrian mountains... exploring London's lost underground and the secret roof spaces of St Paul's cathedral... These and many others form a kaleidoscope of amazing memories which I'll treasure forever.

I used to say that it was impossible to imagine a BBC without *Blue Peter*. I'm not sure if that is still true. The pace of change in the media continues to accelerate and surprise. *Blue Peter* is no longer just a television programme. It is a 'brand'. Its audience is less captive than at any point in its history and is getting steadily less so.

But despite everything, the needs and interests of 21st-century children are not really a million miles from those of the children who sat down to watch back in 1958. They still look for knowledge, adventure, friendship. They still want to collect, to be creative, to help others. They still love animals and pets. Above all, they still love good stories, well told.

Over the decades, the comings and goings of presenters, the scandals and the triumphs of the world's longest-running children's programme have fuelled countless conversations in playgrounds, pubs and dinner parties. *Blue Peter* and its associated terminology is constantly referenced on television and the internet, and in books, magazines and stand-up comedy. It is part of the DNA of Britain, unique, eccentric, a cultural phenomenon shared in, laughed at, loved and remembered by generations of children everywhere.

Presenter Profile
LIZ BARKER

JOINED: 23 June 2000

LEFT: 10 April 2006

MEMORABLE MOMENTS: Tightrope walking; Canary Wharf window-cleaning; brake woman in the British Bobsleigh Championships; lots of acting and dancing, including *The Quest* and several pantomimes; trips to Spain, Vietnam, Morocco, Brazil, India, Vienna, USA, Ghana and Belize

Liz Barker was another presenter who never intended to present. She was working on the production team of an early BBC digital programme with a tiny audience and budget. Liz was occasionally called on to appear in front of the camera. Nobody knows exactly who sent a tape of her making these fleeting appearances in to *Blue Peter*, but it was enough to get her an interview.

1 Liz used to joke that nobody knew who she was because she changed her hairstyle so often. This made keeping her photo-cards up to date a challenge.

Editor Steve Hocking was looking for '...someone who you could imagine children wanting to invite round for tea' and it was Liz's girl-next-door quality that got her the job. She later said: 'I was so stunned that I didn't reply straight away and they thought I didn't want it. All my friends and family were flabbergasted. I was such an unlikely candidate.'

On her first show, she had to be pushed on. There was a continual conflict within Liz's personality. One side thoroughly enjoyed the limelight, but the other was shy and hermit-like. She veered between the two extremes, sometimes within the space of a live show. She was intuitive about people and highly sensitive to atmosphere. I asked her why she'd called the singer Craig David 'David Craig' on air. A hunted look crossed her face: 'The drummer was looking at me funny.' She could easily be put off by aggressive or unresponsive guests, and it took her a while to accept that they were on her patch and not the other way around.

Chameleon actress

Liz was a gifted actress with one of those chameleon faces that could be transformed, as required, from vamp to old hag. She was fabulous in character parts and always joked that she played more queens than any other *Blue Peter* presenter. She had a point. Elizabeth I and a record three versions of Queen Victoria were among her gallery of monarchs. When she played Mary Queen of Scots, I persuaded her husband to make a cameo appearance as her lover, Lord Bothwell. They had to kiss in a set filled with hundreds of flickering candles. It was the closest *Blue Peter* had ever got to a love scene and I thought it might help if the real-life husband and wife played the parts.

Liz had very particular ideas about what she wore. During one Christmas spectacular, she was bedecked as a Latin American dancer, all frou-frou and feathers. She looked magnificent, but wasn't happy. Already tall, she felt that the towering headdress made her ridiculous next to the others. 'I look like Big Bird', she wailed. Not for the first time, we seized the scissors and did some impromptu alterations, trimming the biggest and most exuberant feathers until she felt confident.

Clothes were always a good barometer of Liz's mood. Whenever she turned up in something black and voluminously baggy, you knew she was feeling down and wanted to hide. When she was on form, she always managed to look fashionable without trying too hard.

Liz surprised herself with some of her achievements. She won a bronze medal as the brake woman in the British Bobsleigh Championships. When we started filming her as a rowing cox, we were in despair. She just couldn't find the voice or the power essential to inspire her crew. Then, in the

2 Costume designer Debbie Roberts dashes in for a last-minute adjustment of the royal underclothes when Elizabeth B became Elizabeth R in 2003.

3 About to go for a take on location in Bath. Liz was a natural actress and her gallery of characters over five years was impressive.

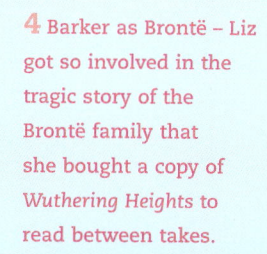

4 Barker as Brontë – Liz got so involved in the tragic story of the Brontë family that she bought a copy of *Wuthering Heights* to read between takes.

actual race, she suddenly transformed herself into a shouting she-devil, driving her crew to victory.

Liz had an extreme fear of heights and yet she allowed herself to be tormented on several occasions. Once, halfway through shooting a tightrope-walking challenge (dressed entirely in yellow), overcome with terror and nerves, she stormed off in her car for a couple of hours. Typically, she then pulled herself together, came back and finished the job.

Valerie Simpleton

We were all fond of Liz. She was generous, enthusiastic and had a boundless ability to laugh at herself. The boys teased her unmercifully. She was far from stupid, but could drift off into her own dream-like state of mind. I nicknamed her Valerie Simpleton and she just laughed. When she focused, she rewarded directors with excellent performances.

She'd just signed a two-year contract when she came to tell me she was pregnant. She didn't want to leave and this felt like an opportunity. I was keen that we no longer implied that having a baby necessarily meant the end of a woman's career. But I wanted to be realistic too. We couldn't predict how Liz might feel once she'd given birth. Long filming trips away from home were obviously out of the question. We were about to go five times a week as well.

That's why I decided to introduce a fifth presenter. It helped with the workload, but upset the balance of the team. When Zöe Salmon was cast, Liz felt in some way that she had been replaced before she'd even left. Ironically, viewers only loved Liz even more now that we were regularly featuring her cute baby son, Dexter.

Being a mother is hard enough without criticism and Liz was very upset when we had complaints. One eccentric claimed that Liz was promoting life as a single mother, because her husband was rarely featured. Others attacked her for bottle-feeding Dex.

When the rest of the team jetted off to Japan on the summer expedition, Liz stayed behind. It was bad psychology. We had arranged a busy filming schedule for her in Britain, but when Liz returned from a trip to HMS *Illustrious* and asked to see me, I knew what was coming. She'd been horribly homesick. She felt that anyone doing her job should be loving every moment, not feeling sad and faking enthusiasm.

She left the following spring after being awarded her own gold badge and quickly built a new life in the country with her family. She had another baby, a beautiful daughter called Poppy, and later wrote to me, 'I had the most fun working with you – and want to thank you for all the happy and wonderful memories.'

BLUE PETER 50th Anniversary

Presenter Profile
ZÖE SALMON

1 Zöe's smile hides determination. She once explored the sewers of Paris in a white skirt and gold sandals and, against all expectations, emerged spotless!

2 Fresh-faced and ready to fly over Niagara. Zöe shot several *Blue Peter* films before making her first appearance in the studio.

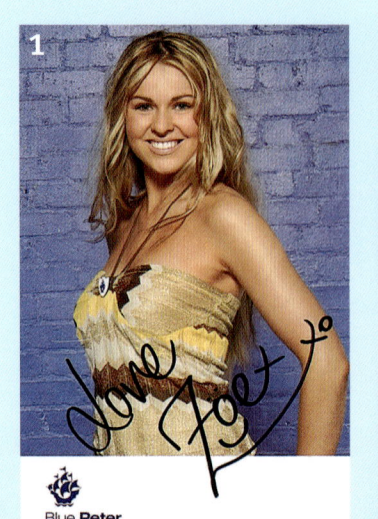

JOINED: 23 December 2004

LEFT: 25 June 2008

MEMORABLE MOMENTS: Running the London Marathon; joining the cast of *Riverdance*; having a painting exhibited at the Royal Academy; her I'll Try Anything Once challenge series; trips to Austria, Switzerland, Iceland, Japan, USA, Bolivia and the Bahamas

When Zöe came in for her very first interview, she was so carefully dressed and made up that it was a bit off-putting. Her eye-shadow even matched her handbag. But we thought there was somebody interesting under all that slap, so I called her and said, 'Come back, but this time wear jeans and a T-shirt. And no make-up.'

Zöe duly returned and there had been a transformation. 'And you are?' enquired someone who'd met her during the first interview. Zöe sailed through the second round and did a brilliant studio audition.

Until now, the tradition on *Blue Peter* was for new presenters to start within days of their audition. Haunted by the memory of Matt Baker's terror when he was shoved in front of the cameras for the first time, and bearing in mind that our new girl had no television experience, I decided it was time for a change. We contracted her for three months before her planned debut. This way she could get used to living in London, work with her new colleagues and do lots of filming before the pressure of being on screen kicked in. We realized that there was no way we could keep her appointment secret that long and so we'd have to announce her arrival long before viewers would actually see her.

Zöe took up her position on the time-honoured trampoline. The studio was heaving with photographers and the next day the coverage was phenomenal. Former Editor Lewis Bronze emailed me: 'Beauty queen *and* a law degree… what more could one ask?… central casting if I ever heard it. She looks divine. And another Irish girl… couldn't be better.'

The audience finally got to meet her on our Christmas show. She emerged from a giant gift-wrapped box, an idea I nicked from my childhood memory of watching a Christmas *Top of the Pops* in which Cherry Gillespie was unwrapped to join the legendary dance group Pan's People. We made a behind-the-scenes film about her first live show, just like those which covered the arrivals of Janet, Diane and Romana.

In the firing line
Unfortunately, Zöe had hardly started before she was engulfed in a storm of controversy. In January 2005, we launched a competition for viewers to create a design on the theme 'Best of British'. The winning entry would be emblazoned along the side of a British Airways plane. To help inspire children, each presenter gave an example of what 'Best of British' meant to them. Zöe's choice, in consultation with the producer and her dad, was the Red Hand of Ulster, a symbol commonly used in Northern Ireland on flags, buses, tax discs and by sporting teams and Irish dancing groups.

This meant we were surprised when, after transmission, a sociology professor from Strathclyde University angrily accused us of sectarian bias, telling the *Guardian*: 'Like the swastika, the Red Hand is a symbol that has been misappropriated. It is the symbol of the unionists.'

The BBC took advice and issued a response: 'The symbol was used in good faith and it certainly wasn't our intention to be provocative or promote sectarianism. We realize that the context in which we were referring to the Red Hand was inappropriate and mistaken. We'd like to apologize for any upset or concern we have caused.'

This apology unleashed a further flood of emails and letters. Now people from across Northern Ireland's communities were up in arms. 'Spineless', 'Wrong', 'Unbelievable', 'Hurtful and derogatory' and 'Apologize to Zöe' were just some of the comments flying around.

The debate raged in the press and the House of Commons, where a motion was signed by a group of MPs that stated: 'This House notes the events that followed a

3 The press call for Zöe – there was huge coverage in the next day's newspapers.

4 The Polaroid taken before Zöe's very first interview for *Blue Peter*.

5 Zöe performs 'Material Girl' in 2005's *Totally Blue Peter*. Critics didn't seem to realize she was playing a part!

suggestion made by a Northern Ireland-born presenter that the innocent and perfectly legitimate symbol, the Red Hand of Ulster, be one of a number of symbols to adorn an aircraft, and repudiates entirely the complaint to the BBC from a professor at Strathclyde University who attempted to portray the Red Hand as a sectarian symbol.'

It was a difficult time for Zöe and the whole team, who were bewildered by the sheer ferocity of the arguments. It was an eye-opener for us all to the simmering tensions that still remain within politics in Northern Ireland. The BBC's Belfast Political Editor came to brief the team on some of the pitfalls.

It wasn't to be the last time that Zöe found herself in the media firing line. I'd warned her that the way she looked meant some people would write her off as a bimbo. She has a passion for style and fashion, but there is a great strength of purpose beneath the surface and she has yet to refuse a challenge. She has a sharp brain and a legally trained one at that. She has learnt to be suspicious of people's motives, not surprisingly considering the way that some people have treated her.

In January 2006, under the heading 'Hello Boys', the *Guardian* women's pages launched a searing attack on Zöe, calling her a 'full-size Barbie doll', 'insincere and fatuous' and 'self-interested and steely cold'. It all added up to a spiteful character assassination in an article peppered with inaccuracies. Zöe was attacked for being a beauty queen and for her figure. Her shape apparently helped to make her a bad role model, despite the fact that she was appreciably curvier than her co-presenters, Konnie Huq and Liz Barker, both praised in contrast as 'wonderfully normal'.

The 'steely cold' Zöe was actually devastated. Bad press is part of the territory, but this piece had come out of the blue and was painfully personal. I wrote to the *Guardian* pointing out that we had no complaints about her from the audience. Indeed, whenever there were sizeable groups of children in the studio, they would flock to be near her. Long blonde hair appeals to lots of little girls, but it is not enough to make someone a popular presenter.

Trying everything once

Zöe dried her eyes and got on with the job, one of the benefits of which is that there is little time to brood. On her first programme, she had confidently stated that she'd 'try anything once', and putting that promise to rigorous test, we created a series of action challenges for her called I'll Try Anything Once. Among many others, she jumped off Bognor Pier in a man-powered flight competition, helped to 'flush' London's sewers and worked with a crew of Camden bin men. Other triumphs have included skydiving, paragliding, achieving her childhood dream of dancing in the Royal Variety Performance, singing in Comic Relief's Celebrity Fame Academy and joining the cast of *Riverdance*. She also grabbed the chance to re-create a formative *Blue Peter* memory of Caron Keating barnstorming on a biplane.

Zöe says: 'I'm the 30th presenter and 30 is now my lucky number. I feel blessed by God to be part of *Blue Peter* – a British institution. I treasure my badge! I stayed as excited pinning it on throughout my time. It's taken me to places I never thought I'd see, introduced me to people I never dreamt I'd meet and made me do things I never thought I could. Life on *Blue Peter* was one continuous highlight.'

Presenter Profile
GETHIN JONES

JOINED: 26 April 2005

LEFT: 25 June 2008

MEMORABLE MOMENTS: Royal Marines Commando Yomp; Have a Go Geth sporting challenges; presenting *Blue Peter* in Welsh; playing the violin at the Proms; playing a Cyberman and a Dalek in *Dr Who*; trips to the USA, Japan, Namibia, Bolivia, China and Finland

1 Gethin 'in the moment'. This shot was actually an out-take but when I saw it, I thought it was so natural that we issued it as his photo-card.

2 Geth loves all sport but rugby is his first love. We used to tease him that he had a rugby ball sewn inside his head!

Gethin had by far the longest wait of any presenter to get the job. He first came to see me months before we'd even announced that Simon Thomas was leaving, but I liked him enough on that first meeting to invite him to come down to the studio, watch rehearsals and meet the current team. This was a test in itself – it always proved tricky for potential presenters. Play it too cool, and they come across as arrogant and lacking interest, but too keen is equally off-putting. Gethin got it just right.

Some months later when our audition process began in earnest, Gethin was invited back. He had a lot going for him – Welsh, warm, sporty, musical and good-looking. He had experience too, presenting children's programmes on S4C, the Welsh language TV channel. Because of this, I paired him with a girl who had no experience whatsoever. I hoped that she would help him to feel relaxed and confident and that he'd help her to step up to the required level. The girl was Zöe Salmon and to our surprise she did better than him.

Nevertheless Gethin had done well enough to go through to the all-important studio audition. This time the stumbling block was the make. Technically, it was fine, but as television it was deadly dull. Konnie Huq and Liz Barker were enthusiastic, but from the sidelines, Matt Baker observed: 'He's too good-looking. We don't want a male model.'

The weeks passed as we kept Gethin in reserve and carried on looking. His interest in working for this audience was clearly genuine. But I still had doubts. It was nearly Christmas and I decided it might be fairer to part company before the start of the holiday period. Calling candidates who've got this close with bad news was always one of the worst aspects of the job. Harder for them, of course. There were often tears and anguish.

Not so with Gethin. He reacted with dignity and unexpected, surprising determination. Displaying passion, conviction and energy, he convinced me to look at another of his tapes. To be honest, the video that arrived a couple of days later was largely irrelevant. Everything had suddenly clicked into place. I invited him back to Television Centre, this time to offer him his dream job, at long, long last.

Just like Zöe, we started his contract three months before his first on-screen appearance. For his photo-call, I asked costume designer Debbie Roberts to create a *Blue Peter* rugby kit. It was cold, dark and pouring with rain as Gethin set out to the garden to meet the press, but he couldn't stop beaming.

Rising to the challenge

Unfortunately, the next few months were anything but easy. We soon learnt that Gethin was a hard worker, but also one of life's worriers, tying himself in knots with every mistake. Understandably, to begin with, there were plenty of them. After a bad show, his head would go down and his voice would slow to a mumble. By being so busy beating himself, he would shut out crucial notes and feedback designed to help him improve.

Concentration was a big problem. Gethin would put so much effort into making sure that children visiting the studio were having a great time that he'd forget to focus on his own performance until too late. Often, he'd do fine until we cut to a close-up. Then he'd instantly fluff or forget his words. It was toe-curling and started to become a habit. Struggling to find a way to help, I seized on something

Presenter Profile GETHIN JONES

3 The trenches of Television Centre. Gethin tried hard to live up to Matt's high standards and expectations but they were very different people.

4 Weightlifting, diving and boxing – some of the tough Have a Go Geth challenges. Jokers in the office called them 'Have a Go at Geth'.

5 Photo-call in the pouring rain – but Gethin couldn't stop smiling.

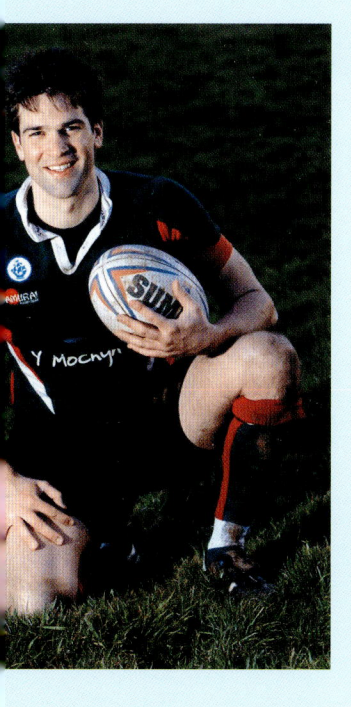

I thought a guy who'd nearly become a professional rugby player might understand. I told him to think of close-ups as needing the same focus as the crucial kick in a match. It did the trick.

A remarkable early achievement was training and completing the gruelling 30-mile Royal Marines Commando Yomp. The Marines never doubted his physical ability, only his mental attitude. Gethin loves flying, but at first every airborne film ended with him being violently sick. A stomach-churning formation flying exercise was next. I called in expert help and the therapist gave him a useful new mantra: 'What the mind believes, the body achieves.'

Gethin kept this thought and his lunch to himself.

He's certainly got courage. In interviews, we always asked, 'Do you have any phobias?' Gethin had admitted to a serious fear of the dark. This is shared by so many children that I suggested we used it in a film. It was a daunting one. He was to spend the night in the London Dungeon, completely alone. But he'd be in constant two-way communication with a psychologist who would give him techniques to combat his fear, sharing them in the process with our audience.

It was tough, but he triumphed and we decided to show the film in our Hallowe'en programme. It started with the presenters pulling spooky clues about that day's content from a bubbling cauldron. Matt Baker borrowed an oversized shirt from Wardrobe, and on the dress rehearsal, produced it with a flourish. 'Oh look!', he grinned, 'It's a big girl's blouse. It must be yours, Gethin.' It was a joke, but the damage was done. Gethin's fragile confidence was crushed and the transmission that followed was unfortunate.

A new double act

In the end, it took around 18 months for Gethin to really find his feet. The turning point was the arrival of Andy Akinwolere. Gethin wasn't the new boy any more. Now he not only had to fill the big gap left by Matt, but also support the latest arrival. Happily, his warmth and generosity was reciprocated by Andy and soon *Blue Peter* had a strong male double act again.

Gethin went from strength to strength and began to blossom away from *Blue Peter* as well as on it, taking part in the 2007 run of BBC1's hugely successful *Strictly Come Dancing*, in which he was partnered with Camilla Dallerup.

In April 2008, Gethin announced that he was leaving *Blue Peter* at the end of the season in June. He says: 'When I left *Blue Peter*, I left the best job in the world. There were times when I had never felt more alive. I've been privileged to meet some truly inspiring people, from Olympic champions to a llama farmer in Bolivia. You feel like you've lived five lifetimes. You do have to make a lot of sacrifices, especially with friends and family, but it was all worth it. I couldn't have given it more. Words can't describe how wonderful it has been.'

Presenter Profile

ANDY AKINWOLERE

JOINED: 28 June 2006

MEMORABLE MOMENTS: Helicopter bungee jumping; puppy walking Magic; stilt-walking in the *Lord of the Rings* stage show; trips to the USA, Malawi, Sweden, Bolivia, Oman, Egypt, Nigeria and China

1 Andy says: 'Sometimes I wake up wondering where I am and what I'm doing. Then I realize I'm sailing on yet another unforgettable adventure with this ship.'

Chance has always played a part in becoming a *Blue Peter* presenter. When we started the exhaustive search to find someone to take over from Matt Baker, little did we know that the best candidate was sitting under our noses.

First and foremost, we were looking for a contrast and somebody with whom little boys could identify and look up to. We interviewed scores of people. One of the most important questions in the interviews was designed to identify any skeletons in the cupboard. 'Is there anything in your life that you would be uncomfortable with your family and friends reading about in the national press?' is how we usually put it. It's almost impossible to impress upon a young hopeful how much scrutiny they will be under if they get the job. Within hours of Simon Thomas's arrival, reporters turned up in his local pub asking searching questions. When Zöe Salmon was introduced to the press, journalists posed as her mates on the Friends Reunited website trying to dig the dirt. An ex-boyfriend was offered £20,000 for a story. Greatly to his credit, he refused. But these are the realities and it would be irresponsible not to explore any potential pitfalls. It meant the end of the line for one promising auditionee when he cheerfully admitted to having taken a lot of soft drugs and that, as a joke, mates often took his photo when he was high.

With time running out, two strong candidates emerged. Joe Crowley was a bright young actor and highly likeable on camera. But bizarrely he had a look of Matt about him and his impressive song-and-dance skills only compounded the comparison. Likewise, another actor and former rugby league player, Matthew Landers, could have been very good. Matt had just been pipped at the post by Gethin Jones the time before, but when we saw his latest audition, we realized that his 'laddishness' and sporting skill would mean we had two presenters competing for the same material.

Andy Akinwolere was working as a runner in CBBC. Runners are right at the bottom of the production ladder. As the title suggests, they fetch and carry, and take on all the jobs nobody else wants to do. Long hours and low pay are the name of the game, but it is an entry into the industry and the best runners swiftly move up. One hot summer's day, Andy was having a drink with some of his colleagues in the BBC Club. Among the group was Catherine Paterson, an assistant producer who'd recently worked on *Blue Peter*. Andy was entertaining everyone, effortlessly holding their attention, and this made her wonder if he might have something. The next morning she popped her head round my door.

She was so enthusiastic that I phoned Andy up and asked him to come in for a chat with me and the Deputy Editor, Jack Lundie. A typically frantic *Blue Peter* day followed, so by the time Andy arrived, neither Jack nor I had given any thought to the obviously nervous young man now waiting outside my office.

It was stuffy in there and we were tired. We sat down and asked the first bland questions with little or no expectation. Then Andy started talking. He didn't stop for the next hour or so. He was confident, charming, interesting, funny and he completely re-energized us. As soon as he'd left the room, we knew we had to audition him.

2 Andy in Malawi for the Shoebiz Appeal. When he got back, he called me: 'I didn't really get *Blue Peter* until this trip. Now I do.'

3 Andy demonstrating a remote-controlled Dalek during his audition. We showed his tape to children and they loved him.

A new star

Andy was born and lived in Nigeria until he was eight years old, then his parents had moved the family to France before settling in Birmingham. He had graduated from Sheffield with a media degree, determined to break into the industry in some way. Because of his upbringing, *Blue Peter* didn't mean that much to him, and I think he was as surprised as we were that he was now in the running for one of British television's top jobs.

His first audition was what you'd expect from someone who has never presented in a big studio before. But as well as the fear, the hesitancy and the rolling eyes, there was still a glimpse of the charm and spirit that had been so evident in his interview. I called him back for the final audition, where he was up against Joe Crowley and Matthew Landers. Although both delivered better technical performances, Andy definitely had the edge. We took the tape to several schools across the country and the result was a landslide in his favour. I'd also asked the brilliant coach and drama teacher Kate Marlow to conduct in-depth interviews with each of the boys. Kate's methods dig deep into the psyche. She concluded, 'Well, it's obvious. It has to be Andy.' Kate found him warm, natural, curious and emotionally connected – a perfect match with our first impressions.

The fact that he was black was a bonus. I'd made no secret of the fact that I wanted to cast the programme's first male black presenter. It was high time. Even so, I would never have cast anyone on the basis of their colour alone. Andy absolutely got the job on merit.

Originally, the plan was for him to appear only in silhouette, as a teaser, right at the end of the last programme of the season. In the event, after the run-through, I discovered we were several minutes light, so the silhouette business was abandoned and at the very last minute Andy's arrival became a full-scale item. It was a nerve-racking introduction to the demands of live television.

Fast learner

Because of his lack of experience, the first year was always going to be hard work. To begin with, Andy was constantly exhausted. The rigid self-discipline required to be on time all the time was a skill he had to acquire. He also tended to treat his lines as though they were boiling hot coals – tossing them away as quickly as possible. To help him, we brought back autocue. Luckily Andy was a fast learner and within months he was on top of what he was doing. Now his special qualities are shining through the screen. For *Blue Peter*, his serendipitous arrival was another fantastic stroke of luck.

BLUE PETER 50th Anniversary

Special Assignment
FAMOUS FACES

From pop stars and actors to prime ministers and royalty – they've all appeared on *Blue Peter*. The incentive is not just the opportunity to reach the audience of children, but also the genuine kudos of getting a badge for themselves.

1 Jon Pertwee drove his futuristic Whomobile into the *Blue Peter* studio several weeks before it made its debut in the *Dr Who* story 'Invasion of the Dinosaurs'.

2 Former Beatle Ringo Starr brought his groovy, ultra-modern designer table to the studio. John Noakes was suitably impressed.

1973

1971

1965

1975

178

Special Assignment FAMOUS FACES

3 Actor Jack Warner, or PC George Dixon in the long-running BBC series *Dixon of Dock Green*, switched studios to give viewers a closer look at Dixon's dog.

4 Ex-dancer Lesley Judd copies the Funky Gibbon, as performed by Bill Oddie, Graeme Garden and Tim Brooke-Taylor, aka The Goodies.

5 Just like The Goodies, Mike Batt's Wombles strutted their stuff on *Blue Peter* several times during their 1970s heyday.

6 David Cassidy pre-recorded his appearance, in which he helped to judge *Blue Peter*'s Keep Britain Tidy poster competition.

1975

1973

179

BLUE PETER 50th Anniversary

1 ABBA visit the studio for a chat, a mark of their status as the 1970s were an era when pop guests were unusual on *Blue Peter*.

2 This was the first of two appearances made by Kenneth Williams to promote *Willo The Wisp*, for which he provided all the voices.

3 Writers Jimmy Perry and David Croft created a special script so that John le Mesurier and Arthur Lowe could appear in character as Wilson and Mainwaring, to inspect a *Dad's Army* collage sent in by viewers.

1978

1973

1982

1973

Special Assignment FAMOUS FACES

4 Another *Blue Peter* coup – securing the fork- and spoon-bending sensation Uri Geller for his first major British TV appearance.

5 Elton John appeared with his verdict on Peter Duncan's single, 'Cold As Ice'. Elton was complimentary but the record wasn't a hit.

6 Veteran British comedian Arthur Askey played Baron Hardup in the very first *Blue Peter* pantomime, Cinderella.

5

1983

6

1973

181

BLUE PETER 50th Anniversary

1 Bob Geldof was presented with the Outstanding Endeavour award for helping to bring the desperate plight of Ethiopia to the world's attention.

2 Pelé, one of the most famous footballers of all time, showed off his skills and talked about his glittering career.

1

1985

3

1981

2

1983

4

1980

182

Special Assignment FAMOUS FACES

3 Curly-permed British football hero Kevin Keegan wisely didn't comment on presenter Simon Groom's choice of kit.

4 The stars of *Star Wars* – Mark Hamill and Carrie Fisher – were bemused at the prospect of 'Star Wars stew', one of the recipes from the *Book of Gorgeous Grub*.

2005

1993

2006

5 Dawn French appeared as Bunty, a character she played in one of the *Murder Most Horrid* series, set behind the scenes on a show suspiciously like *Blue Peter*.

6 Ewan McGregor guested throughout *Blue Peter*'s 4,000th edition, 14 March 2005. He told of the bird-cake recipe he'd sent in as a boy.

7 Gold-badge winner David Beckham donated a pair of boots to the Shoebiz Appeal. He credits *Blue Peter* with inspiring him to go football training when he was a boy.

BLUE PETER 50th Anniversary

1 The relationship between *Dr Who* and *Blue Peter* has endured. David Tennant helped to judge the phenomenally successful design-a-monster competition which had 43,920 entries. The winner was nine-year-old William Grantham, whose Abzorbaloff subsequently appeared in the story 'Love & Monsters'.

2005

Special Assignment FAMOUS FACES

2 On completion of the Harry Potter saga, J.K. Rowling was awarded a gold *Blue Peter* badge. She was moved to tears by the honour.

3 Catherine Tate ad-libbed her way through one show as Lauren, the stroppy teenager. Some of her caustic comments caused complaints.

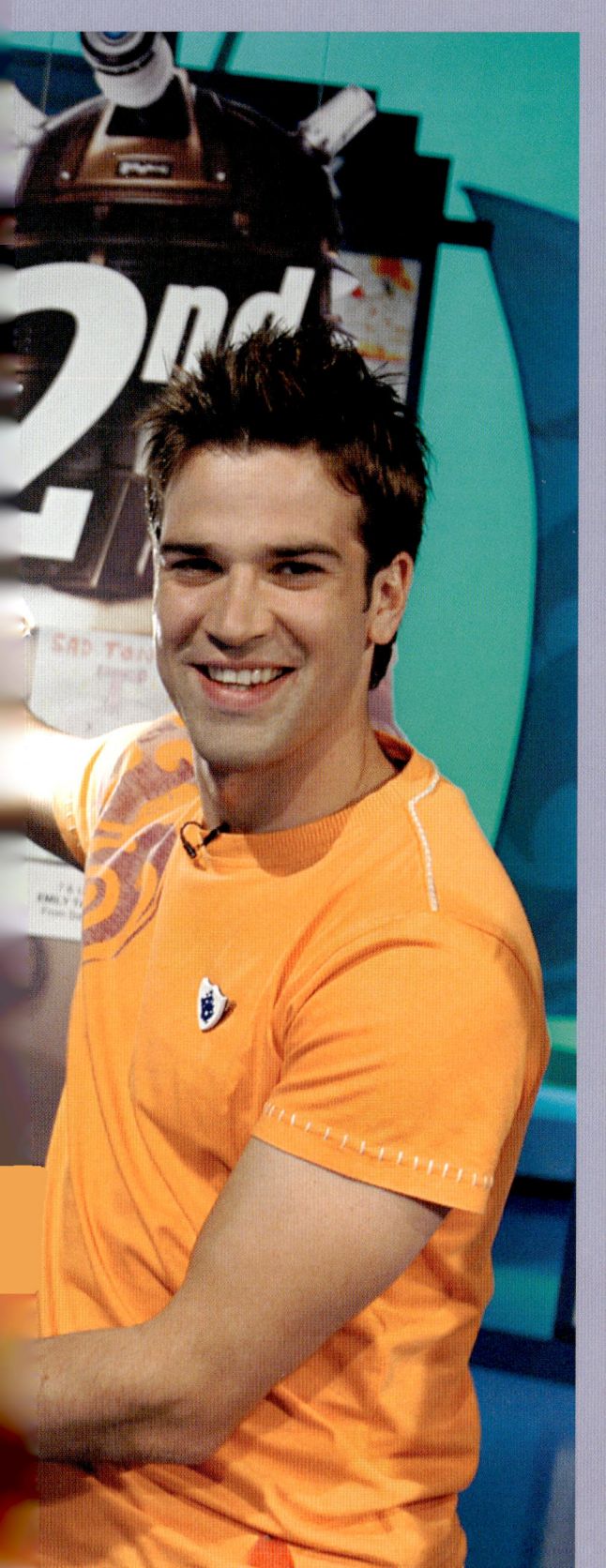

2007

2006

INDEX

Page numbers in **bold** refer to main features.
Page numbers in *italics* refer to illustrations/captions.

A

ABBA 123, 180
Acapulco 126–7
Adcock, John 63, 75
African stories: series 16
Akinwolere, Andy 29, 175, 176–7
    pets 30
    profile **176–7**
Aldred, Sophie 120
All Your Own 11
Allcroft, Britt 46
Anderson, Miss 64
Andrew, Prince 64
animals:
    birthdays 33, 34–5, 72
    handlers 26
    small: mini-series on 16
    stars **24–35**
Anne, Princess 64, *64*, 65
annuals 88–9
appeals **150–5**
    Cambodian 44
    Double Lifesaver 79
    Ethiopia Famine 150, 152
    Malawian AIDS Orphans 152
    RNLI 154
    Romanian Orphans 114, 115, 152, 154–5
    Shoebiz 177, 183
    Well Water 131
Ark Royal 71
Armstrong-Jones, Antony 15
Askey, Arthur *181*
Assisi 166
Atkinson, Rowan 121
audience research report 15
auditions 22
Australia 60, *129*
Austria 145
autocue 111, 114, 133

B

'Back in Time for Christmas' 23, *23*
Bacon, Richard 111, 115, 126–7, 128, 136, 144
    profile **142–3**
Bad Boys Inc 123
badges 42, **118–21**, *119*
    privileges 120–1
    sale on eBay 120–1
    winning 6
Badham, Mollie 45
BAFTA awards 101, 123, 128, 143, 149
Baker, Matt 8, 35, 129, 145, 146, 147, 152, 160–1, *161*
    caricature *167*
    in Christmas show 164
    pet 34
    profile **148–9**
Ball, Zöe 142, 149
Band Aid 19, 150
Barker, Liz 9, 16, 31, 83, 107, 145, 160, 161, 163, 170–1, 174
    caricature *167*
    in Christmas show 163, 164–5
    on location 60
    pets 30
    profile **170–1**
    in *Quest* 156
'Barnacle Bill' (theme music) 12, 72, 124
Barnes, Edward 6, 7, 16, 18, 19, 28, 37, 51–2, 52, 58, 92, *167*, 168–9
    becomes producer 45
    in Children's Programmes 63
    as director 64
    leaves programme 96
    partnership with Biddy 38
Barney (parrot) 25, 30
Bath: story of 44–5
Baverstock, David 38
Baverstock, Donald 118
Baxter, Biddy 6, 7, 8, 19, 24, 28, 30, 33, 38–9, 95, 96–7, 166, *167*, 168–9
    appointment 16, 37
    BBC career 37
    becomes Editor 45
    'Biddyisms' 101
    as child 37
    defending programme 91–2
    ideas 41, 49
    introducing appeals 150
    introducing badges 118
    joining *Blue Peter* 37–8
    leaving programme 96–9
    name 37
    notes to presenters 99
    organizing book material 88
    partnership with Barnes 38
    presenters' views of 99
    resisting use of autocue 111
    in schools' programmes 37
    selecting presenters 54, 56, 76, 80, 82, 91, 101, 104, 108, 109, 110, 114
    standards 74, 92–5
BBC:
    Lime Grove: Studio E 12
    technicians' strike 15
BBC Enterprises 88
BBC Worldwide 88, 89
Beckham, David 183
    football boots 33
Big Breakfast 143
Billy Bunter 11
birthday celebrations:
    20th 21
    25th 19, 94–5
    35th 21, 49
    40th 21, 23, *23*, 128, *128*
Bishop Rock Lighthouse 75–6, *76*
Blair, John Hunter 6, 12, 13, 15, 20
    death 46
    ideas for programme 21
    illness 16
Blake, Darrol 42, 72
Blake, Quentin 167
Blount, Captain James 166
Blue Peter:
    badges 42, **118–21**, *119*
        privileges 120–1
        sale on eBay 120–1
        winning 6
    books **88–9**, *88–9*, 100, 141
    in colour 63
    content 15, 16
    Correspondence Unit 118
    frequency of transmission 18, 45–6, 124, 161, 165–6
    garden **84–7**, *84–5*, *86–7*, 157
    gold medallion 121
    logo 42, 118, 165
    name 12
    opening titles 12
    ship 95
    theme music 12, 72, 124
    transmission time 12
    tree 157, 158
    videos 96
    website 127
Blue Peter Flies the World 165
Blue Peter (locomotive) 47, 131

INDEX

Blue Peter Unleashed 165
Blunt, James 166
Bolan, Marc 123
Bond, Michael 45
Bonnie (dog) 32, 33, 33, 34, 111
Bonnington, Chris 56
books **88–9**, 88–9, 100, 141
   annuals 88–9
Bowden, Lucy 23
Boyd, Tommy 49
Bradley, Clare 85–6, 86, 87, 117, 143, 158
Brazil 76
breaking news 71
bridge-swinging 117
Brigade of Guards: mini series on 16
bring-and-buy sales 150, 150–1, 154–5
Brint, Simon 124
British Bobsleigh Championships 170
Bronze, Lewis 6, 44, 61, 67, 79, 92–5, 114, 125, 131, 133, 167, 168–9
   appointing presenters 108, 116, 130, 132, 134, 138, 140
   commissioning new version of theme music 124
   leaving programme 127
   taking over from Biddy 99–100
Brooke-Taylor, Tim *178–9*
Broomfield, Robert 'Bob' 44, 45, 88
Brown, Gordon 145
Brownies: mini-series on 16
Bruinvels, Peter 107
Brunei 75
bungee-jumping 116
Burdis, Ray 80
Burrell, Paul 41
Bussell, Darcey 117
Buttons (guide dog) 30

C

Caldwell, Bridget 115, *168–9*
Camber Sands 18, *19*
Cambodian Appeal 44
Canada 103, 141, *141*
Cansdale, George 27, 45, 96
Capital Radio 143
Caribbean 131
Carrickfergus Castle, Northern Ireland 100
cartoons 15, 16
Cassidy, David 179
Casualty 102
catchphrases 42
cats 31–3
   Cookie 33
   Jack and Jill 25, 31
   Jason 24–6, *25*, 31
   Kari and Oke 30, *31*
   Ragdoll breed 33
   Smudge 31–3, *33*
   Socks 31, *33*
   Willow 31, *31*, 32
Cawston, Richard 64
CBBC 163, 165, 176
CBEEBIES 165
CBTV 102
Centre for Alternative Technology 124
Ceylon *see* Sri Lanka
Channel 1 112
Chase, Leonard 37, 51
children: in 1958 11
Children's Department 46–9
Children's Ward 134
China: Great Wall 138–9
Christmas Shows 66–7, 67–8, 83, 107, 113, 150, 163–5, *164–5*
   At the Club *Blue Peter* 163–5, *164–5*
   'Rock 'n' Roll Christmas 145, 149, 163, 165
Cinderella 181
Cindy (guide dog) 30
Clothes Horse Race 30
Clothes Show 135
coins: mini-series on 16
collections: silver paper 150
Collector's Lot 102
Collins, Chris 87

Comerford, John 123, 129, 141, 146
competitions:
   in books 88
   Christmas stamp designs 42
   design-a-monster 184–5
   introducing 16
   Whose Shoes? 166–8
computer games 11
Concorde 71
Cooke, Dave 83
Cooke, Jemma Victoria 82–3, *83*
Cookie (cat) 33
cooking 40–1, *41*
Corners 130
Coronation Street 130
Correspondence Unit 118
Crackerjack 11, 161
Cragg, Marina 33
Cresswell, Luke 124
Croft, David 180
Crompton, Matthew 142
Crossroads 23
Crowder, Chris 85, 86
Crowley, Joe 176, *177*
Crufts dog show 72
Curry, Mark 28, 85, 95, 110–11, *112*, 113, 114, 141
   profile **110–11**
Cutty Sark 12

D

Dad's Army 180–1
Daily Mail 107
Daily Mirror 109
Dale, Jim 20
Dallerup, Camilla 175
Dancing on Ice 102, 135
Danger Man 23
Dangerfield 135
Dangerfield, Grahame 45
D'Annunzio, Romana 140–1
   profile **140–1**
Darwin, Charles 139
Dead Sea 129
Dethick farm 90
Dixon, Anne 168–9

dogs 33–4
   birthdays 33, 34–5
   Bonnie 32, 33, *33*, 34, 111
   Buttons 30
   Cindy 30
   Goldie 25, 30, 72, 107
   guide dogs 18, 24, 30
   Honey 18, 24, 30
   Lucy 28, 33, 34, 163
   Mabel 28, 33, 163
   Magic 29, 30
   Meg 34, *35*
   Patch *26*, 27, 54
   Petra 6, 24, 26, *26*, 27, 34, *34*
   Prince 30
   Shep 6, 27–8, *29*, 34, 54, 68, *68*
   washing 32
dolls: collecting things for 15
Double Lifesaver Appeal 79
Dr Finlay's Casebook 30
Dr Who 56, 102, 107, 184–5
drama:
   serials 11–12
   Quest 52, 57, 102, 146, 156, 161, *161*
Dreamy Daniel 16
Duncan, Lucy 105, *105*
Duncan, Peter 61, 81, 95, 101, 104, 113, 141, 148, 157, 158
   on Biddy Baxter 99
   cooking 41, *41*
   in garden 84
   joins programme 91
   on location 103, *109*
   outfit designed for 93
   profile **104–5**
   return for Queen's visit 162
   turning down job on *Blue Peter* 80
Duncan Dares 61, 105

E

Eason, Ursula 19, 46
eBay 120–1
editors 167

Edmond, Terence 46
Edward, Prince 17, 64
Edwards, Jez 87
Egmont World 89
Egypt 82
elephants:
   Lulu 50, *50*
   Packi: stories about 15
Elizabeth II, Queen: visit to studio 162–3, *162–3*
Ellington, Ray 22
Ellis, Janet 8, 58–9, 60, 61, 85, 92, 93, 95, 106, 141, 157
   on Biddy Baxter 99
   pets 31
   pregnancy 107
   profile **106–7**
   return for time capsule 158
Ellis-Bextor, Sophie 107, 120
Emmerdale 135
Ethiopia 79
Ethiopia Famine appeal 150, 152
Etna, Mount 71
Eureka! 102
Evening Standard 161
experts 45
Expo '70: balloon 42

F
Faking It 141
Falklands 117
Farley, Trey 139
Farnsworth, Gillian 46
fashion 95
Fax! 28
Ferguson, Bob 91
Fielding, Yvette 21, 58, 61, 99, 100, 111, 112, 113, 114–15, 132, 152
   profile **114–15**
Fiennes, Jake 139
fire-bucket chain 02
First World War film 136–7, *137*, 145
Fisher, Carrie 182
Fisher, Sarah 33
flags:

Blue Peter 12
   mini-series on 16
Forte, Michael 91
Forth Road Bridge 56, 57
Fowlds, Derek 76
Fox, Paul 58, 64
Frank, Anne 71
Frank, Otto 70–1, *71*
Franklin, Mark 134
Fred(a) (tortoise) 24, 25, 26, 32
Freeman, Derek 45, 96
French, Dawn 183
Furness, John 16

G
Gabell, Terry 72, 76
Ganges, HMS 55
garden 84–7, *84–5*, *86–7*, 157
Garden, Graeme 178–9
Garrard, George 108
Gaydar Radio 137
Geldof, Bob 19, 182
Geller, Uri 71, 181
George (tortoise) 27, *27*, 84
Germany 145, *145*
Ghostwatch 102
Gill, Rosemary 'Rose' 6, 18, 38, 45, 46, 56, 76, 84, 150
Gillespie, Cherry 172
GMTV 135
Go For It! 87
Go With Noakes 28, 105
go-karting on ice 115
Godwin, Joe 124, 129
Going Live! 102, 114
Goldie (dog) 25, 30, 72, 107
Goodies 123, 178–9
Grant, Linda 104
Grantham, William 184
green topics 100
Greene, Laura 94
Greene, Sarah 8, 27, 91, 92, 94, 95–6, 101, 104, 110, 120, 161
   on location 102, *103*
   profile **101–2**
Griffith, Melanie 79
Groom, Simon 61, 74, 78–9,

93, 95–6, 101, 104, 106, 142, 152, 157, 183
   on Biddy Baxter 99
   first programme 80
   on location 60, 78–9, *103*
   nerves 72, 74
   pet 30, 34, *72*
   profile **78–9**
   return for time capsule 158
Guardian 137, 172, 173
Guide Dog Association 30
guide dogs:
   Buttons 30
   Cindy 30
   Honey 18, 24, 30
   Prince 30

H
Hallowe'en special 141
Hamill, Mark 182
hang-gliding 149
Harington, Joy 22
Hart, Tony 15, 16, 22, 42, 118, 120, 165
Hawcutt, Robert 165
Heath, Tina 72–4, *74*, 82, *82–3*, 94, 101
   profile **82–3**
Hedron, Tippi 79, *79*
Heggessey, Lorraine 127, 129, 143
Heidi 75
Hellings, Sarah 70
Henman, Tim 126
Heston, Charlton: stand-in 18
Hicks, Tony 27
Hill, Katy 124, 127, 128–9, 136, 137, 138–9, 140, 142, 144, 158, 159, 168–9
   profile **138–9**
Hill, Kevin 165
Hocking, Steve 6, 102, 129, 137, 148, 161, 165, 167
Holiday 102
Hollies 43
Home, Anna 44, 96, 127, 132, 138

Honey (guide dog) 18, 24, 30
Horne, Sandra 143
houses: cost: in 1958 11
How Other Children Live 16
Humphries, John 82
Hungary 115
Hunniford, Gloria 112
Hunt for the Blue Stone 102
Hunter Blair, John *see* Blair, John Hunter
Huq, Konnie 8, 129, 142, 144–5, *160*, 161, 174
   profile **144–5**

I
India 60, 131
insurance 55
internet 11
Italy 52
ITV 11–12
Ivanhoe 12
Ivory Coast 61

J
Jack & Jill (cats) 25, 31
Jacobs, David 112
James, Sally 76
Japan 61
Jason (cat) 24–6, *25*, 31
Jennings, Helen 121
Jet (pony) 30
Jigsaw 106
Jim (tortoise) 26, 27, *27*
Joey (parrot) 30, *30*
John Bull 46
John, Elton 181
Jones, Catherine Zeta 117
Jones, Gethin 33, 149, 168–9, *174–5*, 176
   profile **174–5**
Jordan, Diane-Louise 61, 115, 116, 125, 130–1, *132–3*, 134, 140
   profile **130–1**
Judd, Lesley 8, 9, 27, 40, 64–7, *67*, 68, 72, 75–7, 120, 178–9
   first programme 80
   interviews 70–1, *71*, 123

INDEX

letter to 6
on location 57, 75–6, 76
profile **75–6**
Junior Points of View 56
Junior Showtime 110
Junior Sportsview 12
Just the Two of Us 107

K
Kari and Oke (cats) 30, 31
Keating, Caron 41, 95, 99, 100, 111, 112–13, 114, 132
 profile **112–13**
Keegan, Kevin 182
Kenya 58–9, 64, 65
 elephant relocation project 124
Kibble, Derek 72
King Cinder 104

L
Landers, Matthew 176, 177
Langford, David 15
Langtry, Lily 139
le Mesurier, John 180–1
Leger, Alex 72, 78, 80, 99, 114, 116, 168–9
 on Biddy Baxter 99
Legs and Co 72
Leslie, John 58, 98, 114–15, 116–17, 120, 124, 125, 132–3, 134, 143, 168–9
 profile **116–17**
 return for Queen's visit 162
letters: numbers received 6
Lewis-Smith, Victor 161
Light Lunch 76
Lindsay, Charlie 113
Lindsay, Gabriel 113
Lindsay, Russ 113, 132
'Little Eagle' story 45
Live Aid 19
Live and Kicking 139, 142
Lizzie Dripping 82
location filming 16, 18, 42, 124
logo 42, 118, 165
London:

Big Ben: cleaning 104, 105
Natural History Museum 128, 128
Nelson's Column 55, 55
sewers 173
Tower Bridge 79
Trafalgar Square Christmas tree 131
London Marathon 104–5, 116, 117
London to Brighton veteran car run 127
Look East 19
Lovejoy, Tim 142
Lowe, Arthur 180–1
Lucy (dog) 28, 33, 34, 163
Lulu (elephant) 50, 50
Lundie, Jack 176
Lutterworth Press 88

M
Mabel (dog) 28, 33, 163
Macfarlane, Oliver 6, 23, 81, 99–100, 127, 128–9, 130, 140, 143, 144, 167
McGregor, Ewan 144, 183
Macmillan, Harold 11
Macmillan (publishers) 88
Madoc, Philip 116
Maggie (tortoise) 26, 27, 27
Magic (dog) 29, 30
magic tricks:
 going wrong 18
 mind-reading 15
Magpie 49, 84, 110, 123
'makes' 38–9, 39, 41, 129, 133, 133
Malawi 177
Malawian AIDS Orphans appeal 152
Mallet, Timmy 163
Malone, Hazel 75
Margaret, Princess: wedding 15
Margrie, Kez 168–9
Marlow, Kate 177
Marshall, Noel 79
Marson, Richard 6, 8, 8–9, 167, 168–9
Mary Rose: dive to 102, 102

Mayall, Rik 120
Meg (dog) 34, 35
Menezes, Edith 26–7, 26, 28, 31, 101
merchandising 88
Mexico 62
Michaels, Sandra 'Sandy' 46
Mike Flowers Pops 141
Miles, Stuart 23, 126, 127, 131, 134, 136–7, 141, 142, 143, 144
 profile **136–7**
Milkshake 144
Mills, Adrian 80
mind-reading magic trick 15
mobile phones 11
model railway 15
 serial based on 16
Mongolia 139
Moore, Henry: programme on 99, 100
Moore, Roger 12
Morocco 50, 58, 61
Moscow 100
Moscow State Circus 112, 124
Most Haunted 115
Mountbatten, Lord Louis 64
Mr Pastry 11
Mudd, Fred 20
Mudlarks 20
Multi-Coloured Swap Shop 76
 Awards 81
music:
 mini-series on 16
 theme 12, 72, 124
Music Box 116
Musical Youth 19

N
Nanny McPhee 166
National Cat Club 33
 Show 102, 103
National Childbirth Trust 83
National Youth Music Theatre 144
Natural History Museum 128, 128

Nealon, Jasmin 113
Nettleton, John 44
New York Marathon 135
New Zealand 115
News of the World 142
Newsround 134
Niagara Falls 141
Nickleodeon 138
Nigeria 58
Noakes, John 9, 19, 36, 43, 47, 49, 67, 72
 acting 54
 cooking 40, 41
 dangerous feats 55, 55
 with elephant 50, 50
 first programme 80
 free-fall parachute jump 68–71, 69
 on *John Bull* 46
 joining programme 19
 letter to 6
 on location 48–9, 55, 57, 58, 61, 62, 68, 69
 pets 26, 27–8, 29, 54, 54, 55, 68, 68
 profile **54–5**
 return for time capsule 158, 161
 waxwork 28, 29
Noakes, Mark 28
Noakes, Vicky 28
Norway 49, 58

O
Oddie, Bill 178–9
OK! magazine 137
Oldfield, Mike 72, 73, 124
Only in America 61
Orient Express 145
Outstanding Endeavour awards 19, 100
Owen, Rhodri 148
Oxfam 150

P
Packi (elephant): stories about 15
Pan's People 77, 172
pantomimes 111
 Cinderella 181

parachute jumps 136, 136–7
   free-fall 68, 69, 106
Paras log race 149
Paris 63
   sewers 172
Parkhurst, Clive 16, 21
Parnell, Margaret 38–9, 39, 162
parrots 30
   Barney 25, 30
   Joey 30, 30
Patch: (dog) 26, 27, 54
Paterson, Catherine 176
Paul VI, Pope 64
Pedigree (publishers) 89
Pelé 181
Perry, Jimmy 180
Pertwee, Jon 178
'Peter the Great' story 44
Peter Palette (puppet) 16
Peters, Andi 132
Petra (dog) 24, 26, 27, 34
   birthday 34–5
   letter to 6
   statue 34, 157
   training 26
petrol price: in 1958 11
Philbin, Maggie 94
Philip, Prince 87
Pickard, Nigel 161, 163
Pickles (dog) 56
Pocock, Leonie 34, 163
ponies 30
   Jet 30
   Rags 24
pop acts 165–6
Porter, Gail 140
Posh Frocks 102
Powell, Peter 132, 135
presenters:
   advertisement for 167
   profiles **18–23, 51–61, 75–83, 101–17, 130–49, 170–7**
     Akinwolere, Andy 176–7
     Bacon, Richard 142–3
     Baker, Matt 148–9
     Barker, Liz 170–1

     Curry, Mark 110–11
     D'Annunzio, Romana 140–1
     Duncan, Peter 104–5
     Ellis, Janet 106–7
     Fielding, Yvette 114–15
     Greene, Sarah 101–2
     Groom, Simon 78–9
     Heath, Tina 82–3
     Hill, Katy 138–9
     Huq, Konnie 144–5
     Jones, Gethin 174–5
     Jordan, Diane-Louise 130–1
     Judd, Lesley 75–7
     Keating, Caron 112–13
     Leslie, John 116–17
     Miles, Stuart 136–7
     Noakes, John 54–5
     Purves, Peter 56–7
     Salmon, Zoë 172–3
     Singleton, Valerie 51–3
     Sundin, Michael 108–9
     Thomas, Simon 146–7
     Trace, Christopher 18–19
     Turner, Anthea 132–3
     Vincent, Tim 134–5
     Wenner, Christopher 80–1
     West, Anita 22–3
     Williams, Leila 20–1
Prince (guide dog) 30
Princess Diana Memorial Committee 131
Prior, Dorothy 165
producers: interview boards for 16
Purves, Peter 9, 34, 36, 43, 46–9, 47, 50, 56, 67, 72
   on Biddy Baxter 99
   first programme 80
   on location 48–9, 50, 56, 57, 57, 58, 61, 62
   pet 24, 27
   profile **56–7**
   return for Queen's visit 162, 163
   return for time capsule 158, 161

Q
Queen Elizabeth (liner) 71
Quest 52, 57, 102, 146, 156, 161, *161*

R
Radio Essex 138
Radio 5 Live 143
RAF 58
   Falcons 136
   mini-series on 16
Ragged Child 144
Rags (pony) 24, 30
Railway Children 11
Randle, Frank 50
Record Breakers 68
recycling 150–2, *150*
Red Arrows 139
Reed, Owen 15, 16, 37, 38
rehearsals 20
Reilly, Gilly 12, 16, 17, 20
Reilly, Peter 16
Return to Oz 108
Riding for the Disabled Association 30
Ringpress 88
RNLI 127
   appeal for 154
Roberts, Debbie 171, 174
'Rock 'n' Roll Christmas 145, 149, 163, 165
Rogers, Chris 134
Roland Rat 41
Roman banquet 94
Romanian Orphans appeal 114, 115, 152, 154–5
rowing 170–1
Rowling, J.K. 185
Royal Ballet 102
Royal Marines:
   Commando Yomp 175
   Endurance Course 117
   potential recruits course 149
Royal Navy Field Gun Race: training for 105
Royal Safari 64, 65
RSPCA 33
Russell, Alan 92
Russia 100, 148–9, 149

Rye, Renny 79

S
Saint 23
St Clair, Isla 94
St Petersburg 148–9, 149
Salmon, Peter 91
Salmon, Zoë 152, 171, 172–3, 174, 176
   profile **172–3**
Salvation Army 67
Sandhurst: Royal Military College 142, 143
Saturday Disney 134
Saturday Picture Show 110
Saturday Superstore 102
Save the Children 64
Sawyers, Jake 41
scan: antenatal 83, *83*
Schofield, Phillip 110, 132
Scott, Daniel 48, 49
Scott, Stephen 48
Scott, Sylvia 49
Scum 80
Seaview 114
Shearing, Gillian 39
Shelley (tortoise) 26, 27
Shep (dog) 6, 27–8, 29, 34, 54, 68, *68*
Sherlock, Paul 150
Shoebiz appeal 177, 183
signature tune ('Barnacle Bill') 12, 72, 124
Silver Sword 11
Sims, Monica 46, 49, 58
Singleton, Valerie 9, 18, 19, 19, 22, 23, 36, 39, 45, 49, 51, 52, 54, 72, 121, 157
   awards 52
   with Jason 25
   on location 50, 51, 52, 53, 58, 61, 62, 63
   missed by children 75
   profile **51–3**
   return for Queen's visit 162, 163
   return for time capsule 158, 159, 161
   Special Assignments 51–2, 64–7, 64–5

INDEX

Six-Five Special 20
Sketch Club 11, 12
Sky Sports 145
Smith, Dorothy 24, 42–4,
    44–5, 88, 96
Smith, Mike 102
Smudge (cat) 31–3, 33
Socks (cat) 31, 33
songs: mini-series on 16
Songs of Praise 131
Sooty 11
sound effects 44
South Africa 131
Space; 1999 23
Spain 115, *161*
Sparky and the Talking Train 15
Special Assignments 51–2, 57, 64–7, *64–5*
Spencer, Peggy 45, 74, 96
Splendid Spur 11
Sport Aid 19
Sri Lanka (Ceylon) 49, 53, 58, *60*
Stableford, Howard 110
Stage 116
Starr, Ringo 178
Stephens, Doreen 45, 46
Stopwatch 57
storytelling 44–5, *44–5*
Strictly Come Dancing 175
strikes 67
  technicians' 15
Studio E 11
studios:
  allocation 42
  backcloth 42
  for colour transmissions 63
  floor 42
  lighting 42, 95
Sundin, Michael 105, 108–9
  profile **108–9**
Sweetbaum, Annie 106
Swish of the Curtain 101

T
Take Two 102
Tate, Catherine 185
Taylor, Ann 15
telegraph poles: climbing 111
television:
  channels 11
  children's programmes:
    in 1958 11–12
Tennant, David 184
Thames Television 49
That's Life 80
Theakston, Jamie 142
This Morning 102
Thomas, Simon 9, 129, 145, 146, 159, 160–1, *161*, 168–9, 176
  caricature 167
  in drag 147
  in garden 86
  joining programme 137
  on location 147, *161*, 166
  meeting Queen 162, *163*
  pet 34
  profile **146–7**
  in *Quest* 156
Thomas the Tank Engine 46
Thompson, Emma 166
Thompson, Roy 92
Thrower, Percy 84, 85, 96
Thunderbirds' Tracy Island 133, *133*
time capsules 157–61, *158–9*
Time Out 137
Times 49
Timyn, William 45, 88, 157
Tomorrow's World 95, 110
Top of the Pops 77, 134, 143, 172
tortoises 72
  Fred(a) 24, 25, 26, 32
  George 27, *27*, 84
  Jim 26, 27, *27*
  Maggie 26, 27, *27*
  Shelley 26, *27*
Trace, Christopher 10, 18–19, 38, 46–9, 54
  conducting interview 16
  death 30
  dress style 14–15
  interview for job 18
  leaving programme 19
life after *BP* 19
opening first programme 12–15
with pets 25
as presenter 15
profile **18–19**
rapport with Leila 20
resignation incidents 18
at toy fair 16
Trace, Jonathan 120
Tracey, Hugh 16
transmission:
  frequency of 18, 45–6, 124, 161, 165–6
  time of 12
Traveller in Time 78
Treasure Houses 110
Tripods 106
Truebridge, Liz 81
Turkey 61
Turner, Anthea 122, 125, 130–1, 132–3, *134*, *135*
  profile **132–3**
Turner, Darren 93
Turner, John 12

U
Universal Studios 124
USA 100

V
VE Day commemoration 124
Versailles 63, 166
Victoria Cross: story of 18
videos 100
Vincent, Tim 124, 127, 131, 134–5, *136*
  profile **134–5**

W
wages: average: in 1958 11
Wallenda, Karl 70, *71*
Warner, Jack 178–9
Warwick Castle 124
Watch with Mother 11
water-skiing *135*
WaterAid 131
Waugh, Tina 113
website 127
Well Water Appeal 131
Wenner, Christopher 72, 74, *74*, 80–1, 104, 108
  first programme 80, *81*
  on location 80, *81*
  profile **80–1**
West, Anita 16, 22–3, 51
  profile **22–3**
whale: riding on 109
Whately, Kevin 81
What's Up Doc? 115
'When *Blue Peter* Became ABBA' 107, 137
Where Are They Now? 19
white-water rafting 115
Williams, Kenneth 180
Williams, Leila 10, 19, 20–1
  disagreement with Clive Parkhurst 21
  dropped from programme 16
  interviews for job 20
  as presenter 15
  profile **20–1**
  at toy fair 16
Willow (cat) 31, *31*, 32
windmill: presenter going round on sails 111, *111*
wing-walking 141
Wogan 96–7
Wombles 123, *179*
woodwork: mini-series on 16
Woolacombe 124
World Books 88
Wright Stuff 107
Wurzels 123

Y
Yentob, Alan 124
Yes/No People 124
Young Generation (dance group) 75
Young Ones 120

Z
Zimbabwe 58
zoo: day at 48

ACKNOWLEDGEMENTS

Author acknowledgements

Thanks to the following for granting me interviews: John Adcock, Matt Baker, Edward Barnes, Biddy Baxter, Bob Broomfield, Romana d'Annunzio, Rosemary Gill, Simon Groom, Tina Heath, Alex Leger, Gillian Reilly. Bridget Caldwell, Annie Dixon and Jack Lundie were a huge help and support and I'm grateful to them. Steve Hocking, Oliver Macfarlane and Lewis Bronze gave invaluable feedback and comments. I'd also like to thank John Comerford for his input – and for bringing me into *Blue Peter* in the first place.

I made extensive use of the unexpurgated interviews filmed for the 40th anniversary, as well as my own earlier interviews with Caron Keating, John Leslie and Peter Purves. My notes, emails and diaries were also invaluable. Some of the best photographs in this book were taken by Chris Capstick, Adrian Homeshaw and Alex Leger. I'd like to thank the BBC Written Archive Centre, BBC Information and Archives and, from the *Blue Peter* office, Sarah Courtice, Clemmie Chamberlain and Lucy Morris for all their dedicated hard work. Finally, thanks to the excellent team at Hamlyn: Trevor Davies, Fiona Robertson and Darren Southern.

Picture acknowledgements

Hamlyn would like to acknowledge and thank the following for supplying images for publication in this book. All images copyright BBC with the following exceptions:
Edward Barnes pp.44–45 above centre
Michael Barrington-Martin p.22
Quentin Blake p.167 above right
Tim Graham p.7
Adrian Homeshaw p.145 left, p.149 centre, p.156, p.161 below, p.166 above, p.171 centre
Alex Leger p.99 above, p.115 right, p.135 right, p.139 right
Richard Marson p.83 right, p.86 above left, pp.86–87 below, p.126 above, pp.128–129 below, p.137 centre and right, p.139 centre, p.143 left and right, p.145 right, p.147 left, centre and right, p.149 left and right, p.160, p.161 centre, p.165 above, p.166 below, p.171 left and right
Robert Opie p.88 above, p.89 above
Gillian Reilly pp.12–13 main picture
The Stage 24.06.04 p.167 above left

Publisher acknowledgements

The publisher would like to thank Tim Levell for his assistance.

Executive editor: Trevor Davies
Senior editor: Fiona Robertson
Executive art editor: Darren Southern
Senior production controller: Martin Croshaw